# RETAIL
## management
### FOR SALONS & SPAS

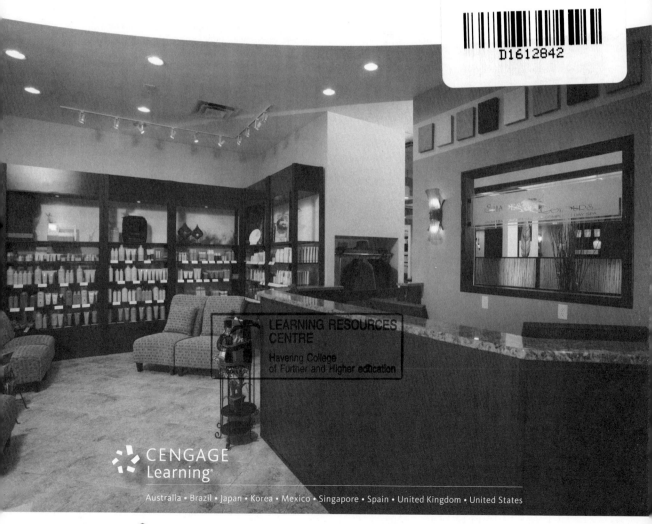

CENGAGE
Learning·

Australia · Brazil · Japan · Korea · Mexico · Singapore · Spain · United Kingdom · United States

International SPA Association and ISPA Foundation

**Retail Management for Salons and Spas
International SPA Association (ISPA)
Foundation**

Vice President, Milady & Learning
Solutions Strategy, Professional:
Dawn Gerrain

Director of Content & Business
Development, Milady:
Sandra Bruce

Senior Acquisitions Editor:
Martine Edwards

Product Manager:
Maria Moffre-Barnes

Editorial Assistant: Sarah Prediletto

Director, Marketing & Training:
Gerard McAvey

Marketing Manager:
Matthew McGuire

Senior Production Director:
Wendy Troeger

Production Manager:
Sherondra Thedford

Senior Content Project Manager:
Stacey Lamodi

Senior Art Director: Benj Gleeksman

Cover and title page photo:
© Milady, a part of Cengage
Learning

For product information and technology assistance, contact us at
**Cengage Learning Customer & Sales Support, 1-800-354-9706**

For permission to use material from this text or product,
submit all requests online at **www.cengage.com/permissions**.
Further permissions questions can be e-mailed to
**permissionrequest@cengage.com**

Library of Congress Control Number: 2012941337

ISBN-13: 978-1-111-54077-7

ISBN-10: 1-111-54077-2

**Milady**
5 Maxwell Drive
Clifton Park, NY 12065-2919
USA

Cengage Learning is a leading provider of customized learning
solutions with office locations around the globe, including Singapore, the
United Kingdom, Australia, Mexico, Brazil, and Japan. Locate your local office at:
**international.cengage.com/region**

Cengage Learning products are represented in Canada by
Nelson Education, Ltd.

For your lifelong learning solutions, visit **milady.cengage.com**
Purchase any of our products at your local college store or at our preferred
online store **www.cengagebrain.com**

Visit our corporate website at **cengage.com.**

**Notice to the Reader**
Publisher does not warrant or guarantee any of the products described herein or perform any independent analysis in connection with any of the product information contained herein. Publisher does
not assume, and expressly disclaims, any obligation to obtain and include information other than that
provided to it by the manufacturer. The reader is expressly warned to consider and adopt all safety
precautions that might be indicated by the activities described herein and to avoid all potential hazards.
By following the instructions contained herein, the reader willingly assumes all risks in connection with
such instructions. The publisher makes no representations or warranties of any kind, including but not
limited to, the warranties of fitness for particular purpose or merchantability, nor are any such representations implied with respect to the material set forth herein, and the publisher takes no responsibility with respect to such material. The publisher shall not be liable for any special, consequential, or
exemplary damages resulting, in whole or part, from the readers' use of, or reliance upon, this material.

Printed in the United States of America
2 3 4 5 6 7 17 16 15 14 13 12

# Contents

Preface                                                                vii

Chapter 1.  THE ART AND SCIENCE OF RETAIL                                 1
            Importance of Retail                                          3
            Retail Partnerships                                           8
            Chapter Summary                                              12
            Learning Activities                                          13
            Review Questions                                             13

Chapter 2.  RETAIL PLANNING                                              17
            Why Retail Planning Is Important                             18
            Defining Your Business Vision and Mission                    20
            The Core Values                                              22
            Who Are Your Clients?                                        28
            Creating Retail Classifications                              30
            Sales Planning                                               33
            Compensation                                                 39
            Chapter Summary                                              45
            Learning Activities                                          45
            Review Questions                                             46

Chapter 3.  PURCHASING                                                   49
            Purchase with a Plan                                         49
            Create a Vendor Structure                                    56
            Vendor Selection                                             57
            Vendor Partnerships                                          70
            Creating a Private Label Product Line                        72
            Marketing                                                    79
            Chapter Summary                                              80
            Learning Activities                                          81
            Review Questions                                             82

| Chapter 4. | INVENTORY MANAGEMENT | 85 |
| | Supporting the Plan | 86 |
| | Basic Retail Management | 89 |
| | Advanced Retail Management | 95 |
| | Manual Recordkeeping | 107 |
| | Shrinkage | 114 |
| | Chapter Summary | 117 |
| | Learning Activities | 118 |
| | Review Questions | 119 |
| Chapter 5. | EVALUATING FINANCIAL PERFORMANCE | 123 |
| | Key Business Indicators in Salon and Spa Retail Operations | 123 |
| | Cost of Goods Sold/Cost of Sales Percentage | 131 |
| | Inventory Turnover | 142 |
| | Salon and Spa Retail Budgeting | 145 |
| | Chapter Summary | 156 |
| | Learning Activities | 157 |
| | Review Questions | 158 |
| Chapter 6. | SALES AND SERVICE | 161 |
| | A Unique Opportunity | 161 |
| | Maximizing the Total Environment | 163 |
| | Seize the Sale | 165 |
| | Retail Challenges for the Salon and Spa Manager | 165 |
| | Retail Challenges for Front Desk and Other Salon and Spa Staff | 167 |
| | Retail Challenges for Service Providers | 170 |
| | Massage Therapists and Retail | 172 |
| | Retail Challenges for Retail Consultants in Spa Environments | 175 |
| | Education and Training for Effective Selling | 178 |
| | Value-Added Customer Service | 186 |
| | Chapter Summary | 188 |
| | Learning Activities | 188 |
| | Review Questions | 189 |
| Chapter 7. | VISUAL MERCHANDISING | 193 |
| | Basic Store Planning and Floor Layout | 193 |
| | Floor Layout and Product Positioning | 203 |
| | Presentation and Display for Skin, Body, and Beauty Products | 206 |

Presentation and Display for Apparel
    and Apparel-Related Products                        217
Merchandising Tips: Putting
    It All Together                                     225
Chapter Summary                                         229
Learning Activities                                     230
Review Questions                                        230

Chapter 8.    MARKETING                                 235
What Is Marketing?                                      235
Preparing a Marketing Plan                              242
Delivering Your Message                                 253
Internal Marketing Pieces                               263
People Make Marketing Happen                            264
Putting the Plan into Action                            267
Marketing Promotions                                    267
A Year of Promotions                                    269
Evaluating the Salon and Spa's Marketing Efforts        275
Chapter Summary                                         276
Learning Activities                                     277
Review Questions                                        277

Chapter 9.    SALON AND SPA RETAIL OPENING              281
A Systematic Approach to Planning                       281
Six Months from Opening                                 284
Four Months from Opening                                300
Two Months from Opening                                 307
Four Weeks from Opening                                 310
The Final Countdown Checklist                           312
Chapter Summary                                         313
Learning Activities                                     314
Review Questions                                        314

Appendix 1.    RESOURCES FOR FURTHER STUDY              319

Appendix 2.    REVIEW QUESTIONS ANSWER KEY              322

Glossary                                                323

Index                                                   329

# Preface

For more than 20 years, the International SPA Association (ISPA) has been recognized worldwide as the professional organization and voice of the spa industry, representing health and wellness facilities and providers in more than 70 countries. Members represent the entire arena of the spa experience, from resort/hotel, destination, mineral springs, medical, cruise ship, club and day spas to service providers such as physicians, wellness instructors, nutritionists, massage therapists, and product suppliers. SPA advances the spa industry by providing invaluable educational and networking opportunities, promoting the value of the spa experience, and speaking as the authoritative voice to foster professionalism and growth.

In the mid-2000s, ISPA and the ISPA Foundation recognized that with the rapid growth in the spa industry, education was extremely important for clients to receive a quality spa experience and for the industry to continue to thrive. To advance education, ISPA and the ISPA Foundation partnered to create *Retail Management for Spas*, the first of several educational resources developed in collaboration with the American Hotel & Lodging Educational Institute (EI). This textbook was designed to provide spa professionals with the retail skills needed to succeed. In 2011, Milady approached ISPA about adapting the content of *Retail Management for Spas* to create a salon-specific version of the book to provide salon professionals with the same strong foundation in retail knowledge.

Retail is a critical component for both salon customers and spa-goers. From a profitability standpoint, successful retail practices can provide many financial rewards to owners of salons and spas. This textbook provides information on retail strategies, planning, management, and administration—all of which can help salon and spa owners achieve even greater financial performance. However, many salon and spa professionals are involved in the salon and spa industry for a higher purpose and, while being profitable is important, it is not the only goal. Retail can also play a substantial role in this higher purpose as well.

The "selling" of retail products and the "higher purpose" of the salon and spa experience may seem in direct opposition to each other. But balance is a key word that is often used in the salon and spa industry. With the right balance, you can provide a mutually profitable retail experience with your salon and spa experience and still provide an overall comfortable environment. Ultimately, your guests can decide, with your guidance, whether they need any of these extensions that you provide—things they can take with them into their home, or provide to family and friends to share just a bit of their experience. This textbook provides you with information on not only the science of retail, such as inventory management and how to determine cost of sales, but also the art of retail with approaches to balancing this dichotomy to provide a valuable, lasting experience for your guest—and your salon or spa.

## HOW TO USE THIS TEXTBOOK AND NEXT STEPS

*Retail Management for Salons and Spas* has been carefully designed to provide education through a variety of learning techniques. The educational material provided in the chapters is complemented by quizzes, learning activities, salon and spa success stories, exhibits, key terms, retail formulas, and articles. The textbook provides valuable education on the very broad subject of salon and spa retailing.

At the beginning of each chapter, you will find a list of learning objectives that will assist you in determining areas that you need to concentrate on the most. Chapter review questions at the end of each chapter will help you determine your understanding and mastery of each chapter. These quizzes are multiple-choice questions based on the chapter competencies. The answer key can be found at the back of this textbook, in Appendix 2. Score yourself on your knowledge of the chapter, making note of your incorrect responses. Go back and review those parts of the chapter that discuss the material you missed. This will help to strengthen your knowledge of the subject matter.

Each chapter also includes learning activities that will offer opportunities to put the concepts and techniques of the chapter into practice.

# STUDY TIPS

While this textbook presents a variety of learning activities and methods, there are some common study tips that you may find helpful. Although you may already be familiar with many of the following study tips, they are useful reminders as you begin studying this text.

- Set up a regular time and place for study. Make sure you won't be disturbed or distracted.
- Decide ahead of time how much you want to accomplish during each study session. Remember to keep your study sessions brief; don't try to do too much at one time.
- Before you read each chapter, read the chapter learning objectives.
- Carefully read, focusing on the material included in the objectives and asking yourself such questions as:
  - Do I understand the material?
  - How can I use this information now or in the future?
- Make notes in the margins and highlight or underline important sections to help you as you study. Read a section first, and then go back over it to mark important points.
- Keep a dictionary and other reference materials handy. If you come across an unfamiliar word that is included in the text, look it up in one of your references.

# FOR FURTHER STUDY

ISPA and the American Hotel & Lodging Educational Institute (EI) have developed a series of courses designed to prepare spa professionals for management responsibilities in the spa environment. Four spa-specific courses that include a 100-question final examination, along with a more general hospitality supervision course, make up a five course program culminating in the Spa Management Certificate of Specialization. Along with *Retail Management for Spas*, the other courses in the program are *Supervision in the Hospitality Industry, Spa: A Comprehensive Introduction, Financial Management for Spas*, and *Risk Management for Spas*. In addition, ISPA and EI offer a nine-workbook series, *Supervisory Skill Builders for the Spa Industry*, which prepares professionals to take the Certified Spa Supervisor (CSS) examination. For more information on any of these programs, please contact ISPA at 1.859.226.4326 or visit www.experienceispa.com.

# The Art and Science of Retail

© Milady, a part of Cengage Learning.
Photography by Yanik Chauvin.

Chapter 1

## INTRODUCTION

Successful salon and spa technicians understand the importance of providing excellent customer service and solving problems. They understand that the service experience does not end once the client walks out of the door. It is the responsibility of the technician to recommend the appropriate tools and products to support the results experienced in the salon or spa so the client can maintain their results when they go home. For example, if your client had a problem with dandruff, and you provided a scalp treatment to relieve the issue, wouldn't you want to recommend a special shampoo to maintain the results at home? Perhaps a client has received a color service for the first time and the hair products used at home are not designed for color-treated hair. If the client uses these products, the results achieved in the salon will not have the longevity promised. Therefore, suggesting the appropriate products to maintain the color and health of the hair is looking out for the best interest of the client and in line with the role of a professional service provider.

In a spa environment, clients not only have the goal of receiving a skin or body treatment to solve problems, they also want to focus on their well-being and feel rejuvenated. Guests may wish to reduce stress, and may only have an hour or two for a visit.

For this reason, retail becomes an essential part of the spa experience. If a guest can only visit the spa for a short time, it is the responsibility of the technician to send the client home with the tools to maintain their results or to create an opportunity for relaxation. The technician may recommend a special skin cream to maintain

## LEARNING OBJECTIVES

After successfully completing this chapter, the reader will be able to:

- Explain why retail is an important extension of the salon and spa's services.

- Describe what the retail selling process looks like in the salon and spa environment.

- Identify the roles that various people play in creating a successful retail environment.

1

hydration, or an aromatherapy candle that creates that sense of calm. The salon and spa's retail offerings help recreate the experience or maintain results at home.

When salon and spa technicians solve problems and provide an excellent service experience, clients look upon them as trusted advisors and experts. Although true retailing is more about serving the client than *selling*, it can seem very daunting for technicians. The very word "selling" can create negative images in the mind of the technician, and prevent them from fully serving the client. Fully serving the client means taking care of their needs in such a way that they feel good about buying the products that are recommended. This type of "selling through service" approach will create good feelings within the client because the technician has recommended a solution to their problem. The good feelings the client experiences through expert advice will bring about customer loyalty and referrals.

Oftentimes, fear of being perceived as appearing "too pushy" or lack of product knowledge will prevent technicians from recommending retail products. Professionals must become aware of their responsibility in educating their client about products and making valid recommendations for home care. This text explores the art and science of retail and provides essential information by teaching retail strategies and systems. It also uses a variety of case studies, examples, and stories, which help illustrate the concepts and approaches being presented.

Understanding and implementing the planning, systems, and tools presented in this text will help make the life of the salon and spa professional easier and will enable the business to run smoother, while also maximizing revenue and the contribution of the retail department.

# IMPORTANCE OF RETAIL

Retail is an essential component of a salon and spa for many of the following reasons:

- Retail extends the benefits of services and treatments.
- Retail provides a one-stop shop for the client's needs.
- Retail fulfills client desires to shop.
- Retail promotes the **brand identity** of the salon or spa.
- Retail supports the salon and spa with additional revenue at higher margins than services.

**brand identity.** The philosophy of a business that is communicated and experienced through the staff, service models, and decor.

## Retail Extends the Benefits of Services and Treatments

People are increasingly turning to professionals to find ways to help live a more balanced, meaningful life. In record numbers, people are going to fitness trainers, life coaches, psychologists, and personal shoppers to find answers. These personal care professionals support the client during their sessions and provide resources and guidance for the client after their sessions so goals can be achieved. Fitness trainers not only guide clients through an exercise session, they also provide advice on nutritional needs and often recommend a particular diet. A life coach may focus on a particular challenge during a client appointment, and then recommend exercises and tools for self growth outside of the

session. People come to salons and spas for the same reasons they visit coaches, trainers, and personal shoppers, and expect the same level of professional advice. They also want services that provide benefits lasting long after their visit so their goals can be achieved.

In thinking of the above examples, if a client is told by a personal trainer to buy a certain hand grip exercise tool to build the strength in their hands, the client is not only likely to buy it, but they will appreciate the suggestion. In the same way, if a hair stylist tells his or her clients that they have split ends and should use a certain type of conditioning treatment, they will likely buy it because they want to look and feel better about themselves, and in turn, appreciate the suggestion.

In the beauty and wellness arena, retail selling is prescriptive by nature; estheticians do not suggest an eye cream because the guest has been looking for an eye cream. Instead, they are prescribing an outcome: "If you use this eye cream, you will tighten the skin under your eyes and will look better." Not recommending products you know will solve a beauty and wellness challenge is doing a disservice to the client in the long run. Imagine going to the dentist for a cracked tooth. You get a crown to preserve the tooth, yet the dentist does not inform you that you missed your regularly scheduled cleaning. Wouldn't you think your dentist would take note and remind you?

A successful technician recognizes that recommending product is addressing the ongoing and continuing needs of the client.

## Retail Provides a One-Stop Shop for the Client's Needs

A well-planned, easily accessible retail space can become reason alone for visiting your salon or spa. Carrying multiple lines can offer your clients product offerings that meet their specific needs. Carrying tools and accessories such as hair dryers, brushes, tweezers, and bath sponges can eliminate the need for clients to go elsewhere to purchase these items. According to the American Salon Online Survey in 2010 and 2011, salons have expanded their retail offerings to include boutique type items such as jewelry, clothing, fragrances, accessories, and books. Spas, on the other hand, have been known to offer non-treatment-related items such as robes, blankets, candles, and relaxation CDs. In either case, providing an opportunity for a one-stop shop experience for clients will encourage them to think of the salon or spa after they leave and perhaps repurchase consumable items on their next visit.

### DID YOU KNOW?

Retail products are the home care version of the service or treatment received in the salon and spa. Who would go to the dentist to have their teeth cleaned every 6 months but never brush their teeth in between visits?

A large-scale retail space can become a destination unto itself; such is the case for many spas and salons. Many salons and spas allocate about half or more of the entire space to retail. Some even have a separate space for the retail store with the salon or spa located across the breezeway. In these instances, a dedicated person is usually assigned to manage the retail operation. Product offerings are usually large, with many visitors to the retail portion never crossing over to become salon clients. Retail profits are often equal to or more than services profits. As a business owner, this design can be quite lucrative, especially when the reception desk is located within the retail space. Clients are tempted to purchase on an impulse while waiting for services or check out. As a salon or spa client, this design is quite convenient, as the vast amount of retail offerings can often rival a standalone gift shop.

## Retail Fulfills Client Desires to Shop

Many people like to shop and receive emotional satisfaction by merely browsing and engaging their senses of sight, smell, and touch. For these people, there is something magnetic about walking through a retail area, something that ignites their curiosity and satisfies a desire to absorb both new and familiar information through the things that surround them.

Salons and spas are the perfect environment for creating an emotional reaction to merchandise. People who are early for their scheduled appointment will likely take a look at the retail space while waiting to check in. By nature, products within the salon and spa environment create a wonderful opportunity to engage the curiosity of the client through a well-designed retail area filled with testers and inviting visual displays (Figure 1-1).

## Retail Promotes the Brand Identity

The tangible products that guests take home from the spa are continual reminders of the services they experienced. They are tangible connections to the salon or spa that can increase the likelihood that guests will return.

For salons and spas, private label products increase the brand awareness and become a take-home advertisement. This helps maintain loyalty and encourages repeat visits. Clients come back not just to re-experience the services, but also to refill the products that they purchased or to try something new.

Carrying a single product line or having a large suite of products from one line can also promote brand identity, especially if

### HERE'S A TIP

New products or those with low sell through can gain more movement by becoming a "Feature Item." Train all staff on the product, assure service providers are using it in their treatments, as appropriate, and feature it at the front desk. For example, a new hand cream can be used in manicures, massages, and facials, and can be offered to clients during hair services. It can even be made available in restrooms and given out as samples.

Figure 1-1
Recommending the appropriate products to clients is crucial to your professional appearance.

## SALON AND SPA SNAPSHOT 1.1

### An Invitation to Explore
### At the Eco Salon...

At The Eco Salon in Oceanside, California, the reception area could be mistaken for a well-appointed boutique. Clients enter the front doors and are welcomed into a large foyer. An oversized round table stands in the middle of the room and is arranged with multilevel displays calling attention to the latest fragrances and room scents. The overall look of The Eco Salon has great visual impact, and testers are liberally available for most items offered. The receptionist is strategically positioned at the far wall of the room, and is well versed on all of the products. Mirrored trays and fresh cut flowers provide a showcase for the various items, many of which can be found in upscale department stores. The walls are lined with unique hutches, each carrying a distinctive line of hair care and bath and body products. All displays have mirrors and tissue, and manufacturer shelf talkers are replaced by custom-made signs within sleek picture frames. The signs call out key product ingredients and benefits, and also prompt guests to touch and sample the enticing jars and bottles. For example, "This silky cream is made with almond oil and smoothes the driest skin. The fresh scent is instantly uplifting. Go ahead; try it on your feet or elbows."

Marilyn, the owner of the salon, made the transition from a small wall of retail shelving units to a more dedicated boutique type atmosphere a year ago and has experienced a steady increase in retail sales. "By enlarging the space, I have allowed for more opportunity for clients to browse and unwind before moving into their appointment. Because of the generous use of testers and 'try me' type signage, awaiting clients become instant shoppers as they are encouraged to experience the benefits of products firsthand."

the brand is nationally recognized. Most national brands have a strong marketing strategy and cooperative advertising for retailers so they can gain increased exposure. In addition, the manufacturer's website may also include the salon or spa in the database of retailers, accessible from the website.

## Retail Supports the Salon and Spa with Additional Revenue

Retail is an integral part of the business of salons and spas. Retail revenue supports the overall business by increasing the financial sustainability so that it can continue to provide or expand its services. Retail offers a greater profit margin simply because of the mark-up potential.

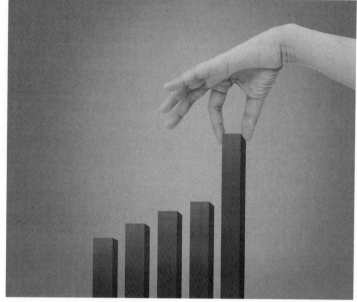

© jannoon028/www.Shutterstock.com

Example:

If a spa can purchase an eye cream for $35 and then sell it for $79, the gross margin on the sale is nearly 56 percent. The margin will be called a **gross margin,** as this is the profit before expenses such as shipping and payroll are deducted. To find the gross margin, simply divide the profit from the item by the selling price.

$$\$79.00 - \$35.00 = \textbf{\$44.00} \quad \text{(profit)}$$
$$\$44.00 \div \$79.00 = \textbf{55.6\%} \quad \text{(gross margin)}$$

**gross margin.** The profit derived from sales after the cost of goods sold and before payroll and other expense items are deducted. It is calculated by subtracting the Cost of Sales percentage from 100.

The topic of profit margin and evaluating financial performance on retail will be covered in more detail in Chapter 5.

Lower labor costs are the reason there is a higher margin in retail versus services. In a salon, there is typically one technician dedicated to each client, with limited support staff. Labor costs are lower and profit margin on services is relatively high—but not as consistently high as profit margins for retail. A 2011 American Salon Readers survey reported an average profit margin on services to range from 10 percent all the way to 50 percent in some services. Margins for retail averaged steadily between the 35 to 40 percent range, with shampoo, conditioner, and products for thinning hair representing the most common products purchased.

The 2011 Global Spa Summit research found that spas get an average of 14 percent of their total revenue from retail, with most revenue from skin care products. The other 86 percent of revenue is from spa services. In a spa, there is one employee dedicated to each client or guest plus all of the support staff it takes to run a spa. This means that labor costs can run between 45 and 60 percent of total revenue. Some spas run a labor cost even higher. This cost makes it very difficult to generate a net income percentage that can ensure financial sustainability on services alone.

## Retail Philosophy

**retail.** The sale of physical goods or merchandise directly to consumers.

**Retail** can be defined as the sale of physical goods or merchandise from a fixed location—such as a department store, boutique, or kiosk, or by mail—in small or individual lots for direct consumption by the purchaser. The word "retail" covers a broad expanse of businesses. It can cover anyone who sells anything in small quantities to the person who will consume those items.

**philosophy.** A statement of the main beliefs conveying what a business stands for.

Salons and spas experience the greatest amount of success with their retail when the retail is in sync with the salon and spa **philosophy**, or what a business stands for and the main beliefs. Philosophy guides the retail practices of the business and coincides with the mission and core values. There are different retail philosophies for different people and different businesses. For example, perhaps the philosophy of one salon and spa is that the business exists to provide a service, not products. In that case, any sale of products is a bonus, but not its primary business. For another salon and spa, its philosophy might be to provide a service that extends beyond the life of the treatments. That salon and spa would have a stronger retail focus and philosophy.

The greater the synergy between the salon and spa's philosophy and the retail philosophy, the more likely the retail is to be embraced by clients and staff alike.

# RETAIL PARTNERSHIPS

When it comes to retail, there are a lot of players who contribute to making it a success. There are partners, such as the media, financial institutions, local businesses, and charitable organizations, all of which can help a salon and spa business grow and succeed.

Salon and spa retail exists through three primary partnerships; each is equally important.

The three primary partners in any retail operation are staff, vendors, and clients. Think of retail as a three-legged stool and each leg of that stool represents one of these partners. If any of these legs are removed, or if one is weaker than the other, the stool will not be stable. Strength in these partnerships is essential in maintaining a well run profitable retail operation.

© Andresr/www.Shutterstock.com

In a perfect world, the seam between the services and its retail product would be so minute that guests would never know that they had moved from one place to the other. The service side of the sale would be so strong, the passion for the product so great in the heart of the person sharing the information, that the guest would feel compelled to try the product because his or her care provider believes so strongly in it. That is a perfect partnership of staff, vendor, and client, and provides an easy harmony and rhythm.

On the other end of the spectrum is the situation where the technicians do not believe in retail—or they believe in retail, but not in the products that are carried. In this scenario, the technicians provide the service without ever mentioning the retail—or if they do mention it, they send guests elsewhere to purchase products that they do believe in. The guests might browse the retail area of their own initiative—unless the service provider is ushering them straight to check out.

## The Staff

Few salons and spas have personnel devoted solely to retail. Rather, the tasks are part of a larger job description of such spa professionals as the front desk receptionists, the technicians or therapists, and the manager.

One of the more challenging decisions a business must make is to determine who does the selling. Is it the front desk receptionist? Is there someone dedicated fully to spa retail management? Is the primary responsibility for the promotion of products in the hands of the professional experts? In reality, all of these people will play a role in the success of the retail shop and in the way the salon and spa retail philosophy is carried out.

Managers must also think of ways to work with their staff to give them the sense that it is to their benefit to help grow the business. The motivation could be financial, but it can also be more basic than that. Sometimes having a manager tell a staff member that he or she is really proud of the employee can mean more to the staff than a cash bonus. Managers need to tell their staff how important they are to the success of the spa.

Managers can look for creative ways to motivate the staff and create opportunities for staff to become more acquainted with the products. This is where a partnership with the vendors can become a valuable resource. Some vendors send monthly samples to all of the staff so that they will have personal experience with each item they sell. Vendor partners can also create and support an incentive program that gives each employee a free full-size product for every three product combinations that he or she sells, for example. This increases sales while simultaneously providing opportunities for firsthand product experiences. Any number of methods can work as long as they are based on what motivates the staff.

Some of the key benefits to retail sales that managers can share with their staff include:

- Increased financial incentives for the employee—more take-home pay.
- Increased financial incentives for the business, which allows the business to continue to grow.
- Increased client loyalty to the technicians and therapists by educating their clients on ways to extend the service experiences or create a healthy lifestyle.

## Vendors

Salons and spas need to partner with vendors with whom they have synergistic philosophies. The philosophy is interwoven in every product choice and vendor selection.

It is also important that vendor partners understand and respect the needs of their client and openly communicate. There will be times when the salon and spa professional needs the vendor's help; for example, when product knowledge classes are needed or when internal campaigns require the presence of a vendor. The vendor will also need the help of the salon and spa at times. For example, product manufacturers will need support in launching new products or elevating sales for certain products. In return, **spiffs** or special rewards are often given to the staff. Therefore, establishing a good relationship with your vendor will create a win-win outcome for both parties.

 Reputable vendors will stand behind their products, provide support, such as product knowledge training, sampling, product brochures, and displays. Selecting vendors and products to carry in the retail department requires careful planning and consideration. It is also a decision in which professionals should consider the opinion of their other two partners, staff and clients. Their input into these decisions can be a key factor in the overall success of this partnership trio. Chapter 3 contains a more detailed discussion of vendor selection and relationships.

**Spiffs.** Vendor rewards provided to staff to recognize sales achievements.

## Clients

Understanding the needs and desires of individual clients can sometimes be the most difficult challenge. It is easier for a salon and spa to understand what frequent clients are looking for and what is important to them, but more challenging to understand the same about first-time guests. So how does the salon and spa professional understand the needs of each client regarding retail? The process may take the form of an in-depth consultation by the service provider, a detailed intake questionnaire, or a combination of the two.

 In the salon environment, the nature of the service is built upon relationships and consultative selling. The client visits the salon because they want to look better and feel more confident. The client need is highly emotional in nature and, therefore, the technician must ask questions and listen. Through a client consultation, needs and desires are discovered and solutions to problems are recommended. The service is conducted while a conversation is carried out between the client and the technician. In fact, products are typically discussed throughout the service as they relate to the solution of problems. Because the service is not carried out in silence, there is more opportunity to discuss retail products and gauge the interest level of the client throughout the engagement.

 In the spa environment, the method of conducting treatments is quite different. A guest will make an appointment for a treatment and then a client intake form is usually completed for a first-time client. Needs are discovered quickly through this process and a consultation prior to the start of the treatment establishes rapport and further pinpoints needs. Then, the session is carried out as a relaxing experience, with little to no conversation taking place between the guest and the service provider. This may become a challenge in discovering a client's interest level in retail because this dialogue usually takes place at the end of the service prior to check out.

In both cases, the service provider must gauge the interest level of the client in terms of retail and then guide the conversation accordingly. Even though salon and spa consumers may be highly interested in retail products, the retail environment still needs to be in sync with the customer's mood. If salon and spa professionals are pushy or technicians give guests the wrong prescription for their needs, the consumers are going to resist further purchases and be turned off by the salon and spa. That is why it becomes so important for the retail offerings to be aligned with the salon and spa's philosophy and clientele.

# CHAPTER SUMMARY

- It is the responsibility of the technician to recommend the appropriate tools and products to support the results experienced in the salon or spa. This helps the client to maintain their results when they go home.
- The "selling through service" approach will create good feelings within the client because the technician has recommended a solution to their problem.
- Retail supports the overall business profitability because of the high profit margin.
- The staff can become motivated to support the retail operation in ways other than financial compensation. Client loyalty and product perks and other recognition are effective motivators.
- Vendors are partners in the retail operation and contribute to its success by connecting product offerings with the philosophy of the salon and spa.
- Clients are partners in the retail outcomes because they communicate their needs to the technicians, who in turn recommend appropriate products.

# LEARNING ACTIVITIES

## Learning Activity 1-1: Reflecting on Success

Get a blank journal that you will dedicate to the activities and information in this book. Write in it at least three times a week. Record things you've learned, observations you've made, ideas that you have. Use it to note improvements in your salon or spa or to praise yourself for those things that you are already doing well. Use it to experiment with concepts in this text that are new to you or that you want to try out in a different way. Make notes to yourself about things you'd like to research further or discuss with a mentor or another salon and spa professional.

## Learning Activity 1-2: Purposeful Work

Select three to five products that your salon or spa sells in its retail area. For each product, write a description of how that product can enhance the life of the person who uses it. Does it have the ability to change someone's life? How? Include that in the description.

# REVIEW QUESTIONS

1. Which of the following statements about the benefits of retail is FALSE?
   a. Retail helps extend the benefits of treatments and services.
   b. Retail enables the technician to build client loyalty.
   c. Retail has a lower profit margin than spa services.
   d. Retail markets the salon and spa and its services.

2. Which of the following statements would demonstrate a massage therapist promoting retail products to a guest?
   a. "We have an esthetician here who really recommends the sea algae serum to remove puffiness under the eyes."
   b. "Have you considered using a cuticle cream? The spa has a cream that works wonders on cuticles."
   c. "We offer a magazine on ways to self-style medium-length hair."
   d. "There's a lot of tension in your right shoulder muscles. We've got a vitamin E rub that could help you relax and can be used daily."

3. Why have salon and spa professionals traditionally resisted selling retail products?
   a. They do not want to be seen as salespeople.
   b. Salons and spas have not traditionally extended sales commissions to therapists.
   c. They do not want the home treatments to replace the services they offer.
   d. They have not resisted selling retail products and instead have been the most enthusiastic supporter of retail offerings.

4. What type of reaction are most guests seeking from their shopping experience?
   a. Physical
   b. Medical
   c. Knee-jerk
   d. Emotional

5. Which of the following statements about retail revenue is false?
   a. Retail brings in more revenue than services.
   b. Retail has a higher profit margin than spa services.
   c. Retail has a far lower labor cost than services.
   d. Retail costs are roughly lower than salon and spa services costs.

6. Titus is designing a retail-training program for the soon-to-be-hired staff at a salon and spa that will have its grand opening in three months. He's preparing a flip chart page listing the reasons why retail is so essential to the operation of the salon and spa. As he finishes the list, the owner walks by and glances at it over his shoulder. "Get rid of that one," he says, pointing at one of the bulleted items. Which one of the following bulleted points was it likely the owner wanted deleted?
   a. Retail helps extend the benefits of spa treatments.
   b. Retail creates an attractive room for clients to pass through on their way to treatment.
   c. The retail experience fulfills an emotional need for clients.
   d. Retail markets the salon and spa and its services.

7. Which of the following is the BEST way to motivate the staff to support the retail operation?
    a. Providing full-sized product
    b. Recognition
    c. Coaching and feedback
    d. Managers sharing the benefits of retail such as client loyalty and providing product perks

8. Which of the following is NOT a service that salons and spas can expect from their vendor partners?
    a. Product knowledge training
    b. Gift promotions
    c. Displays and brochures
    d. Definition of the salon or spa's philosophy

9. Which of the following statements is TRUE?
    a. Retailing is a necessary evil.
    b. Retailing is an integral part of providing exceptional service.
    c. Technicians and therapists cannot be expected to sell retail.
    d. The role of vendors in a salon and spa's retail environment is limited to the provision of retail products.

10. Keith is the manager of an upscale men's salon. The salon's philosophy is to provide full-service grooming in a one-stop shop. Keith is considering expanding some of the salon's retail offerings. Which of the following products would best align with the salon's philosophy?
    a. Shaving cream and accessories
    b. Aftershave and a face treatment
    c. A manicure kit
    d. All of the above

# Retail Planning

## INTRODUCTION

Chapter **2**

**W**hen looking at the overall business operation, there are three simple questions that will lead the way through the planning process of a salon and spa:

1. Where is the business now?
2. Where do you want it to go?
3. How are you going to get there?

The first question, "Where is the business now?" is the foundation of your plan. This is where you look at the current state of your business, and consider aspects such as retail sales volume, profit, product offerings, the target market, and so forth. All of these factors combine to describe the current state of your business. The second question, "Where do you want it to go?" is somewhat more difficult to approach. This describes your goal of what could possibly be. It is your vision of success. As a manager, you must be completely open and honest with yourself and be willing to investigate your markets, your environment, key trends, threats, and your opportunities. This will help you determine the future direction of your business and help mold your vision into a reality.

The third question, "How are you going to get there?" describes the framework of success, or the detailed task of deciding all of the things necessary to achieve your vision. These tasks include determining retail classifications, calculating the cost of sales, and planning both your annual and monthly sales.

## LEARNING OBJECTIVES

After successfully completing this chapter, the reader will be able to:

- Explain the importance of planning.

- Monitor and identify trends.

- Answer important questions related to his or her overall salon, and related to the spa and retail departments.

- Create retail classifications.

- Plan annual and monthly sales.

- Develop a compensation plan that drives retail sales.

**SALON AND SPA SNAPSHOT 2.1**

## At the Seasons Salon and Day Spa...

Jazmine melted onto the bamboo mat, and applied moisturizer onto her arms as she prepared to meditate. It was the end of her first day as director at the Seasons Salon and Day Spa, a resort/hotel amenity with a medical emphasis built into a beautiful beachfront destination resort.

As she began reviewing the day's events, she remembered a whole shelf of "clearance" items marked down so low that Seasons would be lucky to see any profit from them at all. Nor did it help when one of the resort guests asked whether there was any chance the aromatherapy massage oils would move to the clearance shelf before the end of the week.

Jazmine took out an incense stick and lit it, thinking about how everything in life—whether it is starting a diet, managing a salon and spa, or creating a retail venue in a business—needs a plan. She wouldn't be able to get Seasons where she wanted it to go if she didn't have a plan.

She'd asked the retail manager, Kendra, about the retail plan and was told there wasn't one. She had been surprised. She pointed out to Kendra that every week she had to create a schedule for technicians and therapists. She couldn't just say to them, "Here are the hours that we're open, come in when you feel like it." The same was true of the retail store. The only way they'd succeed was if they had a plan.

# WHY RETAIL PLANNING IS IMPORTANT

Like all business professionals, salon and spa professionals succeed by establishing a solid retail plan. This plan is like a road map so you can plot your footsteps, track your progress, and make changes to reach your goal. There is no universal plan that can be used for all salons and spas. No one can say, "If you put tab A into slot B you'll always be able to increase retail sales by 15 percent." However, all of the chapters within this text will guide you through the journey of the planning process. This chapter will provide you with a beginning, through the discussion of the key elements of retail planning.

## Key Elements That Define a Retail Plan

The key elements of a retail plan are:

- Synchronizing retail with your business philosophy
- Watching and understanding trends
- Identifying customers and target markets

These three areas are the cornerstone of a salon or spa's plan and set the course for its journey. While the philosophy is the compass that guides the business, trends and customers are the winds and current that may redirect its path. It is important that you synchronize your business components, including retail, with the overarching salon and spa philosophy. The philosophy is the reference point for all that you do, and if you don't continually monitor trends and your customers, you may end up way off course without even realizing it.

## Synchronizing Retail with Your Business Philosophy

The most successful salons and spas succeed by anchoring all they do into a solid operating philosophy. The philosophy provides the road map for the decisions you make every day; from the environment you choose, to the people you hire, to the type of retail product you sell, and to the education that you supply to your staff and clients.

The retail products chosen for your business should coincide with the philosophy, which is part of your mission and core values. There needs to be a link between the philosophy and everything the salon or spa presents to its clients, which includes:

- Product offerings/product mix
- Visual environment
- Treatments offered
- Language used by the entire staff
- Type of technicians hired and their values and image
- Approach to service/education

When a salon or spa builds its philosophy, it is creating an extension of its brand through the retail environment. It is this extension of the brand that makes it necessary for a salon and spa manager to create a theme for the environment and stay away from an eclectic or haphazard approach. This further strengthens the clarity of the brand to both its clients and the staff. For example, if a salon has a philosophy of being an eco-friendly environment, than the retail products carried should also follow that same philosophy. Retailing products that are known to contain harsh chemicals would send a mixed message and be inconsistent with the salon's philosophy and brand.

The following are ideas that can help you define or select a theme:

- Geographic influences: High desert, northern lake, ocean, Asian, elevated mountains, etc. For example, a salon or spa on an ocean may want to consider sea algae products or items such as a sea salt scrub in its retail selection.
- Overall theme: Asian, Eastern, Native American, holistic, sports focused, modern, geared toward hip Generation Xers, etc. For example, a salon with a sports theme may want to consider offering specials during March Madness or football season and offering TV channels showing sports.
- Focus on a core business component: A tie-in with the ocean, golf, natural springs, mineral springs, retirement communities, country club communities, alternative or holistic medical practice, adventure, hiking, mountains, etc. For example, in a country club community, a spa may want to consider private labeled apparel such as golf shirts or visors and hats.

**FYI**

Ensuring your service offerings and themes are in sync with your salon or spa philosophy creates a point of difference between your salon or spa and the competition.

The more complete an approach is, the more likely there are to be clear points of difference, or things that make your salon or spa unique. This makes it easier for clients to refer business to you because they will know how to describe what you stand for and how you are different. As for staff, the clearer the points of difference, the simpler it is to hire individuals aligned with your business philosophy.

Finding and defining this philosophy begins with the definition of your salon or spa's vision, mission, and core values. This must be the first step because these should be the touchstones that salon and spa professionals return to when establishing and updating their retail plans.

# DEFINING YOUR BUSINESS VISION AND MISSION

The following questions will guide you to develop an explicit statement about your vision, mission, and culture:

- What is the ideal vision of success for your business?
- Who are the target clients and what is their profile?

- What are the target clients looking for in choosing a salon or spa?
- What does your business represent to you?
- How do you want your business to be perceived?
- What are the core values of your business?

© TerryM/www.Shutterstock.com

## A Vision of Success

The vision of success represents what the salon and spa wants to be known for in the future. It is that lofty aspiration or dream once all of your goals are achieved.

Visioning is a creative process. When envisioning the ideal future state of your business, it is helpful to learn from other businesses that you admire. What attributes do you want to incorporate into your salon or spa? How do you want to be different? For example, if you know you want to be an elegant day spa catering to busy professionals in a business park, look at other successful businesses with a similar niche. As you look at other businesses in your category for ideas, don't forget to look at industries other than your own. For example, if a restaurant in a business area offers express service during lunch and has free Wi-Fi, you can offer these things as well.

## The Mission Statement

The **mission statement** sets forth the purpose of your salon or spa. It articulates what and how your business will deliver your service, the quality customers can expect, and how you will operate. A mission statement provides the foundation for the choices made in the retailing area: what products will be purchased, how they will be promoted, how they will be displayed, and how they will be sold to guests.

**mission statement.** An explicit statement that sets forth the purpose of the business that is publicly communicated and part of the brand and core values.

### Seasons Salon and Spa Mission Statement

"We will provide proven treatments that yield scientific results to combat the effects of aging. Our quality products and services will deliver long-term results that focus on healing and ageless beauty. Our professional and knowledgeable staff will focus on building rewarding and enduring relationships with every guest that visits our salon and spa."

# THE CORE VALUES

**core values.** The key principles that support the mission statement and guide decision making.

Your mission generates the **core values** of your business. These core values are the guiding principles that channel the decisions that you and your staff make.

Core values are simply the behaviors the salon or spa wishes to encourage in its staff to support the mission and bring it to life. Core values give your team the boundaries in which to operate.

Using the Seasons Salon and Spa as an example, its mission states that it wants to be known as an establishment that uses only scientific practices that have been thoroughly tested to achieve long-term results. The perception would be that the staff researches and becomes an authority on the products and services they offer. The research behind the products and services and the knowledge of the staff creates a point of difference.

Seasons Salon and Spa wants to be known for creating ageless beauty; therefore, all decisions must embody that principle. It states it would offer only treatments that were scientifically proven. This principle would mean they would only offer treatments and products that were guaranteed to deliver results, such as healing the body. Another core value of Seasons' would be to offer only product lines that align with the mission. Science-based or dermatology-based products would be the preferred offerings. For example, products that are proven to regenerate hair growth or skin cell renewal are appropriate products that align with the mission of Seasons.

## Retail Trends

When figuring out a retail assortment strategy, it is important for the salon and spa to monitor current trends that the industry has to offer. With so many products on the market today, it can seem a little overwhelming when first considering your retail assortment strategy. But there are some guidelines that transform the process of monitoring trends into second nature. The result? You are able to offer customers the "in-demand" products they want to buy, which creates a win-win situation for your business and customers alike.

Trends represent what is going on in the industry. By nature, trends can change rapidly and retailers have to be aware of what product trends exist. What was considered a hot breakthrough last year may be old news today. Salon and spa professionals need to know some basic information about trends, as well as what to watch and track, both inside and outside of their walls. By constantly updating yourself and getting a handle on what is out there, you are able to know that you are offering your customers the best products available.

## Life Cycles of Trends

Retail sales patterns happen in cycles and often coincide with what is going on with the season, popular culture, or influences in mainstream television or fashion magazines. Typically, a trend has four stages that can last for varying lengths of time:

- Introduction: The trend becomes a buzzword and related images begin cropping up in the media and on the streets.
- Growth: The message spreads and there is an increased awareness that this trend exists.
- Maturity: Variations on the trend can be seen, including copies and "knock-offs," and the trend is commonly known.
- Decline: The trend begins to lose its luster, is viewed as somewhat outdated, and is replaced by a new trend.

Retail classifications, which are explained later in this chapter, help to determine where a particular item fits within trend patterns and life cycles. Knowing what stage a particular item is in helps you to plan for the life cycle of the item, and helps when developing a sales forecast and merchandising strategy. Typically, trends can be identified as belonging in one of these four categories:

- Fad: A trend that sweeps in and out quickly, generating a large amount of sales in a relatively short amount of time.
- Fashion: Typically, a fashion trend lasts for several seasons, depending on the market. The younger the market, the less time the fashion trend will last.
- Staple: An item for which there is a continuous demand over an extended period of time and that is a part of most people's lives.
- Seasonal item: An item that appeals only during the season for which it was created.

## Social and Cultural Trends

Major social trends are those that are of most use and help you to plan. The highly successful trend spotters look for those trends that have a deep and lasting effect on society. Then they identify which of those trends they can either take advantage of or test. For example:

- Concern for wellness: Organics, alternative medicines, herbs, healthier products, chemical-free
- Social consciousness: Heightened sensitivity to environmental and social issues, green products
- Agelessness: A demand for a youthful appearance
- Customization: Consumers crave individuality
- Self-gratification: A focus on affordable luxuries

## Know What the Customer Knows

To the customers, you and your technicians and therapists are consultants and industry experts. They may come in with questions about certain product trends, trusting that if anyone would have an educated opinion on the subject, it would be an expert within your four walls.

© wavebreakmedia ltd/www.Shutterstock.com

As an industry professional, you have access to unlimited amounts of data and information. You can attend trade shows, subscribe to industry-related websites or newsletters, read magazines, and network with other professionals. All of these activities keep you current on trends and forecasts that the average consumer may not be privy to yet.

On the other hand, your customers are flooded with messages on a daily basis about products and trends through magazines, television, and social media. It is in your best interest to tune into popular TV shows and other forms of media so you can become more aware of these influences. By doing so, you will be able to speak with credibility about trends and offer opinions and education. Doing so establishes you as the credible expert and your customers come to trust your opinions when they are offered.

Just as important as it is to stay current on trends, it is also vital to know the pulse of your industry and expectations of the consumer in general. This will allow you to anticipate your own customer needs and prepare for potential variations in your business. In 2011, Green Book published a report containing the following consumer salon and spa trends:

- There is still an increase in male clients visiting both salons and spas.
- Salons reported a reduction in frequency for regular client visits.
- Four in 10 salons reported an increase in revenue since 2010.
- Women were more likely to cut back on services than men on visits.
- Retail product offerings in salons have become more focused on hair care items.
- Massage is the strongest revenue earner (2011 Global Spa Summit).
- Revenue is up from 12.3 billion in 2009 to 12.8 billion in 2010.
- Skin care is an important source of revenue due to add-on services (such as ampoules) and retail home care products (2011 Global Spa Summit).

## Keep Track of What Is and What Is Not Working

A great way of knowing what your customers like and respond to is to keep a careful eye on what is actually selling from a retail mix and what is not. If a product you thought would fly off the shelves is actually just sitting there day after day, in spite of the fact that your staff is promoting it effectively and it is displayed well, it is clear that the product is not aligned with your customer. Conversely, even if an item is not the latest, greatest "in style" product but the customer keeps buying it, you will reorder based on rate of sale. When the rate of sale drops below the standards you have set for the item, then is the time to drop it, even if it takes months or years after you personally grow tired of the item and prefer something new.

There are several questions that you can ask during a product investigation to determine *why* a product is not working. For example, how does it differ from other products that *do* sell? Is the packaging different? Has the product itself, or a key ingredient, recently gotten a bad rap from the media? Noting the characteristics of a product that fails on the shelves can help you to avoid similar situations in the future.

Similarly, you may find that you are unable to keep one certain hair treatment in stock because it sells out the day you get the shipment. When this happens, you can ask yourself what trend that product represents, then watch for similar products that your customers may also find appealing. You should note these things,

Compare what moves quickly and what does not, then find the patterns and buy accordingly.

and, by all means, order a larger shipment. Not having enough of a hot product is a quick way to lose customers, who will rush to the competition if your shelves are out of what they are looking for.

By truly tracking what sells and what does not, you will have a better idea of how to buy for your retail space in the future and avoid similar mistakes.

## Talk Less, Listen More

The importance of listening is huge when talking about retail buying and trends. Listening to the media is obviously important, as the media is the ultimate reporter of trends. But even more important, managers need to listen to the messages that their customers give them.

If a manager keeps getting calls from customers about whether or not he carries a certain product or line, he pays attention! His callers are giving him valuable tips about what interests them. If the staff is buzzing about a new trend, salon and spa managers should not ignore their opinions. Your staff is a great resource when it comes to deciding which trends to follow and which to pass up.

You will always have your own opinion about which retail products are best, which work, or which you would choose for yourself. But as a retailer, your responsibility is to bring in a product mix that represents what the customers would choose for themselves. What the customers are buying far outweighs your personal opinion or desire for a particular item.

You may or may not always have products that represent a certain trend your customers are asking about. When your salon or spa doesn't have an item, you and your staff need to know which of your products offer similar results. For example, if a customer tells her hairdresser that she read an article about the benefits of sea kelp, the hair designer should feel free to discuss that trend with her, even if none of your retail products contain sea kelp. The hair designer can carefully listen for the clues the client gives on why she is looking for sea-based products and what motivated the question. Then, the hair designer can let her know that she understands and appreciates her interest.

The conversation can be an opportunity to offer an alternative product and introduce her customer to the new soy-based product line, for example, which provides similar benefits or accomplishes the same goal. Customers count on your service staff to introduce them to products they know will work for them.

## At the Urban Salon and Day Spa...

Reuben, the director at the Urban Salon and Spa, twiddled his ring thoughtfully. He'd just reviewed his monthly sales figures. They still had not sold a single one of the "Beauty from Head to Toe" packages they'd begun stocking four months ago. He had been certain those would fly off the shelf.

The set included hair care products, spa sandals, a honeysuckle scrub, and two different aromatherapy oils and body cream. Reuben had worked closely with the product's manufacturer to create a wall display that was directly in the path of customers as they left the pedicure stations and styling chairs and went to the check-out desk. He was pleased with the way it had fit with the rest of his retail display. To assure everyone could have first-hand knowledge of the products, Ruben conducted a 20-minute training session with each of his staff and gave each of them a sampler of the products to try. Everyone had seemed enthusiastic about it.

After all of the preparation, there sat the "Beauty from Head to Toe" packages with no sales. Reuben decided he needed to do some investigation. He began by talking to each of his staff members. He then visited several local boutiques and department stores. He also talked to one of the salon and spa's regular customers when she came in for her monthly services. He then came back and reviewed his findings:

- A local department store was selling a similar package, and the store had featured it in a full-page newspaper ad they had run. To make things worse, their package—while not offering any aromatherapy oils—was $10 cheaper.
- Colby, one of the pedicurists, sheepishly mentioned that since Reuben had excluded it from the bonus incentive program, he hadn't been mentioning it.
- The customer said she hadn't been interested in it because it didn't have a deep penetrating conditioner in it.
- Delia, a hair designer who had missed the original training, said that she didn't care for the scent of the aromatherapy oils.

When Reuben expressed his frustration later in the week to one of the other managers on staff, she smiled sympathetically. "Well, Reuben," she said, "we are paid to make mistakes. I know our boutique is pretty much in line with the average retail operation— we have a 20 percent markdown rate. You did mark the package down to clear it out, didn't you?"

In this example, the hair designer can communicate information regarding customer requests to the retail manager. If the retail manager is aware of what clients are asking for, he or she can track products that have had multiple requests and investigate further.

# WHO ARE YOUR CLIENTS?

**WEB RESOURCES**

As you transition into your new career in the beauty and wellness industry, let us continue the journey with you. Be sure to check out www.miladyednet.com to prepare for your State Board Exam and gain access to additional resources to hit the ground running as a licensed professional, ensuring long-term success no matter where your career may take you.

Knowing your clients is quite possibly the most important thing you can do to achieve retail success. Understanding what your target client's needs are, and meeting those needs will be integral to choosing the most appropriate retail offerings. Ultimately, you will draw most of your clients from your immediate surroundings. For example, are you situated in an upscale mall with clients looking to spend their disposable income on high-end products? Or are you near a college campus, where penny-pinching students will likely be the bulk of your clientele?

You can gain further insights about your clients and potential clients by looking at the role your salon or spa plays in the location. Is your business serving a niche clientele or a certain purpose? Perhaps you have partnered with the local boutique in your small town, where people are close-knit and they trust you to help them find the right products for personal care. Maybe you are the "new guy in town," and you hope to make a name for your salon by introducing the area to cutting edge hair products that no one else is offering.

Noting trends in client demographics offers other insights into your customers. Simple questions to ask include:

- What is the average age of your client base?
- What percentage of your clients are women versus men?
- What do your customers do for fun?
- What are their buying habits?

When you start to think about who your clients are, you gain insight into the types of products that they will be excited about.

For a new business, determining who the potential clients will be might entail a bit of guesswork. For an established business, however, you will gather this information every day as you interact with clients; with your therapists, technicians or hair designers; with support staff; and even as you visit other stores in the neighborhood and read magazines.

## Customer Surveys

Surveys are a useful tool that can provide a wealth of information to establish a more definitive view of your clients. Surveys can range from a quick paper survey that guests complete at the time of purchase to a more lengthy online survey they can complete at home. The following are some types of information salon and spa professionals collect during surveys.

## General Demographics

Some of this information can be collected through the forms clients fill out when they first visit with you. Defining who from your client base is purchasing products and who isn't can be challenging. However, this is still a good base of information. You can learn a great deal about your clients when they provide such demographic information as:

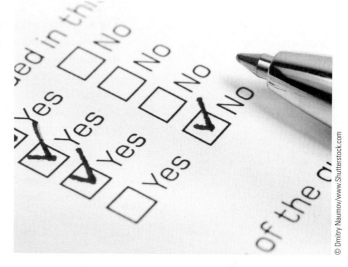

© Dmitry Naumov/www.Shutterstock.com

- Age range
- Gender
- Educational background
- Estimated income
- Marital status
- Number of children
- Employment
- Average number of years as a client

## Survey Outcomes

As you are developing survey questions, always consider what outcome you want from the survey. Possible outcomes include:

- How guests validate their retail purchases made with you.
- What types of purchases they are making, why they make them, and how they make their purchases.
- Who they are shopping for (themselves, friends, specific family members).
- Alternate locations where they purchase similar products in a particular category.
- Whether similar products in that category sold at grocery and drugstores and on television shopping networks are more popular than products sold only at salons and spas. Why?
- Buying habits for retail products offered in salons and spas.
- What role products play in creating a positive experience.
- When consumers would prefer to be informed of the benefits of a salon or spa product.
- Effective merchandising in the retail area.
- Perceptions of private label items versus other brands.
- Emerging product and shopper trends.
- Barriers to product sales in a salon or spa.

## Data Sorts

The ideas given below can be found in salon and spa databases and internal reports. These data sorts are a way of looking at the information in slightly different ways to spot trends and set benchmarks that professionals can use in evaluating their customers' habits.

- Number of clients
- Number of visits
- Average number of retail purchases in general and by product classification
- Average number of retail purchases per client/per visit
- Average number of retail purchases by retail square footage
- Types of guests (first time, frequent, infrequent) and their purchasing frequency
- Key group clients (wedding parties, corporate groups) and their purchasing frequency

## Consider the Target Market

Using the example of the Seasons Salon and Spa, which is located in an upscale metropolitan city, Jazmine, the director, might choose female clients between the ages of 45 and 65 with household income greater than $75,000 as a **target market**.

As a business manager, you need to determine what that target market wants and determine whether those wants are being fulfilled by your service and retail offerings. Going back to the Seasons Salon and Spa, its purpose is to produce ageless beauty. Seasons has to determine whether it can attract enough women between the ages of 45 and 65 who are interested in such a concept.

**target market.**
A specific group of people with something in common to whom you are selling, or wish to sell, your products and services.

# CREATING RETAIL CLASSIFICATIONS

If defining the business philosophy, mission, and core values are the art of retail, then the science of retail might be the planning, the nitty-gritty detail work of crunching numbers, and creating practical budgets.

During the retail planning stages, you determine what the **retail classifications** are going to be. These classifications will form an important part of retail planning as sales forecasting

**retail classifications.**
A grouping that identifies merchandise with a similar end use.

is done for each individual department's classifications. Sales forecasting will be the key to providing you with information for selecting and purchasing products.

The breakdown of classifications provides a far more practical tool than attempting to plan merchandise purchases from a total, salon and spa-wide planning budget. It is easier to spot and track trends when managers can pinpoint sales for types of items.

So the first step in sales forecasting becomes listing the classifications that will be offered in the retail area. Classifications identify merchandise with a similar end use. For example, skin care items are separated from hair care items. Customers purchase each of those types of items for different reasons, and different trends and factors will affect sales.

While each salon and spa will want to develop its own classifications based on its computer system and merchandise selection, there are some common major categories that have been established in the salon industry. These are:

- Shampoo
- Conditioner
- Styling products
- Hair appliances
- Thinning hair/regrowth treatments
- Nail care products
- Skin care products
- Cosmetics
- Bath/body products
- Jewelry
- Hair accessories
- Tanning products
- Fragrances

Spas, on the other hand, are more complex than salons. They tend to have a gift shop with a broad range of retail items to continue the spa experience at home. Standard retail classifications have been set forth in the *Uniform System of Financial Reporting for Spas.* The broad categories for spas are given as:

- Footwear
- Men's/unisex, robes and terry items
- Women's robes and terry items
- Books and media
- Fashion accessories
- Home goods
- Bath and body products

- Hair products
- Makeup products
- Nail products
- Private label products
- Skin care products
- Snacks and beverages
- Sundries

Depending on the merchandise mix and number of vendors, many salons and spas will create classifications based on vendor, or use a combination of product classifications and vendor classifications. The model they use will depend on what is most efficient for them and what information is going to be most helpful for them. A sample vendor classification might look like this:

Vendor Alignment: Body Products

10 Vendor A
11 Vendor B
12 Vendor C
13 Vendor D
14 Vendor E

© VIPDesignUSA/www.Shutterstock.com

In retail planning, you will use these classifications along with your knowledge of your merchandise selection to build a list that provides the most meaningful records and the most usable purchasing plan. While making the choices for classifications, think ahead, and realize that each classification will form the basis for purchasing and will also determine how easy it is to pull specific sales information. As the budget is created, you will set aside money for each individual classification.

This also helps you determine how much business you want to do in any given classification. For example, Jazmine at the Seasons Salon and Spa may find that skin care is a good classification. Once she knows how much money to spend on skin care, she breaks her purchases down into cleansers and serums. Since she wants still more information, she might break it down into **subclassifications.** For example:

**subclassifications.**
Defining retail classifications further to show variables such as price, type, or brand.

Subclassifications by Price:
- Serums to $75
- Serums over $75

Or she might wish to divide the subclassifications into:
Subclassifications by Type/Brand:
- Basic serums
- Specialty serums

She will set up her classification structure based on whatever scenario makes the most sense in terms of her purchasing plan.

# SALES PLANNING

Sales planning affects your business in many ways. It can have an effect on:

- Global revenue: Retail sales account for a percentage of the total salon revenue. For example, retail accounts for, on average, 14 percent of a spa's total revenue (ISPA 2011 Spa Industry Study).
- Global profit: The gross margin is typically around 50 percent and a salon and spa's retail sales costs are variable.
- Buying strategy and inventory level: Errors in sales planning can lead to overstock and back orders.
- Income and the motivation of its staff: Accurate sales goals will motivate the staff to retail/earn more. Salon and spa professionals who succeed in their retail business give their staff clear and easy-to-understand retail sales goals.
- Sales forecasting begins after product selection has been made according to price strategy, trends, and the salon and spa philosophy.

## Forecast Sales for the Year

In the salon and spa industry, the primary traffic variable is the **booking ratio,** which is the volume of services divided by the total capacity (in hours). The busier a salon and spa is, the more retail opportunities it will have. A salon and spa can set its retail goals for the year according to its projected booking ratio. For an established business, you would evaluate the sales records for the previous year to estimate the booking ratio. You can then create a forecast for the upcoming year.

**booking ratio.** A customer traffic ratio used for sales planning to determine retail sales opportunities.

Example:

Last year the Seasons Salon and Spa performed 9,544 services and the booking ratio was 32 percent. The salon was open 2,966 hours last year.

Booking Ratio = Volume of services ÷ Total capacity (in hours)
9,544 ÷ 2,966 = 32%

Jazmine knows that the new massage therapist and hair stylists she recently hired have brought over a full book. She also knows the existing staff is becoming more established. Because of this information, she feels she can increase the booking ratio to 50% for her forecast.

For a new business, estimate the average revenue of the retail business compared to the total projected revenue. That is, if a salon or spa has total projected revenue of $750,000 a year and the retail business is projected to total $90,000 for the first year, then the retail will account for 12 percent of the total revenue.

To find the percentage of retail sold, divide the amount of retail sold by the total sales.

Example:
Percentage of Retail Sold = Amount of retail sold ÷ Total sales
0.12 = $90,000 ÷ $750,000
This answer multiplied by 100 gives you the percentage of 12 percent.

When forecasting retail sales, managers need to be conservative and realistic. The industry average is for retail to achieve 15–18 percent of total revenue. It is a number that has one of the greatest potentials for growth in the industry, yet fluctuates due to changes in the economic landscape and other outside factors, such as seasonality.

## Establish Seasonality

Once a salon and spa sets its global sales forecast in dollars for the year, the total sales forecast needs to be broken down by month.

Factors to consider when creating a monthly schedule include:

- Location: Many salons and spas may realize high/low seasons if located in a destination city, or in a resort with a holiday schedule or a slow summer period. For example, for a salon located in a resort catering to families, there may be a drop in traffic when school begins.
- Holidays: Business tends to increase during the holiday season. Anticipate fluctuations in the months right before and after a holiday. For example, right before the New Year, traffic will increase, then slow down.

HERE'S A TIP

The vendor calendar can be aligned with the salon and spa marketing calendar. For example, if vendor A is launching a new bath and body line in September, you can create a special in your retail space that month to promote that product.

- Past trends: For an established business, examine sales records one to two years prior to gauge sales for the forecast.
- The economy: Watch for changes in the economic landscape to be apprised of consumer spending habits.
- The vendors' marketing calendars: Consider the timing of launch of new products or promotions (such as a gift with purchase) or liter-size sales.

All of those factors can affect how your monthly forecast is made. Managers can begin by breaking down their retail calendar by month. They can then contact their vendors and ask them to provide their **marketing plan** for the year as early as possible. By looking at the expected traffic flow, you are then able to lay their seasonality factors out in something like the schedule seen here.

Once seasonality is established, managers can make monthly forecasts that are then put together in yearly sales. A monthly sales forecast for a salon and day spa is shown in Figure 2-1.

To further plan and assure your sales forecast considers the individual categories of products, you will need to break sales down by classifications and subclassifications. The figure established as the annual amount of sales in your forecast is divided among each of the salon and spa's merchandise classifications. In this example, the annual amount is $190,476.

Then each classification is broken down by month according to the seasonality, as shown in Figure 2-2. Since you have established your retail marketing calendar by month, adjust the monthly sales forecast of each classification according to the marketing calendar. Then check to make sure the sum of each classification equals the monthly total (Figure 2-3).

Retail sales do not happen by themselves. Each member of your staff is involved in the sales process at some point. Therapists, stylists, and front desk receptionists all need to know

## HERE'S A TIP

Ask your vendors about upcoming product launches and get your clients excited. For example, nail polish is ever-changing, and new collections are released several times per year. Anticipate these new color launches and pre-order your collection if possible. Announce the upcoming product to your clients in advance through e-mail campaigns, table tents, or in all of your communications to gain excitement.

**marketing plan.** Part of the business plan that gives a detailed strategy about how to promote the business, build a customer base, and make a profit.

Figure 2-1
Monthly Sales Forecast

| | Jan | Feb | Mar | Apr | May | Jun | Jul | Aug | Sep | Oct | Nov | Dec | Total |
|---|---|---|---|---|---|---|---|---|---|---|---|---|---|
| Seasonality (%) | 8 | 10 | 6 | 6 | 7 | 8 | 6 | 6 | 10 | 9 | 12 | 12 | 100 |
| Monthly sales | 15,238 | 19,048 | 11,429 | 11,429 | 13,333 | 15,238 | 11,429 | 11,429 | 19,048 | 17,143 | 22,857 | 22,857 | 190,476 |

Figure 2-2
Spa Seasonality Calendar

| | Jan | Feb | March | Apr | May | Jun | Jul | Aug | Sep | Oct | Nov | Dec | Total |
|---|---|---|---|---|---|---|---|---|---|---|---|---|---|
| My spa marketing plan | Redemption gift cards | Mailer: new facial | | | Mother's day | | | | Back to school | | Holiday | Holiday | |
| My vendor's marketing plan | | | | | | | | | | | | | |
| Skin care 1 | | New sun range | | | | | | | Oily skin promo | | Holiday sets | | |
| Skin care 2 | | | | | | Summer special | | | | | Holiday sets | | |
| Nail product | | | New nail polish | | | | | | | | | | |
| Seasonality (%) | 8 | 10 | 6 | 6 | 7 | 8 | 6 | 6 | 10 | 9 | 12 | 12 | 100 |

that you expect them to sell and generate retail revenue. Setting sales goals for each individual helps ensure the total salon or spa goal, and the individual staff members can track and review their performance and compare it to the sales goals.

One tool for tracking goals is the yearly sales forecast per employee, broken down per month or sometimes per week as shown in Figure 2-4. Planning this in advance allows salon and spa professionals to create a series of incentives for their staff throughout the year and to have tangible evaluation of their performance.

## Evaluate Sales Forecast Accuracy

The sales forecast is a very useful tool to monitor the business and will trigger a series of business decisions in the salon or spa: purchasing, inventory level, etc. Because it is only a forecast, you must analyze your actual sales results against the forecast each month. Wherever discrepancies are found, you will have to:

- Adjust the forecast
- Implement some marketing actions
- Create sales incentives
- Perform retail education for the staff
- Pursue remerchandising

More information on evaluating financial performance is available in Chapter 5.

Figure 2-3
Monthly Sales Forecast by Classification

| | Jan | Feb | Mar | Apr | May | Jun | Jul | Aug | Sep | Oct | Nov | Dec | Total | % of Total |
|---|---|---|---|---|---|---|---|---|---|---|---|---|---|---|
| **Products** | | | | | | | | | | | | | | |
| Skin care | 3,810 | 4,762 | 2,857 | 2,857 | 3,333 | 3,810 | 2,857 | 2,857 | 4,762 | 4,286 | 5,714 | 5,714 | 47,619 | 25 |
| Private label | 762 | 952 | 571 | 571 | 667 | 762 | 571 | 571 | 952 | 857 | 1,143 | 1,143 | 9,524 | 5 |
| Nail products | 762 | 952 | 571 | 571 | 667 | 762 | 571 | 571 | 952 | 857 | 1,143 | 1,143 | 9,524 | 5 |
| Makeup products | 1,524 | 1,905 | 1,143 | 1,143 | 1,333 | 1,524 | 1,143 | 1,143 | 1,905 | 1,714 | 2,286 | 2,286 | 19,048 | 10 |
| Hair products | 1,524 | 1,905 | 1,143 | 1,143 | 1,333 | 1,524 | 1,143 | 1,143 | 1,905 | 1,714 | 2,286 | 2,286 | 19,048 | 10 |
| Bath and body products | 1,524 | 1,905 | 1,143 | 1,143 | 1,333 | 1,524 | 1,143 | 1,143 | 1,905 | 1,714 | 2,286 | 2,286 | 19,048 | 10 |
| **Total products** | **9,905** | **12,381** | **7,429** | **7,429** | **8,667** | **9,905** | **7,429** | **7,429** | **12,381** | **11,143** | **14,857** | **14,857** | **123,809** | **65** |
| **Apparel** | | | | | | | | | | | | | | |
| Footwear | 457 | 571 | 343 | 343 | 400 | 457 | 343 | 343 | 571 | 514 | 686 | 686 | 5,714 | 3 |
| Men's unisex | 457 | 571 | 343 | 343 | 400 | 457 | 343 | 343 | 571 | 514 | 686 | 686 | 5,714 | 3 |
| Robes and terry | 457 | 571 | 343 | 343 | 400 | 457 | 343 | 343 | 571 | 514 | 686 | 686 | 5,714 | 3 |
| Women's | 914 | 1,143 | 686 | 686 | 800 | 914 | 686 | 686 | 1,143 | 1,029 | 1,371 | 1,371 | 11,429 | 6 |
| **Total apparel** | **2,286** | **2,857** | **1,714** | **1,714** | **2,000** | **2,286** | **1,714** | **1,714** | **2,857** | **2,571** | **3,429** | **3,429** | **28,571** | **15** |
| **Gift and accessories** | | | | | | | | | | | | | | |
| Book and media | 762 | 952 | 571 | 571 | 667 | 762 | 571 | 571 | 952 | 857 | 1,143 | 1,143 | 9,524 | 5 |
| Fashion accessories | 762 | 952 | 571 | 571 | 667 | 762 | 571 | 571 | 952 | 857 | 1,143 | 1,143 | 9,524 | 5 |
| Home | 762 | 952 | 571 | 571 | 667 | 762 | 571 | 571 | 952 | 857 | 1,143 | 1,143 | 9,524 | 5 |
| **Total gifts** | **2,286** | **2,857** | **1,714** | **1,714** | **2,000** | **2,286** | **1,714** | **1,714** | **2,857** | **2,571** | **3,429** | **3,429** | **28,571** | **15** |
| **Other retail** | | | | | | | | | | | | | | |
| Snacks and beverages | 305 | 381 | 229 | 229 | 267 | 305 | 229 | 229 | 381 | 343 | 457 | 457 | 3,810 | 2 |
| Sundries | 305 | 381 | 229 | 229 | 267 | 305 | 229 | 229 | 381 | 343 | 457 | 457 | 3,810 | 2 |
| Others | 152 | 190 | 114 | 114 | 133 | 152 | 114 | 114 | 190 | 171 | 229 | 229 | 1,905 | 1 |
| **Total other retail** | **762** | **952** | **571** | **571** | **667** | **762** | **571** | **571** | **952** | **857** | **1,143** | **1,143** | **9,524** | **5** |
| **Total retail** | **15,238** | **19,048** | **11,429** | **11,429** | **13,333** | **15,238** | **11,429** | **11,429** | **19,048** | **17,143** | **22,857** | **22,857** | **190,476** | **100** |

Figure 2-4
Monthly Sales Per Employee

| | Hr/week | Jan | Feb | Mar | Apr | May | Jun | Jul | Aug | Sep | Oct | Nov | Dec | Total | % of Total |
|---|---|---|---|---|---|---|---|---|---|---|---|---|---|---|---|
| **Estheticians** | | | | | | | | | | | | | | | |
| Monica | 40 | 3,352 | 4,190 | 2,514 | 2,514 | 2,933 | 3,352 | 2,514 | 2,514 | 4,190 | 3,771 | 5,029 | 5,029 | 41,905 | 22 |
| Courtney | 40 | 3,352 | 4,190 | 2,514 | 2,514 | 2,933 | 3,352 | 2,514 | 2,514 | 4,190 | 3,771 | 5,029 | 5,029 | 41,905 | 22 |
| **Total estheticians** | | **6,705** | **8,381** | **5,029** | **5,029** | **5,867** | **6,705** | **5,029** | **5,029** | **8,381** | **7,543** | **10,057** | **10,057** | **83,809** | **44** |
| **Massage therapists** | | | | | | | | | | | | | | | |
| Patricia | 40 | 610 | 762 | 457 | 457 | 533 | 610 | 457 | 457 | 762 | 686 | 914 | 914 | 7,619 | 4 |
| Elisabeth | 40 | 610 | 762 | 457 | 457 | 533 | 610 | 457 | 457 | 762 | 686 | 914 | 914 | 7,619 | 4 |
| **Total massage therapists** | | **1,219** | **1,524** | **914** | **914** | **1,067** | **1,219** | **914** | **914** | **1,524** | **1,371** | **1,829** | **1,829** | **15,238** | **8** |
| **Front desk** | | | | | | | | | | | | | | | |
| John | 40 | 1,524 | 1,905 | 1,143 | 1,143 | 1,333 | 1,524 | 1,143 | 1,143 | 1,905 | 1,714 | 2,286 | 2,286 | 19,048 | 10 |
| Amy | 40 | 1,524 | 1,905 | 1,143 | 1,143 | 1,333 | 1,524 | 1,143 | 1,143 | 1,905 | 1,714 | 2,286 | 2,286 | 19,048 | 10 |
| Bob | 20 | 762 | 952 | 571 | 571 | 667 | 762 | 571 | 571 | 952 | 857 | 1,143 | 1,143 | 9,524 | 5 |
| **Total front desk** | | **3,810** | **4,762** | **2,857** | **2,857** | **3,333** | **3,810** | **2,857** | **2,857** | **4,762** | **4,286** | **5,714** | **5,714** | **47,619** | **25** |
| **Stylists** | | | | | | | | | | | | | | | |
| Harry | 40 | 1,524 | 1,905 | 1,143 | 1,143 | 1,333 | 1,524 | 1,143 | 1,143 | 1,905 | 1,714 | 2,286 | 2,286 | 19,048 | 10 |
| Jean Pierre | 15 | 457 | 571 | 343 | 343 | 400 | 457 | 343 | 343 | 571 | 514 | 686 | 686 | 5,714 | 3 |
| **Total stylists** | | **1,981** | **2,476** | **1,486** | **1,486** | **1,733** | **1,981** | **1,486** | **1,486** | **2,476** | **2,229** | **2,971** | **2,971** | **24,762** | **13** |
| **Nail techs** | | | | | | | | | | | | | | | |
| Susie | 40 | 762 | 952 | 571 | 571 | 667 | 762 | 571 | 571 | 952 | 857 | 1,143 | 1,143 | 9,524 | 5 |
| Lucy | 20 | 457 | 571 | 343 | 343 | 400 | 457 | 343 | 343 | 571 | 514 | 686 | 686 | 5,714 | 3 |
| Sally | 10 | 305 | 381 | 229 | 229 | 267 | 305 | 229 | 229 | 381 | 343 | 457 | 457 | 3,810 | 2 |
| **Total nail techs** | | **1,524** | **1,905** | **1,143** | **1,143** | **1,333** | **1,524** | **1,143** | **1,143** | **1,905** | **1,714** | **2,286** | **2,286** | **19,048** | **10** |
| **Total retail** | | **15,238** | **19,048** | **11,429** | **11,429** | **13,333** | **15,238** | **11,429** | **11,429** | **19,048** | **17,143** | **22,857** | **22,857** | **190,476** | **100** |

## At the Beautiful You Day Spa…
## The Quarterly Retail Marketing Calendar

The Beautiful You Day Spa, in Carlsbad, California, leverages the help from product vendors to increase their retail sales potential. All 15 of their major product representatives are committed to making a quarterly visit to lead marketing events that focus on key products. For example, the representative of a product correcting under eye circles does a complimentary mini facial in the demo area and spotlights three key products in the system. She brings in free products for a raffle and has special pricing for the featured products. The event gains a lot of attention and generates sales because the event was marketed in advance. "Save the Date" e-mails were sent out a month in advance and the event was a part of a monthly calendar posted on the website on the store brochure.

# COMPENSATION

How **compensation** is designed will play a key role in the success of the salon or spa's retail operation. The compensation program must support the retail environment and give your staff the opportunity and incentive to make retail sales. In other words, it is important that you balance profitability with paying for performance. Accomplishing this in the retail area will require careful planning and evaluation.

The topic of compensation is a complicated one and the design of the overall compensation program is one that managers put a lot of time and effort into. Compensation encompasses everything from salary and wages to benefits to commissions, training, work environment, and work/life balance.

The biggest challenge for managers is determining which compensation strategy best suits their vision and philosophy. One strategy does not suit every salon and spa and each program affects the business to varying degrees. Typically, the more multifaceted a strategy is, the stronger the impact on business and the higher the level of return. Some businesses prefer a single compensation approach, others prefer a combination strategy, and more and more salons and spas are adopting a team-based solution because it consistently rates high in its ability to produce positive staff behaviors.

However, there are three key questions that you can ask yourself to determine the total compensation strategy. The total

**compensation.** What an individual receives for working in the salon or spa. These include base pay, commission, benefits, training, and non-monetary rewards.

compensation strategy should be straightforward and direct in answering these questions:

- What employee behaviors and results does the salon and spa value and wish to recognize through its compensation programs?
- Why are these behaviors and results to be recognized?
- How should the behaviors and results be recognized?

The answers to these questions can be the blueprint from which you design all of your compensation programs.

Salary and benefits will be part of the overall compensation plan and will rarely be localized in the retail department. However, staff commissions, pay structure, and incentives can have a direct impact on whether the retail operations will succeed and therefore should be carefully planned.

## Compensation Planning

Retail commissions have traditionally been a part of the overall compensation strategy. However, each salon and spa's individual strategy will come into play as managers determine what commission structure works for their business and who it rewards for retail sales.

There are several sources available to gather compensation data for salon and spa retail-related employees, as well as tools to help salons and spas develop a compensation plan. Figure 2-5 is a snapshot of various compensation designs for retail managers within spas and their popularity.

Figure 2-5
Retail Manager
Compensation
Agreement

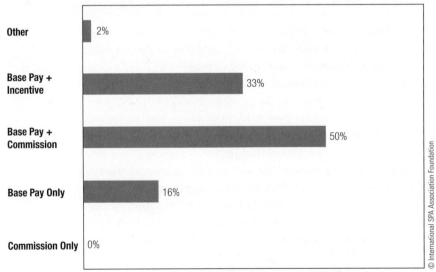

Percentage of Total Responses across All Spa Types

© International SPA Association Foundation

To find out what other salon and spas are paying their retail professionals as a base rate, incentives, commissions, and benefits, you can review industry reports discussing compensation or ask people in your professional network about their structures.

Your compensation structure can also provide the motivation for staff members to behave in certain ways. For example, if you offer a compensation structure with an incentive tied to client retention, your staff will get the message that client loyalty is a top priority for the salon and spa.

**FYI**

Keep in mind that, ultimately, the choice you make regarding compensation will communicate to your staff what the salon and spa's priorities are and what you expect from your staff.

## Commission Structures

There are three main ways to structure a commission program:

- Straight commission
- Tiered commission based on profitability
- Tiered commission based on productivity

### Straight Commission

Until recently, many salons and spas adopted the decades-old straight commission compensation strategy in which staff receives a generous percentage of services performed (40 to 50 percent) and a percentage of the products sold (10 to 20 percent). The percentage remained constant regardless of the treatment provided or the product sold and the staff was not compensated for down time under this model.

However, issuing such impressive commission rates is virtually impossible with today's cost of doing business. A straight commission strategy does not consider fluctuating operating costs or recognize that some services are more profitable than others.

Straight commission can also provide weak employee incentive. While the 10 percent commission on retail sold represents a potentially significant amount of net dollars earned, it does not stimulate sales in most salons and spas. Employees think of retail as an afterthought. They mistakenly regard the retail opportunity as minor, even though it requires no additional time. Your staff may ask why they should focus on retail when they get only a 10 percent commission when they're getting, for example, a 50 percent commission on giving a massage.

It is up to you as a manager to educate employees that retail commission is a perfect opportunity to work smarter, not harder—it takes far less time to make a retail sale than it does to perform a service.

One solution might appear to be to offer higher commissions on retail products. However, many vendors enforce a manufacturer's suggested retail price that allows a 50 percent gross profit. So raising the commission bites into the ability to pay for freight, taxes, display, and marketing—to say nothing of the needed profitability.

## Tiered Commission Based on Profitability

Another solution is to offer commissions on retail lines according to profitability. Products with higher profit margins can carry higher commissions. Lower profit products are commissioned lower.

Under this model, retail commissions might range from 5 percent to 30 percent. To establish a system like this, salon and spa professionals sort their retail products into classes based on product profitability. Figure 2-6 shows an example of how products could be broken up.

Figure 2-6
Tiered Commission Based
on Profitability

| Retail Product Class | Product Cost (as % of retail price) | Commission |
|---|---|---|
| Class I | 32% or less | 20% |
| Class II | 33–42% | 10% |
| Class III | 43–52% | 5% |
| Class IV | 53–60% | Non-commissioned |

© International SPA Association Foundation

For this type of system to work, a salon and spa needs a full-featured, well-integrated point-of-sale or payroll system so that the program can be managed accurately. The system has to let you assign a commission classification to the individual items.

Methods to lower product cost include:

1. Order larger quantities that provide price breaks.
2. Price products higher (increases gross profits). (Warning: Raising prices too high can price merchandise out of the competitive range and decrease its salability.)
3. Use private label as the "anchor" product in the retail mix.
4. Negotiate a lower cost of goods with the vendor.

## Tiered Commission Based on Productivity

This commission compensation strategy has levels, like a ladder, and staff can be motivated to move up the commission ladder. This

## At the Seasons Salon and Day Spa...

The Seasons Salon and Spa offers a tiered commission strategy based on productivity for the spa staff to encourage them to sell more retail.

Jazmine is explaining the commission structure to Daisy, a new nail technician on staff.

"In the first level—which is where you will start—you receive a 5 percent commission on each unit that you sell until the quantity of items sold totals $500 each pay period. In level 2, you will get an 8 percent commission on each additional unit sold until you accumulate $750 worth of items in a pay period. Upon reaching level 3, you get 10 percent commission on any more units sold for that pay period."

Example:

| Sales | Commission Percentage | Employee Pay |
|---|---|---|
| $1–$500 | 5 | $0–$25 |
| $501–$750 | 8 | $40.08–$60 |
| $751–$1,000 | 10 | $75.10–$100 |

"What this means," Jazmine explained, "is that if you make $775 in sales, you'll get 5 percent on the first $500, 8 percent on the next $250, and then 10 percent on the rest—or a total commission of $47.50."

is an established method and offers spas more flexibility than a straight program. Essentially, various commission percentage rates and performance goals are established for differing performance levels. Once staff achieves these predetermined targets, they graduate to a higher level and are entitled to receive a greater commission rate. This format allows you to define performance targets, establish margin objectives, and gives staff well-defined incentives.

Commission tiers are much more complex to initiate than straight commission and are time-consuming to manage without sufficient technology. Once performance goals and commission rates have been assigned, it is extremely laborious to track where staff ranks on the ladder.

## Staff Incentives

In addition to commissions, you can provide other incentives to the staff to promote sales. They might include such things as dinners, movies, gift certificates, and nonmonetary incentives.

Other ideas for staff incentives include:

- Offer a product of the month.
- Hold contests. Don't just focus on staff overachievers, but gear contests toward other members of the staff as well. It might include most sales of a particular category, most improved, most re-bookings.
- Offer paid time off.
- Increase employer-paid benefits.
- Offer small, unexpected rewards.

## At the Seasons Salon and Day Spa...

**SALON AND SPA SNAPSHOT 2.5**

Jazmine sipped a glass of cold pomegranate juice as she reviewed her monthly retail sales figures with satisfaction. Since she took over as salon and spa manager six months ago, she'd managed to dramatically increase the retail area's profitability.

It began with the one-day retreat she had held with her therapists, nail technicians and estheticians two weeks after she was hired. They'd spent the morning identifying what made the Seasons Salon and Spa special to its guests—why those guests returned to the salon and spa year after year.

Jazmine wrote out all of the core values that her staff identified and then began evaluating the products offered in the retail space. She ended up clearing out several products that didn't fit with the salon and spa's mission—products that were insufficiently tested or had little appeal to the guests. She even eliminated, albeit reluctantly, one of her favorite facial masks as none of the estheticians were comfortable recommending it and its packaging clashed with the colors of the space.

She worked with the point-of-sale vendor to reclassify several of the products. They also incorporated an inventory system that allowed her to conduct cycle counts and aggressively track the cost of sales and gross margin of each retail category.

From there, she'd created an annual forecast and broken it down into monthly forecasts by category and by employee. She set aside time on the first Monday of every month to review the forecasts and determine whether she needed to adjust any of her sales strategies. There was still a lot of work to do, but Jazmine was pleased with the results so far.

- Provide staff with thank-you cards for people who help them out.
- Hold special events to inspire team building.
- Trade with local vendors for gifts or rewards (such as swapping spa services with local restaurants for a staff member night out).
- Create games for product education (such as product education trivia, jeopardy, or hot potato).
- Offer $1 to $5 rewards for answering product trivia questions.
- Have a different contest of the day each day to focus staff on a particular goal.

# CHAPTER SUMMARY

- It is important in the planning process to know where your business is now, where you want it to go, and how you are going to get there.
- Your retail plan must be in sync with your salon and spa philosophy.
- Establishing a vision, mission, and core values are important elements in defining your business.
- Knowing your customers is essential in choosing the right retail product offerings.
- Retail classifications are an important part of the retail planning and forecasting process.
- Sales forecasting will help you to make important business decisions regarding purchasing and inventory.
- Compensation structures should encourage the attitudes and behaviors you wish to see in your staff.

# LEARNING ACTIVITIES

## Learning Activity 2-1: Lighting a Fire for Your Staff

Select a product from your retail offerings that has a high margin but isn't necessarily a top seller. Create an incentive program to encourage staff members to sell that item. Find nonmonetary ways to compensate staff for extra sales. Determine whether it would be profitable to change the commission structure on that item.

## Learning Activity 2-2: Shining the Crystal Ball

Prepare a retail sales forecast for the month. Consult three years of past history (if available). Make a list of any special events, promotions by competitors, promotions by the salon and spa, arts and other cultural events, vendor promotions, and weather forecasts (if available).

Create a retail sales forecast that break sales down for the month, by classification, and by employee.

# REVIEW QUESTIONS

1. Which of the following questions is the FOUNDATION of a salon and spa's retail plan?
   a. Where does the business want to go?
   b. Where is the business now?
   c. How is the business going to get where it wants to go?
   d. Where has the business been up until now?

2. Which of the following is a trend that lasts for several seasons, depending on the market?
   a. A fad
   b. A fashion
   c. A staple
   d. A seasonal item

3. The Dew Drop by Salon and Spa focuses on stress relief and restoration. Which of the following products would be most appropriate for it to offer in its retail area?
   a. Trendy women's cell phone totes
   b. A book on the results of recent research into sea algae and beauty products
   c. Workout pants with the salon and spa's logo
   d. Deep scrubs

4. Which of the following is the LEAST common method of compensating your service providers?
   a. Base pay plus incentive
   b. Base pay plus commission
   c. Base pay only
   d. Commission only

5. What does a salon and spa's target market represent?
   a. The entire client base
   b. The core client
   c. The periphery client
   d. The clients who are not yet using the salon and spa

6. What can be found in the salon and spa's mission and core values?
   a. The philosophy of the salon and spa
   b. The salon and spa director's job description
   c. The salon and spa's visual environment
   d. The pricing strategy

7. According to the *Uniform System of Financial Reporting for Spas,* in what subclassification do toners fall?
   a. Skin care
   b. Hair
   c. Nail
   d. Gifts and accessories

8. Ariana has just completed a customer survey gathering more information about the customers who make retail purchases in her salon and spa. She has compiled the information and sorted it into demographics and purchasing information. Which of the following data would be found in the demographics section?
   a. Estimated income of guests
   b. Average number of retail purchases by product classification
   c. Buying habits for retail products
   d. Perceptions of private label items versus brands

9. Which of the following sales forecasting factors would be considered a seasonality factor?
   a. Industry average of retail percentage of total salon and spa revenue
   b. Vendor's marketing calendar
   c. Prior month's sales history
   d. All of the above

10. The Printemps Salon and Spa offers commissions to its entire staff for retail sales. It gives a 5 percent commission on gift items, a 10 percent commission on apparel and skin care sales, and a 15 percent commission on private label products. What type of commission structure does it have?
    a. Tiered commission based on productivity
    b. Tiered commission based on profitability
    c. Straight commission
    d. Unstructured commission

# Purchasing

© Milady, a part of Cengage Learning.
Photography by Visual Recollection.

Chapter **3**

## INTRODUCTION

**P**urchasing often feels somewhat like shopping. You get to browse catalogs and brochures, sample products, and search for the best deals. However, unlike the individual shopper, you have a weighty responsibility on your shoulders.

The salon and spa's retail is a business and the product selection must go far beyond what you or your staff likes on a personal level. Purchasing must be approached with a **retail plan.**

Planning is your key to success, given that the retail operation has the potential to support the salon and spa with its significant profit margins. You or your buyer must make selections that fit with the philosophy of the salon, that successfully market the salon and spa, and that will have the greatest appeal to your guests. Because your retail operation supports your philosophy and is such an important entity, it is essential to form partnerships with your vendors, as they will become integral to your retail success by providing support to you and your staff. You don't want to simply place a catalog order from a nameless and faceless store.

## PURCHASE WITH A PLAN

Effective buying is more than placing orders and receiving inventory. It is having a plan about what merchandise the salon and spa will purchase, the retail mix, the budget, the vendors, the pricing, and how to create synergy between your retail lines. When considering a buying strategy, you may wish to consider the following:

- The philosophy of your salon or spa. Will the products support the message you wish to convey and your underlying purpose?

## LEARNING OBJECTIVES

After successfully completing this chapter, the reader will be able to:

- Describe the planning process for purchasing.
- Explain how to create a vendor structure.
- Research potential vendors.
- Hold productive meetings with retail product vendors.
- Select product lines that are appropriate for the salon and spa.
- Identify the activities that can bolster a salon and spa and vendor partnership.
- Describe the benefits and risks of private label products.
- Implement a private label line in a salon and spa and successfully market it.

## At the Season's Salon and Day Spa...

SALON AND SPA SNAPSHOT 3.1

JaRoss Salon and Resort Spa

Reuben clicked offline after making his plane reservations and went to the printer to pick up the confirmation. He would be leaving for the Salon and Spa Expo in 6 weeks. He was especially looking forward to the Expo as he'd made appointments with two of his vendor partners to discuss their new lines.

He filed away his confirmation and began walking through the boutique, straightening the bottles on the shelves and realigning the tent cards on the table.

Patty, one of his massage therapists, walked up to him as he was rearranging one of the moisturizing creams. "Reuben," she said, "I've been meaning to talk to you about that moisturizer. Can't we get rid of it? The fragrance is way too strong. As soon as I open it, my nose crinkles."

Patty opened her purse as she spoke and pulled out a small bottle of moisturizer. "Why can't we carry this brand instead? My mom brought it home from a spa she visited on vacation last summer and I've been ordering from their website ever since. It's the best stuff I've ever used. And it doesn't make my hands feel slimy like our stuff."

Reuben thanked Patty and wrote down the name of the moisturizer she'd liked so much. Perhaps he would look into it—after all, the moisturizer she was referring to was a slow mover with a lower profit margin than he'd like. The only thing was, Reuben had never heard of the vendor who made that new moisturizer. He'd have to find out more.

**retail plan.** A plan outlining the product lines carried, retail mix, budget, purchasing process, vendors, and pricing.

- Is there a need for the product? Or are you duplicating or competing with your existing lines?
- The quality of the products. Do they deliver what they promise?
- Does the price and brand mix fit with your existing clientele?
- Does the packaging fit in with the theme of your brand and is it appealing?
- Does your staff have positive feedback for the product and will they be able to recommend it with sincerity?

## Know Your Budget

Purchasing begins with effective budgeting and inventory management—topics covered thoroughly in Chapter 4 and Chapter 5. The budget helps you keep track of your reorder capability and what money you will have available to capitalize on trends.

Having determined what financial resources are available, you should remind yourself of the salon and spa's philosophy and key elements of the retail plan. For example, a medical salon and spa would be wise to retail products that focus on results over relaxation. A salon built near a metro area with surrounding businesses could very naturally feature stress-reducing products that are travel friendly.

Salon and spas have the ability to get creative with the items they carry. Keeping the salon and spa's philosophy and plans in mind, you can develop a unique and fun shopping experience. A salon and spa retail operation can strive to accommodate its client from head to toe. For the business focusing on relaxation, you can also consider related products, such as teapots, tea strainers, and honey sweeteners in addition to specialty teas. For a business focusing on business professionals, you can retail products sized for air travel and neck pillows and noise reducing headphones.

Keeping the mission of the retail department in harmony with the purpose of the salon and spa becomes paramount. A salon and spa retail store is not just about merchandising designer belt buckles or trendy scarves. The merchandise is instead selected to align with the purpose of the salon and spa and its work.

## Determine a Retail Mix

Salon and spa professionals are faced with the decision of what merchandise to select within each classification. In some cases, products purchased in one classification may coordinate with products purchased in another classification.

**FYI**

A fatal sales mistake for a salon and spa is to lack a unique mix of products that align with every service on the menu.

## HERE'S A TIP

Maintain a stock of travel-sized products of the most popular brands. Place these by the check-out area in eye-catching bowls. Clients wishing to try a product will be more inclined to do so if a smaller version is available.

**impulse item.** Any unplanned purchase a guest makes upon check out. These are usually small, inexpensive items chosen near the checkout counter.

You will need to carry unique products for therapists, technicians, and stylists, so they can provide recommendations for aftercare. Carrying the right mix of products addressing client needs is a critical part of providing a total service experience. So what are the typical products retailed by salons and spas? As you may expect, shampoo and conditioner and styling products are the main sources of retail revenue for salons. Spas lead with skin care and products such as moisturizer.

A retail error commonly made when purchase planning is for spas to stock only skin care products and salons to stock only hair care items. Salons and spas can bolster sales greatly by offering a wider mix of products such as cosmetics. Offering cosmetics keeps the salon and spa client out of the department, drug, and grocery stores for their beauty needs. Medical spas can benefit by adding cosmetics to their retail line-up for clients recovering from postoperative procedures and featuring products developed to soothe the skin. In this case, offering cosmetics will be a natural fit with the condition that the product line is corrective in nature and designed for postprocedure aftercare. Salons can also benefit by offering makeup applications and retail, as it extends the service offerings to include a total look make-over. The service menu can also include wedding day preparation with a hair and makeup package.

**Impulse items** can also bolster retail sales. Ideal impulse items include bath fizz balls, lipsticks, travel shampoo and conditioner, candles, even small items of clothing. A salon and spa can help boost its sales by stocking a certain number of these and putting them near the check-out counter.

## Developing a Purchasing Plan

It doesn't matter whether a salon and spa is on its first day of planning, six months out from opening day, or whether it has a thriving retail assortment that has been going gangbusters for years. All salon and spas have to take the time to really think through a few key questions before they start to buy. This sort of ongoing basic planning provides the salon and spa with an excellent framework for choosing or updating its product mix.

Some salon and spa managers create an organized plan by considering the following topics:

- Price points
- Product classifications
- Seasonal products
- Pricing schemes

## Price Points

What is the salon and spa's overall range of price points and are all necessary price points covered? You should investigate and/or carefully consider how much your customers will spend on retail products. The key word here is *balance.*

There is a fine line between trying to make customers feel comfortable with the prices of retail items and leaving room for the business to make a profit. Part of the art of retailing is embracing the idea of introducing customers to products that meet their needs, and which they may at first think are "too expensive." If your staff members are excited about the product and feel knowledgeable, they will be able to help customers value the quality of the product first and reduce their price sensitivity. However, salon and spas must also be careful about not overdoing it.

It is very important to know your target audience and their pricing thresholds. Businesses succeed most when they know who their customers are and find products that they know will not overwhelm those customers from a pricing standpoint. For example, they do not choose the most expensive products out there if their typical client is a young college student on a tight budget.

## Product Classifications

What product classifications does the salon and spa expect customers to buy from? One of the easiest ways for you to identify product classifications is to reflect on the treatments offered and choose corresponding retail products that are in alignment.

For example, if a salon's specialty is hair color, a wide selection of styling products to maintain color and bring out shine will be the easiest sell. A spa might highlight facials as a specialty. In that case, it might offer a nice mix of skin care so that its customers can follow up with a skin care regimen at home between visits. If the spa offers yoga classes, perhaps it will choose to also include clothing in its retail selection.

Remember, you must strike a balance between the services you offer and the retail products that go along with these types of services. If only a small amount of your business comes from tanning services, then only offer only a small amount of tanning related retail products. You must also be careful to provide what the clients want to purchase, even if it doesn't seem directly tied to a service. For example, if pedicures are a major part of your business, then carrying flip flops would be a good item to retail.

## Seasonal Products

Will the salon and spa want to include seasonal products? Many retail lines offer special packaging for their existing products and even new products based on seasons and holidays. Because retail salon and spa space is limited, you may find yourself planning for holidays and seasons well in advance of their arrival.

By planning ahead and knowing that certain products will be available only during certain months or times of the year, you are able to make room for the products when they arrive and also plan your promotion of the products.

## Pricing Schemes

What type of products will guests not only desire, but also purchase? Price levels and their relationship to the guest are important to success and sometimes tricky to establish. In general, most retail stores operate on a "good-better-best" pricing philosophy and cover their classifications and key categories with one primary vendor per category as follows:

© Losevsky Pavel/www.Shutterstock.com

- Good: The opening price range for the spa's customer—a price and perhaps brand name (or proprietary signature line) that all customers would be comfortable with in terms of price and ease of use.
- Better: The next level up in terms of quality, price, and exclusivity and may require more expertise when selling or explaining features and benefits to consumers. These items appeal to someone who might know and appreciate new styles or higher-end features such as finer

ingredients. These customers may be willing to spend more to buy those benefits.

- Best: The salon and spa's top line—usually the top 10 percent or less of your customers are the target for the highest end of products you carry. Customers are willing to pay top dollar for such things as exclusivity, newness, special ingredients, or place of origin. This merchandise will require a well-trained staff that is knowledgeable about the "Why should I buy this?" and "What makes this the best?" type questions. The customers for these items are probably well-read and well-traveled and have interests in fashion and luxury products. Because of this, they can be demanding in terms of expectations.

A good-better-best approach to pricing is a useful pricing strategy for many reasons. By splitting lines according to these tiers, you can help avoid duplication at some price levels and missed opportunities at others. You can also introduce your clients to products they would not ordinarily consider purchasing if it weren't for the lower-tiered pricing options. For example, your client may be reluctant to purchase a much-needed serum if he or she were only offered in the "best" category, but might choose a serum offered in the better or best category.

The more you can learn about your clientele, the more likely you are to know their price sensitivity and what ranges have the most appeal. Different types of retail operations have different pricing philosophies.

Example:
Walmart® is going to have a low mark-up with a high volume and a huge selection. A department store is going to have a higher mark-up with a lower volume. Boutiques and most salon and spas fall into this category. They going to have a high mark-up with a low volume and a smaller selection.

The following are some additional questions that may be considered when creating a purchase plan:

- What types of products are in harmony with the salon and spa's philosophy and theme?
- Does the current product line have a proper assortment—color, type, sizes, etc.?

- Will the product groups complement one another?
- Is there a consistent overall appearance in packaging?

# CREATE A VENDOR STRUCTURE

**sell through.** A
product performance
percentage rate to tell you
how well a product is selling.
Weekly Sales ÷
Beginning Inventory for the
Week = Sell Through

Creating a well-thought-out vendor structure can provide continuity and better **sell through,** which tells you the percentage of product sold. There will be more about this topic in Chapter 4, Inventory Management. Dividing vendors into categories, such as key and peripheral, allows you to maximize relationships with vendors and provides a consistent and interesting product mix.

A key vendor represents the majority of purchases that generate sales in a particular category, or is a vendor whose product is represented consistently throughout each selling season. Key vendors allow you to develop continuity in how the retail area looks, quality of products, and pricing. You have to put in a lot of careful thought and research when choosing key vendors, as these vendors will become your partners and support your retail success.

Peripheral vendors represent smaller groups within the product plan. They may or may not have consistent representation on the selling floor. An example of a peripheral vendor might be a company that provides seasonal items. Peripheral vendors allow salon and spas to test new products and vendors, add variety, and give the salon and spa balance. Some of the following questions regarding each company, their products, and their quality levels can also help you choose vendors:

**Company**
- Is this vendor financially stable?
- Who are the principal owners of the company?
- Where is the product manufactured?
- Does this company understand the unique elements of your business?
- Would you feel comfortable working with this vendor?
- How many lines does this vendor produce annually?

**Products/Services**
- Does this vendor offer the products your customers desire?
- What is the depth of selection that this vendor offers in relevant classifications?
- Where does the vendor fit into your price scheme? Low? Moderate? High?

- Does the vendor take an interest in your mission, goals, and philosophy?
- What is the turnaround time for stock item reorders?
- Can this vendor ship the orders on time and complete?
- What are the vendor's return policies?
- Will the vendor provide assistance when problems occur?

**Marketing Support**

- Does the vendor offer co-op advertising and promotional assistance?
- Is the vendor's representative available for support such as trunk shows, fashion shows, product demonstrations, and inventory assistance?
- How many times during the season will a representative visit the salon and spa?
- Does the vendor take an interest in your sell through and assist in product movement?
- Does this company affiliate with or use a portion of the products' sales to support an event or charitable/environmental cause?
- Does the vendor provide research to support effectiveness claims?

**Other**

- Are there any exclusivity arrangements with the vendor?
- How will import restrictions (ingredients, product types, packaging, product description wording) affect the availability and expense of the vendor's products?
- Is the product's packaging consistent with your salon or spa's philosophy and beliefs?

# VENDOR SELECTION

Getting a start on vendor selection can be overwhelming. Whether a salon and spa is planning a new retail space or just rethinking its current one, there are some guidelines for each step that can help a salon and spa professional through this process.

The steps you'll take include:

- Research several vendors
- Attend trade shows

- Meet with vendors
- View the product lines
- Select product lines
- Establish a receiving system

Guidelines for each of these steps are suggested in the following sections of this chapter.

## Research Vendors

Before you choose your vendors, it is important to research several options. There are numerous vendors, products, and merchandise that might or might not work for any given salon and spa. Vendors who have a successful relationship with one salon and spa might not be a good fit for another.

Thankfully, you also have a wide variety of resources that you can draw upon to research vendors and products. Given the wealth of information on the large number of different vendors, you are likely to find it helpful to create some sort of system to organize the information on an ongoing basis. It may be a collection of file folders in which you can save print-outs, ads, articles, and other items. You may want to have everything on a file on your laptop. What's important is that you find what works for you and have an organized collection of information that you can draw upon as needed.

What sort of information are you going to collect for your vendor research about products, or about trends affecting salons and spas? This information can be found in the following ways:

- Trade magazines
- Industry events and trade shows
- Word of mouth
- Direct communication from vendors
- Related industry publications and events

Trade magazines are invaluable sources of vendor information and an easy place to begin research. You can rip out product ads in magazines from vendors that get your attention. You might also find articles about emerging trends.

Salon and spa industry events, such as ISPA's Conference & Expo or the International Beauty Show, are a wonderful place to network with vendors, make business connections, and make new friends. These peers can provide many recommendations and share stories about vendors and their experiences with them. There is also a wealth of vendor information found at trade shows and exhibitions. There are many events to choose from, so careful preplanning will help you use your time most efficiently.

Word of mouth is another source of vendor and product information. You can glean information from current and former customers and vendor staff. Their comments about a product line can alert you to product lines you may not yet be familiar with.

As a salon or spa manager, you will receive direct communication and product samples from vendors. This can include product ingredient information, company information, and sample products for you to review at your leisure.

Finally, related industry events and magazines are also a source of information that may not be directly targeting your industry, yet can provide unique retail options. For example, fitness, hospitality, and other related industries have trade shows and publications that may provide new ideas. While doing research, it is important to find out if a vendor represents one product or a number of products. If a vendor is focused on one brand of product and your account executive has a great deal of product knowledge, he or she can provide in-depth education on the product. This may be important if the treatment requires a certain level of technical expertise, such as a laser machine or a hair extension system.

In some cases, you may work with a distributor, who is a channel of delivery to make products available to businesses. Some distributors are one-stop shopping sources that bring together many lines to offer a salon and spa a complete shopping package. Others may be distributors of a brand, but may not bring with them the guarantees and support, such as education, that the brand itself would offer.

## Attend Trade Shows

Major trade shows are a good place to research and select vendors. Major, national, or international trade shows provide salon and spa professionals with a wealth of information and contacts. An organized and systematic approach to attending trade shows can help you and your staff make the most of your time and travel costs.

At your earliest convenience, determine your annual budget and decide which trade shows members of your salon or spa will attend during the year. This allows you to establish a travel budget for the retail department. It also enables you and your attendees to register early to gain reduced fees and to have more time to prepare.

Before the show, review all the information that you can get to predetermine whether most of the vendors you are interested in will be at this show. Trade shows typically have lists of exhibitors available before the show begins. If there are vendors on the list that you are not familiar with, you can research them through trade publications or on the Internet.

Next, check your current inventory for sell through. Evaluate how your current vendors are performing. While checking inventories for reorders, determine whether you need to adjust the assortment with a particular vendor to get a better turnover. (See Chapter 4: Inventory Management, for more details on evaluating turns.) You might also review new trends that you want to see represented in your retail inventory and perhaps conduct a brief customer survey at this time.

Having done these reviews, you can make a list of questions that you want to have answered at the show—either by vendors or by other attendees of the trade show who have well-established relationships with vendors.

Trade shows can be quite overwhelming, especially when attending an international show where many disciplines are represented. Such large-scale shows may span across several areas of the convention center or hotel. Arriving at a show early gives you time to pick up a trade show book and map out your day, marking each vendor that you want to visit.

There is no set strategy to cover the various vendor booths or seminars. Each person will have a strategy that works best. There are those who recommend first taking a quick walk through the aisles—going row-by-row so that nothing is missed—to allow time to spot new vendors and trends and to make notes as to which vendors to spend more time with. During this initial walk-through, schedule appointments with key vendors, leaving space in your schedule to add smaller or new vendors. Others recommend immediately visiting key vendors, then peripheral vendors, and then walking the show.

Regardless of your approach, one key point in setting appointments is to analyze vendors by classifications. So if you know that you need two or three skin care lines and a hair straightening system, you might set appointments with several vendors in each of these areas representing different quality levels. The advantage to setting appointments in this fashion is that it makes it easier for you to compare products and to analyze the features and benefits of each product.

## HERE'S A TIP

If you have a few members of your staff in attendance, you may wish to ask them to participate in the research. Assign a vendor to each staff member so they can assist you.

After the first walk-through, time can be devoted to scanning the booths and setting further appointments. If the show is large, it is advisable to set appointments by geographic area to save time walking back and forth between appointments. There are several things that you can accomplish while walking a show. You can:

- Look at the total picture by taking time to shop and interpret the market.
- Identify trends, looking at direction changes in areas such as ingredients, fragrances, colors, and purchasing.
- View experts providing treatments or sample new product.

One of the advantages to trade shows is that you can get personal time with potential vendors. It is an opportunity to talk with them and perhaps even learn of special offerings. Many vendors will accept orders at a show—though some experts advise that you mark any orders as "hold for confirmation" and that the confirmation be given after the show.

Ask yourself the following questions to help focus your time:

- What company provides you with your best-selling product?
- What equipment vendors are important to that upcoming project you have this year?

Fill at least 50 percent of your available trade show time with those primary contacts. Then open your schedule up to learning about those products that you may not have considered before. Reach out to vendors you're interested in prior to the show. What are your target vendors offering at the show in terms of opening deals? What new concepts or products will they be showing? If you think it's a possible match for your business outcomes, then add them to your schedule. Finally, leave 20 percent of your time to walk the show and be open to seeing what's new.

## Meet with Vendors

Before adopting products or establishing a vendor partnership, you will want to have a meeting with each potential vendor. This might be at the trade show or at your salon and spa. Many vendors have sales representatives who travel and will bring products in so that you can view the line.

© Milady, a part of Cengage Learning. Photography by Paul Castle.

To do your due diligence, during these meetings, in addition to viewing new lines of products, ask about product claims and assure you receive data on any clinical trials or actual client results. You want to be sure you are bringing in a product that delivers on all promises so your credibility is supported. Always be aware that the sales representative is trained to persuade you to purchase a large starter kit or increase your initial order to get a price break. Evaluate these incentives against your budget and projected sell through. A true vendor partner will balance his or her desire to sell with the interest in your total retail strategy and goals.

When meeting with a new vendor, many salon and spa professionals have found it best to begin the meeting by giving a brief synopsis of the salon and spa and any retail they are currently doing. This is also the time to share with the vendor your salon and spa philosophy, a description of your typical customer, other lines the salon and spa has tried, your price points, and how different products have performed in the past. This helps the vendor direct you toward certain products and begin building a partnership.

As with any relationship, the early stages are spent getting to know one another better. There are several questions you can ask potential vendor partners to learn more about their company and product:

- Where is the company located and/or where will the product be shipped from?
- Where is the product manufactured?
- How many lines per year do they release?
- What range of price points do they offer and do they fit into the salon and spa's model?
- Once an order is placed, what are the lead times for stock items?

- Are reorders generally available and what is the turnaround time?
- Does the vendor have a minimum order dollar amount?
- Is there a vendor representative available in your geographic area to visit the salon and spa for product information, training, or helping check inventory levels to aid with reorders?
- How can the salon and spa establish credit payment terms with this vendor?
- Does the vendor offer any product signage, co-op advertising, promotional assistance, or possibly store fixturing for their products?
- What product ingredients are used and what are their effects?
- Is private labeling an option with this vendor and, if so, what are the costs involved, minimums, etc.?
- If at a trade show, are there any incentives to write an order at the show?

## View the Product Lines

Once the initial discussions regarding product lines are complete, view the product lines with the vendor. You might go through each entire line or focus in on the products that you are most interested in. As you view the line, let the vendor know which products you would like to focus on and which ones you are not interested in.

It may be tempting to focus on products you like or what your staff may favor. It is important to keep in mind the philosophy of your salon or spa and the needs of your customer. Just as product type and quality is important in choosing a line, packaging is also an important component. Salon and spa retail succeeds best when it matches the space and services provided. You will want the retail products you choose to fit into the environment. They should be an extension of the tone and atmosphere you wish to create.

If your salon and spa color scheme can be described as beige, cream, classic, and serene, then a line that features edgy

products in bold, fluorescent packaging may be a bad fit. Similarly, if the space is decorated with clean lines and a minimalist feel, you should choose products that mimic that tone.

The products offered must also match the philosophy and spirit of the staff. Does the salon and spa staff pride itself on a commitment to eco-friendly living? If so, select products and packaging that share this same philosophy. Do you strongly oppose animal testing or do you have a salon and spa with an organic philosophy? When choosing your retail products, it is important to examine your personal philosophy and the message conveyed to customers, and to harmonize those ideas with your retail selection.

During the review process, you can discuss the wholesale price points of products, suggested retail pricing, and how the products fit into your overall retail price objectives. The vendor can also provide input on what the brand's top sellers are by classification, style, and color. Once again, this is part of building a good vendor partnership. The better the exchange of information, the better your product selection should be.

This is also the time to get input from your staff. Gaining input is important because you want commitment from your staff. Although everyone has an opinion, it is ultimately you who must choose the product mix. As the cliché goes, you can't please everyone all of the time. Successful managers aim to please most of their staff most of the time where retail products are concerned.

Gaining support for the products you will carry is important. If your staff uses and likes the products you choose to carry, then they will be your greatest assets on the selling floor. Nothing is more compelling than a personal testimony. If the staff can look their customers in the eyes and say, "I have this lotion in my purse right now because I can't leave home without it," or "I wouldn't skip this conditioner for a day if you paid me to!" or "I love this loungewear set—it's my favorite thing to put on after a long day at work!" then they will likely make the sale.

At this time, you may be ready to have the sales representative write the order, or you may want to view other lines before making a final decision. Before placing the order, though, you may want to once again ask yourself the following questions:

- Is this the correct product for the salon and spa's philosophy?
- Is this the right product for the customers—quality, price, and image?

- How will it complement our merchandise with the other lines in this category?
- How will you display the products?
- How does the delivery of each selection fit into the salon and spa's event calendar, monthly or quarterly budgets, etc.?
- How do you personally feel about working with this vendor? Does the vendor offer a partnership approach to important issues?
- What product knowledge, education, and sampling does the vendor offer?

## Select Product Lines

When selecting product lines, it is easy to become overwhelmed with narrowing down your options. A simple way to approach this task is to start with selecting the product lines that are used for professional treatments. These are the products that salon and spa customers are going to be most interested in and your service staff is going to most support.

If you wish to explore other factors, such as the current market trends, you may want to gain an overall sense of what is selling within your target customer group. Talk with various vendors to learn more, then supplement this information with your own observations and research in comparable salons and spas. This will help you identify what products and types of products will work well over time so you can incorporate these into your product mix. You may also wish to consider the products that your competitors are carrying. Do you want to have the same item as your neighbor? What associations do the salon and spa's guests make with the other businesses that carry the products? Is there a particular product that is working extremely well for a competitor?

Perhaps on an even more basic level, you will want to ask yourself what your customers' needs are, whether you can or should supply those needs, and whether they can make a profit selling the items that meet those needs.

As opposed to exploring multiple lines, you may want to feature one major brand and utilize it in all service areas. Aveda lifestyle salon and spas or Paul Mitchell concept salons are just two examples of a branded salon and spa experience that have profited by this strategy. A single product line offers a strong brand identity and cooperative advertising with the vendor. When considering a single product line, check with your vendor to research any programs they offer for this purpose.

Part of the art of retail is to trust one's instincts after satisfying the steps in the science of retail. The time to sit and write orders is at the end of this research process, while everything is still fresh in your mind. Once you have done all of your homework, and gained trust in your vendor's capability to partner with you, move forward with the ordering process then assure your internal systems are in place.

**SALON AND SPA SNAPSHOT 3.2**

## At the Fathom Salon...
## Vendors as Partners

Fathom Salon in San Diego, California, operates with a distinct philosophy that makes them unique. Every treatment they deliver is marine-based, with products derived from seaweed and algae. The styles that emerge from the salon are natural, soft, and free-flowing. Because of their clearly defined concept, they thought it best to become a single line salon and gain marketing support from the vendor. Before making the decision to sign with this vendor, the owner, Tom, made sure that the vision of the two companies aligned, that they had similar artistic themes in terms of hair design, and that there would be plenty of support resources. The staff is well-trained on the products, they have become advocates of retail, and are motivated toward success. The vendor continually recognizes the team for their high sales volume and provides products for the various marketing events. The power of aligning with one vendor has paid off for the salon, and after just two years, Fathom has been designated as a premier salon with the vendor.

## Establish a Receiving System

Before you can have an order processed from a vendor, you will most likely need to establish credit, as some vendors will not start processing an order from a new company without credit information. This usually takes the form of a credit card on file, or an extension of credit terms from the vendor, or a COD arrangement. Likewise, if the product is going to be a private label, or if the salon and spa's logo is to be embroidered on garments, you must have the graphics sent to the vendor.

After the necessary paperwork is completed and you have placed your order, you will want to create a process to handle the merchandise once it arrives at your salon or spa. Receiving actually begins before product arrives at the salon and spa—it includes making sure that you can track the shipment once it leaves the vendor. You may have a person assigned for this important task, making it his or her responsibility to assure incoming orders are accounted for. An organized receiving system can track purchases and make sure that they are correctly recorded and out on the shelves rather than languishing in a box where they cannot be sold.

Most salon and spas maintain a purchase order log—either manually or using their point-of-sale system. The log includes vendor name, brief description, cost of product, retail cost, mark-up percentage, and a space for comments about special orders or promotions. Many point-of-sale systems will have databases where this information can be input. The dollar amounts of purchase orders are entered into the budget spreadsheets during the month that they are expected to arrive.

Common receiving procedures include:
- Check incoming products against purchase orders or purchase records.
- Check incoming products against standard purchase specifications.
- Check incoming products against delivery invoices.
- Accept incoming products.
- Move accepted products to storage or to the selling floor immediately.
- Complete necessary receiving documents.

You will also need to establish receiving policies for both organizational and control purposes. Policies will cover: late orders, partial shipments, and substitutions.

## Late Orders

What do you do with orders that arrive late? It helps to make the purchase order very clear whether a date is a "shipped by" or a "received by" date, especially when the products are needed by a particular day. If the vendor does not comply with those dates, the person receiving the items needs to know whether to return the merchandise or request a discount or free freight before accepting merchandise. It is customary in the industry to accept merchandise past the cancellation date, but this needs to be negotiated before the merchandise is processed.

## Partial Shipments

Will you accept partial shipments? Partial shipments can increase your freight cost and decrease your margin on merchandise if multiple shipments occur. Economy of scale makes multiple shipments more expensive than single shipments. Partial shipments decrease the salon and spa's likelihood of achieving its sell through standards (see Chapter 4: Inventory Management). For example, if an apparel vendor ships a style with sizes small and extra large, but no medium or large, it will make it difficult to sell because the most common sizes are not represented.

## Substitutions

What do you do about substitutions? If you order shampoo for color-treated hair and the vendor ships shampoo for normal hair, will you accept it? The receiver needs to know in advance what to do if there are deviations from the purchase order. You may want the receiver (if you have assigned this responsibility) to set aside the merchandise so you can make a determination about whether to accept and on what terms. Remember, once the merchandise is processed, ticketed, and paid, your negotiating leverage is minimized. Also, the sooner negotiations occur—usually within 24 to 48 hours from receipt of the merchandise—the more negotiating leverage you will have.

© NAN728/www.Shutterstock.com

Many salon and spas have found it helpful to put their receiving policies in a memo or e-mail and communicate that information to all of the vendors. This memo might include things like—must the cartons be marked with the salon and spa name (something that is common in resorts or other businesses with multiple departments where products may be received in one central location)? Do cartons need to be marked with the PO number? Do invoices need to be included with shipment? Is the billing address different from the shipping address? Should the invoice be billed to a different name than the salon and spa's name (i.e., a parent company)?

While all of these factors are often covered during the initial meeting with the vendor, written confirmation and communication can save potential inefficiencies and headaches down the road.

The person designated to receive the merchandise needs to check the actual shipment compared to the purchase order and the vendor's invoice or packing slip by all available attributes, such as item name, item description, style, size, color, and SKU (stockkeeping unit). While many people think it is acceptable to check at one level, such as style level or item name, to verify items are correct, this does not tell the entire story. For example, if you ordered 12 face creams for antiaging, and you receive 12 face creams for dry skin, you may not notice the substitution if you only check against price and item count. These products could inadvertently be placed on your shelf and go unnoticed for several days, if not more. This may be too long to get replacement product ordered and delivered to meet your customers' needs. As a result, your customers may go elsewhere to purchase the product, and your sell through is adversely impacted. Procedures for ticketing (pricing) also have to be established for each classification of your retail. You must determine whether you are going to use vendor/ UPC bar codes or tickets or whether you will generate your own unique coding. Some salon and spas might require hangtags or price stickers or you may also have a standard place to put the price tags on merchandise.

Many retailers use their own hangtags or price tags to reinforce their brand identity. The tags can contain the salon and spa's logo while clearly and effectively marking the price and other necessary information.

Reorders have the potential for loss of good information if they are not ticketed with the same exact style, size, color, and SKU information and so forth, as original orders. Cross-checking purchase orders for consistency can help you avoid this problem.

After the products have been received, the invoice needs to be processed promptly to pay the vendor within the purchase order terms. Paying bills promptly will go a long way to establishing strong vendor relationships and will help avoid disruption in the receipt of your products. It also helps you to take advantage of any potential discount opportunities that can make your salon or spa more profitable.

After your order has been verified and discrepancies are handled, merchandise can be moved to the selling floor or the designated back stock area. It is important for you to pre-designate the procedure of where receiving is done. Preferably it is not done on the selling floor, as this increases the chance of loss or errors and decreases customer service because of the cumbersome nature of the process. Many salon and spas set standards for the time for merchandise to travel from receipt to the selling floor. These standards are typically 48 to 72 hours from time of receipt of shipment.

# VENDOR PARTNERSHIPS

The relationship between salons and spas and their vendors can go far beyond the simple provision and purchasing of products. The relationship is one that can develop into a partnership—a partnership that is of equal value to both the vendor and the salon and spa. When this happens, the vendor goes from being a seller to being a resource partner.

In these relationships, salon and spas share information with their vendors and vendors help provide training, marketing, and sales incentives. Therefore, you should find

© olly/www.Shutterstock.com

vendors who are willing to train your staff, offer incentives, give specials periodically, and help support your retail venture.

You also need to communicate to vendors who the appropriate contacts are in your salon and spa. Who do vendors talk to when they want to discuss a product, billing, promotions, or training?

It is also important that you and your staff respect the time and expenses of their vendors. If a vendor schedules training and comes to your salon and spa to conduct that training, you need to make sure the training session is well-attended. If it is not well-attended or well-organized and the vendor is required to come back—that may be a factor in future increased costs. It's like eating one or two grapes in the grocery store. If it's one to two grapes, what is the big deal? But if everyone does it, the cost of grapes goes up. If vendors are wasting funds on ineffective/poorly attended training sessions, the cost of that is ultimately passed on to everyone.

Vendors' support comes in the form of: a direct contact person, promotional support, in-store demonstrations, exclusivity, and/or liability insurance.

- Direct contact: Vendors should provide you with a dedicated representative. This is someone you can call directly to discuss all matters that pertain to your retail, including product information, shipments, schedules, and payments. You should be confident that this representative understands your business and will happily answer any and all of your concerns.
- Promotional support: Vendors benefit from you selling their products, and they should be eager to boost your marketing efforts by providing posters, point-of-purchase displays, or other signage to go along with your product order.
- In-store demonstrations: Frequently, vendors have programs that are available to any salon and spa that requests them. They may send a trained representative to do in-store demos with their products or introduce new technology that helps to promote their products. Ask prospective vendors whether they will be able to send a representative to conduct these types of events, which are a great chance for you to get people into your retail space for a fun, hands-on experience with your products.
- Exclusivity: While many salon and spas would like to be included on the vendor's website as the retailer in their area, they do expect vendors to understand their need to provide exclusivity to their customers. Be leery about partnering with vendors who don't pick their market and sell to department stores or directly to the consumer online. You don't want to have to compete with Internet sales direct to the customer.
- Liability insurance: Some vendors offer coverage on their liability insurance in case a customer sues over something related to the product. Normal liability coverage might be $1 million per occurrence with an umbrella of up to $4 million. Vendors will provide you with a document from their liability carrier that you can share with your own carrier to help keep insurance claims and premiums under control or reduced. This is most likely to occur with products that either go on the skin or are digestible. It is less likely to be available for apparel, books, gifts, or accessories.

# CREATING A PRIVATE LABEL PRODUCT LINE

Private label refers to those products that have the salon and spa's name on them. It might be a logo on a sweatshirt, hair care products, or an entire skin and body care line. Few salons and spas will carry only private label items: most will have a mix of private label and branded products.

While 42 percent of salon and spas within the industry have private label products, there is also a direct correlation between the size of the salon and spa and whether it carries private label products. Among salon and spas that make less than $100,000 a year, only 29 percent have private label products. That number climbs to 81 percent among salon and spas that make $3 million or more.

There are a great many benefits and risks to carrying private label and the expenses can often outweigh the benefits for smaller salon and spas. However, having a product that is consistent with the salon and spa's philosophy in every way can contribute to the salon and spa's overall branding and help build loyalty while building the bottom line.

Given that private labeling can be profit-busting for some salon and spas and profit-driving for others, salon and spas must carefully analyze their benefits and risks before making the decision to go with a private label product.

## Benefits of Private Labeling

Private label products create an extension of the overall experience at a salon and spa. The products used by the technicians, therapists, or designers are uniquely associated with the retail offerings and act as an intense sampling experience for them. Products are also a take-home advertisement that helps maintain loyalty and frequent re-visits to either experience the same or different treatments and to purchase products exclusively available at your salon and spa.

The experience is extended to the home as a continuation of the service, creating a continuum with your salon and spa. The client returns to you for more intensive service, for example, a facial or deep conditioner, and to

© Svetlana Lukienko/www.Shutterstock.com

get a refill of the products. When a salon and spa has exclusivity of the product source, it keeps the experience proprietary and maximizes guest loyalty.

Guest loyalty is promoted when you create a unique, quality product. This may be a scent or fragrance, color, texture, or bottle design for your private label. This creation can also enhance the exclusivity component of your salon and spa's marketing plan.

With private labeling, you are using your resources to support your own brand, rather than promoting dedication and loyalty to someone else's brand that is available from many sources.

There is value added in that the product is closely associated with the salon and spa that they have come to associate with wellness, relaxation, and beauty.

Private label products also allow you to create and stock products that are closely associated with your respective markets—products that take advantage of indigenous ingredients or methods. You can add products to your offerings that meet your personal specifications.

In Chapter 1, it was discussed that salon and spa retail fulfills the emotional need that some people have to shop. That emotion, that feeling, is something that private label products cater to. Guests are able to purchase a souvenir that reminds them of the positive experience they had at the salon and spa. Guests are able to closely associate the product with your salon or spa.

Finally, private labeling can add value to your business. The private label merchandise becomes one of the assets of the salon and spa. In the event of a merger or sale of the business, the custom brand is as valuable as the client list. A potential buyer will have to pay for the value that the private label products bring to the profit and loss statement.

**FYI**

The profit margin on the sale of private label products is usually higher than on that of branded items. Since the product is available only at your salon and spa, there is less price competition and guests may be less price sensitive.

## Risks Associated with Private Labeling

Private labeling is not for every salon and spa. For some salon and spas, private labeling can be too costly and require too much of an investment in money and time.

Private label products typically have a six to nine month lead time from the start of the project to the receipt of the products. To keep to this timeline, you must be willing to closely follow and review the development of the products, the packaging, and decoration. Unless you are willing to lead the process yourself, or designate a leader in this process and then allow adequate time to focus on the development, you should not start the process.

There are also different timelines depending upon the type of product being developed. Products that touch the skin or are ingested need significant amounts of time to test for stability and safety.

Skin care and body care lines will take longer than apparel. For example, private label for apparel usually involves sewing on the salon and spa's logo or possibly relabeling an item. Apparel vendors usually require only 24 to 48 pieces to sew on a salon and spa logo. It may take only four to six weeks to get samples approved before production starts.

When considering a private label, it is important to realistically analyze your potential for sale of the products. If you cannot meet a minimum requirement of 1,000 units of each piece per year, vendors probably won't be able to price the products in a way that would allow you to realistically or competitively bring them into the marketplace.

Likewise, a salon and spa is going to be more successful and incur less risk if it starts the private label line with a few (perhaps up to six) of its most frequently purchased products. You should not attempt to take your whole product offering private label until you have tested the market and experience success. Once you have conducted a trial or pilot with your private label, you can strategically bring the rest of the products or new products into the line in intervals that meet the client demand as well as your time considerations. Since the majority of work is completed with the first six products, adding brands with the same vendor is much easier and might require only a six to eight week lead time from the approval of a new private label product.

Salon and spas also need to include their private label products in their back bar. When therapists, technicians, or designers use the product for their services, there can be a better connection between the salon and spa's services and its retail. Your staff more naturally become salespeople for the products and become the best way to initiate a sale.

To ensure the success of private label products, you will need to be willing to create an internal business or marketing plan around the sale of the products. Private label products become an exclusive profit center for the salon and spa and they need to be cultivated the same way that the salon and spa's other resources are. Incentives to your service staff and front desk to sell the products can boost the success of the salon and spa's private label line.

Private label products typically require a substantial investment on the part of the salon and spa. Vendors may require a deposit of $500 to $1,000 per product just to begin development. While this deposit is typically deductible from the first purchase order for the product, it is still a cash outlay that must be budgeted.

In the case of private label products, you may have to purchase a minimum quantity of product initially (i.e., 500 units of each or more) and then a comparable number for each reorder. You can usually purchase branded products in units of 12 or 24 based on the products and the case pack. You will have to incorporate the custom product into the marketing plan to ensure that this investment in creating a product and then purchasing it is sound and consistent with your business plan.

Storage can be an issue with smaller salons and spas. With branded products, you may have had to purchase only a few gallons of back bar and a few pieces of each of the retail items. With a private label, you will have to make sure you have the space to store the minimum purchase quantities that you have negotiated with the vendor. These products may be temperature and light sensitive. The storage area may need to be climate controlled. The products will also need to be otherwise protected. These products are a valuable investment, therefore, they have to be stored in a secured location and inventory control measures must be in effect. Inventory control will also be essential in the reordering process to make sure that you have a continued supply of products.

Private label products may not be an immediate success. The venture may take two years before it can be judged a success or a failure. Repeat purchases of the product and brand loyalty is the same with these products as it is with the salon and spa itself. Promotion, focused marketing, and selling the product is necessary.

## Types of Private Label Products

The types of products that are developed as private label vary. The most common products are bath, body, and skin care, shampoo, and conditioners.

The second most common private label product is apparel. Apparel is one of the easier products to customize. Also, your customer is going to be interested in apparel that has a salon and spa logo on it because it increases the souvenir value of the apparel. This is most commonly true with garments such as basic sweatshirts, t-shirts, and robes or caps. However, when it comes to more sophisticated loungewear, sportswear, and higher-end robes, you may not wish to put logos on these items. Start slowly with logoed apparel as putting the logo on an expensive, nicer type garment can harm sales. Your salon or spa must have some brand identity of its own for anything other than a t-shirt or cap to merit a logo. If it is a well-known entity, then it can be considered a status symbol or souvenir. If the salon or spa is not well-known, the logo will have less appeal. For those salon and spas that are not widely known, the logo should be subtle, tone on tone, almost blending into the garment. Bright contrasting logos on women's apparel in a nice salon and spa can hamper sales more than help.

One of the challenges for you may be to keep product expectations under control. While private label is custom and you can get just about anything you want, a private label can be costly. For example, if you select one of the manufacturer's standard bottle and cap offerings, as opposed to a custom design, the price will be lower.

The remainder of this section will discuss the private label considerations for skin care, cosmetics, and hair care items, as these types of private label projects require a deeper level of detail, including formulations, packaging, and storage.

In considering body lotions, shampoos, conditioners, and so forth, keep in mind that some product fragrance (and all essential oils) can be very expensive and could dramatically add to your cost depending on the final formulation. Be careful of what you ask to be added beyond the minimum expectations. You need to carefully analyze the effect of that addition to the pricing and the effect it will have on the salon and spa's ultimate profitability. Consider that it is always easier to add features to future orders. It is difficult to offer guests less later on.

Packaging is an important element of retail. You should be as creative as you want with the bottle decorations and make it unique, yet in step with your salon theme. As far as the decoration and label itself, you will have to decide whether to use an adhesive label, or silkscreen directly on the package. Silk screening is elegant, tried, and true. In general, keeping the salon and spa's color selection to a maximum of three can help keep silkscreen pricing under control. Each color (or pass) that you add to your decoration will cost more.

It is important to consider how you will store your inventory of products so they remain stable. All products are subject to deterioration and they are especially affected by storage conditions. When placing orders, salons and spas typically place orders that represent less than a year of sales. You have to be cautious where you display the private label products, making sure that they are in a cool location and not in the direct sunlight for any extended period of time. It may be a good idea to ask for empty bottles for display only, if you wish to have products displayed in your window or in areas of the space with an inconsistent climate.

If the salon and spa is carrying a sun care line that includes SPF products, you have to remember that all of these products are delivered with no more than two-year expiration from the date of manufacture. You should not accept these products from the vendor with any less than 18 months dating, nor should they sell them to your customers with any less than six months dating. Since you usually cannot get a return for outdated products from the vendor, you have to be very cautious on ordering and inventory levels for these products.

## Private Label Vendor Selection

Once the benefit and risk analysis has been conducted and you have decided to go with private label, you have to find a vendor. Your business needs and long-term plans will dictate the criteria used in selecting a vendor. You may want to go with a company that specializes in the creation of private label products for salons and spas.

Once a few vendors are selected as having potential, contact them to ask for an overview of their fees, services, minimum order quantities, and approximate prices for various products that you have chosen to customize.

Upon request, vendors can provide a customer list, which you can use to make reference calls and ask how the vendor has performed. Pay especially close attention to customers on the vendor's reference list that you view as equivalent to your salon or spa. To choose a private label vendor, you can also call upon your peers that you have met through networking and ask about their experiences. Sometimes the best resources can be those who are not on the company's reference list but are either former customers or a salon and spa that decided not to go with that vendor.

Part of the research also involves asking the vendor for their representations and warrants for the products. Ask how long vendors will stand behind their products for a refund, replacement, or credit in the event that the products do not perform to the original specifications that you had approved. You will also need to know the lead time expected on new orders and replacement orders. Does the vendor represent and warrant those items?

Freight can be expensive, so always be clear on shipping charges. How is freight calculated? Is it a flat fee or a sliding scale? It is routine in private label manufacturing that the freight is paid by the customer, not the vendor. These shipping and handling fees need to be budgeted, so ask the vendor to estimate what the fees will be.

Many vendors offer a supply agreement that spells out all of your obligations to the vendor and all of the vendor's obligations to you. Such an agreement helps eliminate the surprises. It also outlines how long prices are guaranteed for and in what quantities.

It is also important to know how much it costs to make a change. Usually the earlier in the process it is, the less costly it is to make a change. However, there is typically a charge if the artwork or product changes after development is underway.

Most salons and spas tend to favor entering into longer-term agreements with vendors. It is very difficult to change vendors and start the whole customizing process anew. Likewise, the vendor's terms should improve as the agreement period lengthens.

You will also need to engage the potential vendors in a discussion about their payment terms and try to get terms that best suit your needs. Many vendors will request a 50 percent payment with the purchase order and 50 percent at delivery. The vendors are making an investment in the salon and spa's product as well. They may offer discounts if you pay by credit card and in advance.

Private label, like other retailing, is most successful when you and the vendor become partners. If it is possible, you should visit the vendor's manufacturing and product development facility before making the final decision. You can get a copy of state and federal licenses, quality assurance policies, and standard operating policies for manufacturing and filling.

SALON AND SPA SNAPSHOT 3.3

At the Emerald Salon and Spa...
Private Labeling to Support a Brand

The Emerald Salon and Spa in Brea, California, is a full-service day spa utilizing environmentally friendly, natural products in their services. The owner, Samantha, strives to maintain the integrity of her brand in all that she does, and considers everything from the vendors she chooses to partner with all the way through to the disposal of waste material. Wanting to take more control on the message sent in her retail lines, she decided to create her own line of bath and body products and home scents. These organic, fruit-based creams, scrubs, and candles are not tested on animals and are made without chemicals or artificial scents. The packaging is eco-friendly and she even offers an incentive for customers to recycle the empty containers through her store. She markets her products on her shelves, on her website, and in local boutiques and gift shops.

# MARKETING

The vendor needs to be interested in your business model and be able to offer some form of marketing support. This is especially true in the graphic designs that are created for your bottles, as this is the same art that may potentially be used in other areas of your marketing plan. The vendor's research and development area should be able to provide you with selling points of the product's contents and supply you with data to support this information. This can be helpful in your internal marketing plans to support the sale of the products.

Like the salon and spa services themselves, the private label products need to have a demand created for them.

You can do many things to market your private label items. To be proactive before the launch, you can create marketing and sales hooks for the products while they are still under development. You may choose to add antioxidants, firming agents, or vitamin and nutrient additives. What will your guests be most interested in? What has the most synergy with the philosophy of the salon and spa and its mission? Those are the items that need to be added to the product to make it a good fit for the salon and spa.

Given that the custom products are unique to your salon or spa and are available only through you will maximize this message to support your brand. Sell the point that these products have been developed and manufactured to meet your strict specifications.

To create a streamlined ordering approach for your customers, you may want to investigate a process to take orders by phone, or over the Internet (and fulfill the order by mail). When doing so, you will want to either include the shipping or handling charge to cover their expenses or else use the shipping and handling as an incentive to get guests to return to the salon and spa. For example, a salon and spa might offer to waive shipping and handling charges when a guest books a return visit.

Another technique is to select a product or two that you believe will be the most popular, then use that item as the lead in the marketing plan and the sales initiatives. Positive experiences with these products can lead guests to seek and experience your other signature products.

Displaying the products using tent cards to discuss the features of the products is very important. While in the retail area, guests can "meet" the products and have ample time to ask questions and make a decision to purchase while they are experiencing your salon and spa.

## CHAPTER SUMMARY

- Part of the purchasing strategy process includes a plan covering the retail mix, budget, vendors, and pricing.
- Aligning products with the services you provide is important in a successful retail strategy.
- Consider your target clients and current clients when deciding your retail offerings and pricing structure.
- Carrying different quality and pricing levels of a product classification is a good strategy.
- Before choosing a vendor, conduct a thorough interview to understand the company, the products or services, and marketing support.
- Establish a solid vendor partnership by communicating your philosophy and expectations.
- A good vendor partner will balance the desire to make a sale with the intention of helping you reach your retail goals.

- It is important to establish a receiving system for processing incoming orders and handling returns.
- Private labeling takes a substantial lead time to develop, and you must have adequate resources to dedicate to the project.
- Private label products increase brand identity by creating an opportunity to market your salon or spa.

# LEARNING ACTIVITIES

## Learning Activity 3-1: Who Are You?

Select a salon and spa vendor or consultant that you have not yet done business with.

Research your chosen vendor. Find out who would be the contact person at that vendor, what services they offer salon and spas, who their other salon and spa customers are, and where they are located. Answer these questions about the vendor:

- Does this vendor offer the product the salon and spa's customers desire?
- Is this vendor financially stable?
- Who are the principal owners of the company?
- Where is the product manufactured?
- Does this company understand the unique elements of the salon and spa business?
- Would you feel comfortable working with this vendor?
- How many lines does this vendor produce annually?
- What is the depth of category selection that this vendor offers?
- Where does the vendor fit into the salon and spa's price scheme? Low? Moderate? High?
- What is the turnaround time for stock items?
- Can this vendor ship the product ordered on time and complete?
- Are reorders generally available?
- What are the vendor's return policies?
- Will the vendor assist the salon and spa when problems occur?
- Does the vendor offer co-op advertising and promotional assistance?
- Is the vendor's representative available for support such as trunk shows, fashion shows, product demonstrations, and inventory assistance?

- How many times during the season will a representative visit the salon and spa?
- Does this company affiliate with or use a portion of the products' sales to support a charitable or political event or cause?
- Are there any exclusivity arrangements with the vendor?

Write a three-paragraph summary stating why this vendor would or would not be a good choice as a resource partner for your salon and spa.

## Learning Activity 3-2: Walking the Trade Show Floor

Select a trade show at which salon and spa vendors will be present. Get a copy of the trade show map or look online at the list of vendors they have available. Set up a plan for walking the trade show. Make out a schedule for appointments with core vendors. Establish appointments according to the classification of products you have at your salon and spa.

Then make a list of questions and concerns that you would want to address in a vendor appointment.

# REVIEW QUESTIONS

1. When preparing for a trade show and meetings with vendors, what should salon and spa professionals check their inventory for?
   a. Cost of sales
   b. Sales to stock ratios
   c. Sell through
   d. Open to buy

2. Why is it important to purchase with a plan?
   a. It will create synergy between the salon and spas philosophy and the retail lines.
   b. It is important to know what lines the salon and spa will purchase and what lines will be carried.
   c. It is a way for the manager to create synergy between lines.
   d. All of the above.

3. It is important to discover which of the following when choosing a vendor partner?
   - a. Support, such as education provided and new product updates
   - b. A true interest in understanding your philosophy and needs
   - c. Knowledge of product effectiveness and supporting research
   - d. All of the above

4. Monte is reading an article on noninvasive beauty treatments. He makes notes about some of the products that are gaining popularity with customers. What source is he using for research?
   - a. Trade magazine
   - b. Directory
   - c. Trade show
   - d. Industry event

5. What type of pricing philosophy is a salon and spa boutique most likely to have?
   - a. Low markup with huge volume
   - b. Low markup with low volume
   - c. High markup with high volume
   - d. High markup and low volume

6. What is the advantage to setting appointments with vendors at trade shows based on the salon and spa's product classifications?
   - a. It saves time walking back and forth between appointments.
   - b. It helps to expand the number of key vendors.
   - c. It makes it easier to compare products and analyze the benefits.
   - d. It helps to reclassify products that are slow movers.

7. What is an effective way of beginning a meeting with a vendor?
   - a. Giving the vendor a brief synopsis of the salon and spa
   - b. Providing the vendor with a list of desired products
   - c. Discussing the payment and shipment terms of the vendor
   - d. Testing samples of the vendor's product

8. Why would salon and spas want to artificially narrow the choices available to consumers?
   a. To achieve a higher profit margin
   b. To limit the amount of marketing a salon and spa must do
   c. To avoid overwhelming guests with unfamiliar products
   d. To make products easier for therapists to sell

9. Which of the following statements about private label products is false?
   a. Fewer than one in five salon and spas carry private label products.
   b. The more revenue a salon and spa retail area does, the more likely it is to carry private label products.
   c. Private label products can help promote customer loyalty to the salon and spa.
   d. Private label products often have a higher markup than name brand products.

10. What type of lead time does a salon and spa typically have with a private label body care product from the start of the project to the receipt of the products?
    a. 30 to 90 days
    b. Six to nine months
    c. One year
    d. 18 months

# Inventory Management

## INTRODUCTION

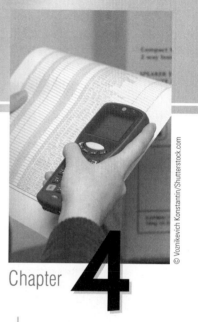

© Voznikevich Konstantin/Shutterstock.com

I n Chapter 2, you gained fundamental knowledge about how to establish a solid retail plan that incorporates product classifications and revenue goals. The next step is learning how to support the plan. This chapter presents the essential concepts and tools for effective retail inventory management. Many of these concepts and methodologies are second nature to those working in traditional retail operations, but are not so intuitive for many salon and spa professionals.

Although your retail operations are important to the success and profitability of your overall business, many managers spend little time applying even the most basic retail management principles to their inventory management. Due to the higher profit margins in retail over services, it makes good business sense to follow a solid retail management strategy. While retail inventory management is not the only contributing factor for increasing your retail sales, it certainly has a direct effect on revenue and costs, and therefore, profitability. Poor retail management techniques (or worse, a lack of any retail management techniques) result in poor retail performance, understocking of popular retail items ("stock-outs"), overstocking of unpopular retail items, increased markdowns, and ever-increasing inventory value.

- How many times have you ever underestimated the popularity of an item and faced the frustration of being out of stock?
- Were you ever excited about a product and ordered in bulk, only to find it sitting on your shelf collecting dust?

Chapter **4**

## LEARNING OBJECTIVES

After successfully completing this chapter, the reader will be able to:

- Describe the purpose of inventory management in successful retail planning.
- Explain the benefits of an automated system for inventory management.
- Define turnover and stock-to-sales ratio and explain their purpose as part of an inventory management system.
- Calculate min/max levels for retail inventory and demonstrate how to set correct inventory levels for a variety of retail situations.
- Apply the concepts of top sellers/ slow movers and inventory aging

*(continues)*

85

## LEARNING OBJECTIVES (continued)

- to salon and spa retail inventory to maximize profitability.
- Explain why the retail method is preferred over the cost method for the purposes of inventory management.
- Describe the concept of open to buy and explain the formula for determining open to buy levels.
- Explain the purpose of a variety of inventory recordkeeping tasks, including markdowns and markups, merchandise received, chargebacks, and transfers.
- Determine causes of shrinkage and list procedures that deter shrinkage.

# SUPPORTING THE PLAN

You will find that using a disciplined approach to retail inventory management will lead to less frustration, stronger retail performance, higher turnover of top sellers, fewer markdowns, and greater profitability. It just takes the application of a few basic formulas to be on your way to better retail results.

## Automation Makes It Possible

Technology has removed much of the drudgery and time commitment traditionally associated with retail inventory techniques and concepts. To calculate many of the necessary numbers and metrics by hand is time-consuming, error-producing, and unnecessary. Face it, most people won't follow through on their inventory management process if they have to perform these tasks manually. By utilizing the capabilities available in most point-of-sale computer systems, you can let the computer generate your reports so you can focus your attention toward keeping your retail plan on course.

## SALON AND SPA SNAPSHOT 4.1

### At the Urban Salon and Spa ...

© StockLite/www.Shutterstock.com

Reuben laughed confidently at the retail consultant's question. "Of course I can tell you our top 20 selling items," he said. "There's our signature line body lotion—we can hardly keep it on the shelf. Then there's the facial cleanser in that same line. And of course, our ginger root hair conditioner. I'd probably say that our Sultry Orchid nail polish is a top seller, ever since a top celebrity mentioned it was her favorite color in a magazine article. That's four, right?" Reuben's confidence began to falter. "Well, then there's our citrus foot scrub, but really, that's only a best seller in the summer ... and maybe the ... no, that used to be, but not anymore ... I give up. I guess I don't know. But that's what you're here for, right?"

continues

## At the Urban Salon and Spa …

continued

The consultant, Kevin, nodded. "I took a look at that sales report by style you gave me last time we met," he said. "I thought it was a phone book at first—35 pages and 712 different items! No wonder you don't know what your top sellers are. But I've come to some interesting conclusions about your boutique based on your report."

Reuben leaned closer to follow along with Kevin's analysis. "The first thing I noticed was that that your top 20 styles had contributed 22 percent of your retail sales, but represented only 7 percent of your inventory. So, theoretically, that merchandise is turning three times faster than the balance of your investment in inventory. Do you ever run out of any of these items?" Kevin asked, showing Reuben his list. Reuben recognized several items, including an anti-frizz hair gel for which he had just placed a rush order that morning. He looked a little puzzled and was confused by some of the terms Kevin was talking about.

Kevin reassured him. "Consistently I am told by the managers and buyers in the salon and spa retail business that they 'know' the top sellers and reorder them as needed, but when pressed they will admit that there are times that they have been out of stock. So you're not alone." He showed Reuben the rest of his report.

"Now, the bottom 20 percent of your 712-item inventory includes 138 items with sales on average of less than $200 in the year, which represents only 3 percent of your sales. What if you were to take the money invested in that bottom 20 percent and invested in your top sellers instead? Do you think you might see an increase in sales, profits, and guest satisfaction?" Kevin asked.

Reuben thought about the call he'd taken earlier that week from an unhappy guest who complained about the spa's being out of her favorite product—again. He'd lost a sale, and was close to losing a customer, too. He turned to Kevin with a resolute glint in his eye. "What do we do?" he asked.

A computer system can be compared to an airplane cockpit. It shows the relevant information about the business in a quick and easy-to-understand format. Therefore, you, as the pilot of your business, can determine if you are off course in a particular area and make some quick adjustments to put the operation back in place. Having the ability to make quick, informed decisions is key to running any successful retail operation. Waiting until the end of the month, or worse, the end of the year, is too late. It's like the

© Mihai Simonia/www.Shutterstock.com

pilot not knowing if there is enough fuel to get to the destination or that is the plane is flying over South America instead of North America. A good point-of-sale computer system will allow you to run real-time inventory reports to determine sales by a choice of variables, including location/classification SKU, what is selling, what isn't selling, and what needs to be ordered. A high-quality point-of-sale computer system will even enable you to generate purchase orders (POs) automatically to the appropriate vendor based on min/max levels. Of course, even the best computer system is only as good as the information configured by the user. To make technology work for retail inventory management, you will want to use a standard or easy-to-manage classification scheme for your retail inventory. Once you choose the right automated system for your business, you can easily run reports and manage inventory levels so you keep your retail plan on track.

## Retail Inventory Management Techniques

Taking a disciplined approach to inventory management will enable you to achieve greater retail success, higher levels of sales, and increased profitability. Making a commitment to a structured approach to inventory management using even the most basic retail management techniques can ensure that you:

- Carry the right inventory
- Carry the right amounts of inventory
- Manage cash flow
- Earn a profit

© Milady, a part of Cengage Learning. Photography by Dino Petrocelli.

While there are some advanced retail techniques that will accomplish the above goals, they involve a commitment of time and effort to grasp the concepts and implement them daily. Many salon and spa professionals often feel overwhelmed by these techniques at first and eventually abandon them. Therefore, this chapter presents inventory management techniques in two formats: basic and advanced.

The basic section will offer some easy concepts, tools, and techniques to get salon and spa professionals moving in the right direction. With these basic techniques alone, you will be able to dramatically improve your retail management effectiveness and boost your revenue and profits considerably. A few minutes a week can make a measurable difference to a retail operation almost immediately. Learning these basic principles will put you on the path to superior retail management, which you can achieve through the advanced techniques discussed later in the chapter.

# BASIC RETAIL MANAGEMENT

When it comes to retail management, two key concepts are fundamental: turnover and stock-to-sales ratio. We will start with these two basic calculations.

## What Is Turnover?

**Turnover** refers to the number of times an **average retail inventory** is sold within a specific period of time, normally for one year. A good turnover rate ensures fresh inventory and an opportunity to change the product mix according to current customer buying trends. A good turnover rate is between three and four. Anything less than three signals problems, while above four is considered very good.

The sum of an operation's average retail inventory is calculated by taking the beginning of month inventory (at retail value) for each month of the previous year and adding the monthly inventories together for the year.

**turnover.** The number of times an average inventory is sold within a specific time period, normally for one year.

**average retail inventory.** The sum of the beginning of the month inventory (retail value) for each month of the year.

---

**Average Retail Inventory:**
Sum of inventory at RETAIL value at start of each month

> Example:
> Jan., $9,000; Feb., $10,000; Mar., $9,000;
> Apr.–Dec. = $92,000. One-year sum = $120,000

**Turnover Rate:**
Retail Sales per Year ÷ Average Inventory (at the beginning of the month)

> Example 1:
> For the sake of simplicity, if Seasons Salon and Spa had the exact same inventory available every month ($10,000 × 12) the average inventory for the year would be $120,000. If sales were actually $600,000 what would the turnover be?
>
> $600,000 ÷ $120,000 = Turnover rate is 5 (which is excellent!)

> Example 2:
> If the Urban Salon and Spa does $300,000 in retail sales in a year, and the sum of its average inventory on hand (at retail price) is $100,000, what would the turnover rate be?
>
> $300,000 ÷ $100,000 = Turnover rate is 3 (which is good)

## Stock-to-Sales Ratio

**Stock-to-sales ratio** is another important concept relevant to retail success. This calculation will help you keep the proper amount of inventory on hand so you don't run out of stock or have items sitting on your shelves, tying up your cash flow.

The stock-to-sales ratio is calculated by taking sales for a month and dividing by the beginning of month inventory (at retail).

**Stock-to-sales Ratio:**

Monthly Sales ÷ Inventory (retail value) at the beginning of the month

Example:
If sales were $10,000 for a month, and the beginning of month inventory was $30,000, the stock-to-sales ratio would be 3:1.

**stock-to-sales ratio.** A calculation allowing you to keep the proper level of inventory on hand. Monthly Sales ÷ Beginning of Month Inventory (at retail) = Sales to Stock Ratio

The ideal ratio is between 3:1 and 4:1. In practical terms, this means the retail operation has between three and four months' supply of inventory on hand. Usually, any less than three months' supply and you will be out of stock, and unable to satisfy the requests of your customers. Any more than four months' supply and the operation is carrying more inventory than needed, which could cause considerable cash management issues and result in higher amounts of "old" inventory.

A rule of thumb is that the longer an inventory item goes without being sold, the less chance it will ever be sold at the current price. In other words, as your products sit on your shelves, you will become inclined to mark them down and sell them at little or no profit.

So the simple plan should be to have a stock-to-sales ratio of 3:1 (three months' supply of inventory), which should result in a turnover rate of between three and four.

The next important concept to managing inventory successfully is knowing how much to buy to maintain the proper stock-to-sales ratio.

## Replenishment Strategies

At this point, you have gained an understanding of the basic principles of retail management. The next section is more advanced and explains sophisticated strategies and methodologies to more precisely replenish retail inventory.

For simplicity's sake, here are a couple of easy-to-implement concepts for replenishment that will help salon and spa professionals ensure that their inventory is in line and that they minimize stock outages and inventory aging, and maximize their inventory investment potential.

## Min/Max

Most point-of-sale (POS) computer systems or inventory control systems provide the capability to identify minimum order point stock levels per retail item. This means that once the "min" stock level has been reached, the system will trigger a reorder. This could be as simple as a notation appearing on a reorder report or as comprehensive as generating a full purchase order, or PO, for each vendor that has items at or below the minimum stock level. The automated POs generate orders for items to bring the on-hand inventory to the maximum stock level desired.

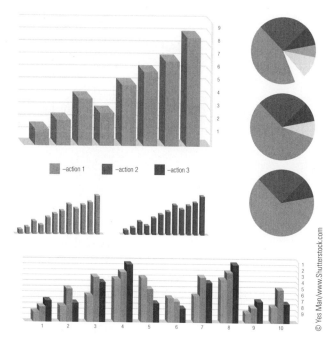

-action 1    -action 2    -action 3

© Yes Man/www.Shutterstock.com

For example, take a salon with a minimum stock level of 6 for its signature brand of hair conditioner and a maximum stock level of 20. When the salon is down to 6 conditioners (the minimum), the automated PO or reorder report would recommend ordering 14 conditioners.

In theory, the maximum stock level should reflect the amount of inventory required (e.g., two months' supply max, but no less than one months' supply) to meet the retail operation's desired stock-to-sales ratio target.

The other element to consider adding to the maximum stock level is the lead time before the product arrives from the vendor. Let's say the average demand for an item is one piece per day and the item takes 5 days to arrive from the vendor. With a minimum level of stock on hand of 6, by the time the order arrives, the store would be very close to a stock-out situation (one item left).

When determining the minimum stock level before reordering, always consider the lead time for the product to arrive from your vendor and leave a buffer of additional product count. The min level or order point should be set higher to avoid a stock-out situation while the order is in transit. In the example above, the manager should probably add at least 4 items to the min order level. That way, even if the order is late or the salon experiences increased demand, there is a buffer to minimize a stock-out situation. Therefore, using the new recommended order point of 10, the quantity on hand should be around 5 by the time the order arrives from the vendor.

The max level should also be set higher to include the desired level of inventory plus the projected inventory demand during lead time.

If you don't have a POS system, you can easily adopt the concept of min/max to a manual system by using a paper and pencil inventory list for your tracking.

## Top Sellers/Slow Movers

The best retailers make a practice of a weekly review of top sellers. Therefore, taking action to reorder and maximize the sales of these items should be one of your top priorities. Studies show that the top 20 items can make up 20 to 50 percent of a store's sales, and on average, contribute to a higher profit margin. This is due to the lower markdown rates, higher markup, and volume of sales. By focusing on maximizing the sales of these items regularly, you can increase sales and profits, and also increase customer satisfaction. Consumers have told the retailer what they like and they are happier when the retailer makes it easy for them to find it.

What defines a best seller? We would need to compare the percentage of inventory needed to sell per week to the sell through rate of a particular item. Using the example of the Urban Salon and Spa, with the goal of turning inventory four times a year, the spa would require an average supply of three months (12 weeks) of inventory.

> **Calculation for weeks of inventory for desired turns:**
> 12 months in a year ÷ Number of turns =
> Required months of inventory
> 12 ÷ 4 = 3 (months)

If the Urban Salon and Spa has 1,000 units of inventory, it would need to sell 83 units a week to make its goal of four turns:

> **Calculation for units to sell per week for desired inventory turns:**
> Inventory on hand ÷ Number of weeks = Units to sell per week
> 1,000 ÷ 12 = 83 units, which = 8.3% per week of their merchandise!

Now that you know the percentage of units to sell per week to meet the desired number of inventory turns, let's look at the sell through rate to determine slow movers and good sellers in the retail area.

**Sell through percentage** is a measure that will give you a view of your top sellers and slow movers. This is based upon units sold, not dollars. Simply ranking items in terms of dollar amounts from high to low will not provide a measure of movement. We want to relate an item's sell through rate to the target of 8.3 percent of their merchandise to sell each week.

**sell through percentage.** A percentage comparing the amount of inventory received from a vendor in units against the units actually sold.

---

**Sell through calculation:**

Weekly sales ÷ Beginning inventory for the week

Example:
Ginger root shampoo had 40 units on hand at the start of the week and sold 5 during the week. So, $5 \div 40 = 12.5\%$ sell through, which is above 8.3%. This product is a top seller!

---

If Reuben of Urban Salon and Spa lists the sales for every item and what their sell through percentage for the week is, he could then draw a line through the report at the items that were at 8.3 percent. Anything above that line is considered a good seller, and below that line a slow mover.

Any product that had 10 percent sell through would probably make the list of best sellers and be a candidate to reorder (depending on the lead time for delivery and seasonal nature of the item, most stores would reorder eight to 12 weeks' supply). By focusing on these top sellers, which many times are also **key items**, several good things start to happen. The store is more focused on what the customer likes and is less **over-assorted**. This allows you to present these items clearly and attractively. The spa staff gets to know these products through training and exposure and becomes more comfortable suggesting and selling these products. The marketing effort gets behind these products for promotion, advertising, direct mail, e-mail, VIP gifts, and group sales. The top sellers drive the retail operation by maximizing sales and service.

At the other end of the spectrum are the slow movers. As Reuben looks at strategies for achieving, the Urban Salon and Spa's 8 percent weekly sell through to achieve his turn goal of four, he must do more than simply reorder the items with more than 10 percent weekly sell through. He must also closely monitor

**key item.** An item that is a consistent part of the store's inventory and which is reordered regularly.

**over-assorted.** Carrying too many styles from a wide assortment of vendors.

HERE'S A TIP

Slow moving products can get more attention if a tester is placed at the cash wrap. Create a small sign to draw attention to the features, advantages, and benefits of the product and encourage all staff members to mention it during their service.

and take action on the inventory that is achieving less than a 5 percent weekly sell through.

Usually, you do not take a markdown after only one week of less than 5 percent sell through, but you will want to watch slow moving products weekly and develop a "hit list" to start the markdown process. This is particularly the case if the item failed to exceed the 5 percent sell through threshold for three to four weeks in a row. In the meantime, you can take action to determine whether you can improve the sell through of the low-performing items. You might examine the following:

- Presentation: Could a change of display position the item more effectively?
- Seasonal issues: Has an unusually warm autumn kept customers from buying sweaters? Has a particularly rainy summer decreased the market for sun care products?
- Merchandise quality: Are there issues with product formulation or performance? Are you getting returns on the product? Is there too much or too little fragrance? Such problems require a call to the vendor.
- Product knowledge: Does the staff understand the product's features and benefits? Are they actively promoting the product?

Ultimately, you must take action to address slow sellers consistently and promptly. Unlike some types of wine (and perhaps cheese), salon and spa inventory does not get better with age! A seasoned retailer will know within the first two weeks after receiving merchandise whether it is a winner or not. Good managers admit their mistakes quickly and take action to mark down and clear out merchandise, so they can reinvest that money in the products that are demonstrated winners.

## Inventory Aging

Inventory is the largest investment that a retail operation makes. While kept as an asset on the books, one thing that is largely overlooked is that this asset is **perishable.** By viewing your inventory much as restaurateurs view their produce and food products as perishable items, salon and spa professionals will become more in tune with one of the major ingredients on how to run a profitable retail business with positive cash management.

In the fashion business (apparel, shoes, jewelry, and accessories) merchandise that is more than 90 days old (from date of receipt in inventory) has a 10 percent chance statistically of selling at regular price. The top tier fashion retailers will start their markdowns as

**perishable.** Goods that lose their appeal over time.

early as three to four weeks after receipt if sell through standards (typically 5 percent to 8 percent per week) are not met. Many salon and spa retailers are now in the fashion business and need to know that this is how the business is run successfully.

What about basic products, such as a signature line and all-natural products for example? Beyond the issues of shelf life and perishability, there is also another reason not to carry beyond what can be reasonably stocked. According to retail industry statistics, merchandise more than six months old is 50 percent more likely to get damaged, lost, or stolen than newer merchandise due to repeated handling, storage, and internal transport/accessibility issues.

Here are the chances that merchandise purchased at regular price will sell after it is received in inventory:

- 0–30 days: 30%
- 31–60 days: 35%
- 61–90 days: 25%
- 91+ days: 10%

By keeping track of inventory aging, you can know when to consider marking down items that haven't moved off the shelves in the past 30, 60, or 90 days.

# ADVANCED RETAIL MANAGEMENT

Basic retail management concepts such as min/max, review of top sellers/slow movers, and sell through can help you improve your inventory management methodology. These applications will certainly improve your retail effectiveness, but there are limitations in terms of how precisely you can hold the operation to its retail plan.

This section gets into a more advanced understanding of retail concepts and techniques that have been employed by traditional retailers for many years to manage their inventory with great precision and control. Some of the topics that were discussed briefly in the previous section (turnover, replenishment, etc.) will be explored in more detail to provide an in-depth understanding on how these concepts interrelate. Specifically, the section discussing "open to buy" will demonstrate how

to keep the proper inventory on hand while ensuring that cash management stays positive.

## Retail Method of Inventory Management

To help achieve effective retail merchandise management and control, traditional retailers use the **retail inventory method** to account for activity and balances of their stock. When the monthly financial statements are prepared, you should look at the value of the retail inventory at *cost* when the entries are booked, to record the cost of goods sold. Otherwise, the inventory is thought of and used at its *retail* value. When traditional retailers total the amount of merchandise scheduled to be sold over a period of time, they always speak in terms of "sold at retail." The plan calculates how much merchandise is on hand and on order to meet those sales projections. Since retail sales are naturally planned using the retail values, you need to compare your inventory and stock on order at retail value. The retail inventory method provides a way to measure the amounts and the percentages of initial markup, markdowns, and shrinkage (inventory loss). It is used for planning purposes and to generate an open to buy—a budgeting process we will discuss in depth later in the chapter.

Knowing whether figures are recorded at cost or at retail can make a huge difference when it comes to calculating various inventory management statistics, such as turnover. For instance, if the financial statement for the year says that the retail revenue for the year was $100,000, and the balance sheet reports that the value of the inventory assets was $25,000, the salon and spa is NOT achieving a four times turnover. The amount reported on the balance sheet ($25,000) is the inventory cost number, not an inventory at retail number.

Assuming a simple 50 percent cost of sales average, the spa retail department has a two times inventory turn, not four times:

$25,000 divided by the cost of sales percentage of 50 percent = $50,000 in inventory value at retail

## Inventory Turnover Goals and Average Turnover

Inventory planning will create:

- Proper timing of merchandise deliveries
- Fresh saleable stock of merchandise at all times
- Cash resources available for restock orders

To begin the inventory planning process, you will work with the total retail inventory and then move on to the individual classifications, as you may choose to use different turnover goals for different classifications of retail merchandise.

The process begins with determining the inventory turnover the salon and spa would like to achieve. Turnover is most simply explained as the number of times an average retail inventory is sold within a specific period of time, normally for one year. The goal is to sell and resell the average inventory investment over and over again.

Salon and spa retail inventory must be thought of as an investment, and like any investment, must provide a return. One of the most basic tenets of retailing is to bring merchandise into the retail space, sell it within a reasonable length of time, bring more merchandise in, sell it, etc. Obviously it is not a matter of selling until the shelves are bare and then bringing in new merchandise, but rather the challenge is keeping a constant flow in and out of the retail space so that the average inventory investment is sold and resold as many times as is reasonable during the year.

**DID YOU KNOW?**

Turnover is the major key to generating spendable retail dollars. Retail profits then support overall salon and spa operational expenses and are used to restock merchandise to generate additional retail sales.

Turnover can be calculated for total inventory or by classification, such as products, gifts and accessories, etc. At the Urban Salon and Spa, Reuben's retail plan within the product classification states that his goal is for his retail sales to represent 50 percent of the total retail sales across all retail classifications within the salon and spa. His sales are approximately $5,000 per month, with annual sales of $60,500.

Figure 4-1 shows Reuben's calculations for average inventory for that product classification and the classification turnover

The average product classification inventory would be the inventory divided by the number of beginning of the month inventory figures. In this case, $195,400 divided by 12 = $16,283.

To arrive at the turnover for the product classification for the year, divide the total product sales for the year by the average inventory just computed. In this case:

$60,500 ÷ $16,283 = 3.7 turns (which is very good)

Here's an example of turnover by product classification for shampoo as shown in Figure 4-2:

Average inventory per month = $31,300 (per year) ÷ 12
= $2,608
$9,885 ÷ $2,608 = 3.8 inventory turns (which is very good!)

Figure 4-1
Urban Salon and Spa Sales Figures

| Month | Product Sales | Beginning of Month Product Inventory (in Retail Dollars) |
|---|---|---|
| January | 5,300 | $15,500 |
| February | 3,200 | $14,300 |
| March | 4,500 | $16,500 |
| April | 5,500 | $18,700 |
| May | 5,000 | $15,900 |
| June | 5,400 | $17,300 |
| July | 5,800 | $16,000 |
| August | 3,300 | $13,500 |
| September | 4,200 | $15,500 |
| October | 4,900 | $15,900 |
| November | 5,500 | $17,500 |
| December | 7,900 | $18,800 |
| Sales Total | $60,500 | Inventory Total $195,400 |

© International SPA Association Foundation

Figure 4-2
Urban Salon and Spa Shampoo Sales Figures

| Month | Shampoo Sales | Beginning of Month Shampoo Inventory (in Retail Dollars) |
|---|---|---|
| January | 900.00 | $3,100 |
| February | 885 | $3,000 |
| March | 920 | $2,900 |
| April | 725 | $3,200 |
| May | 890 | $1,900 |
| June | 720 | $3,200 |
| July | 910 | $1,800 |
| August | 765 | $2,700 |
| September | 480 | $3,000 |
| October | 575 | $3,200 |
| November | 995 | $2,900 |
| December | 1120 | $3,600 |
| Sales Total | $9,885 | Shampoo Inventory Total $31,300 |

© Milady, a part of Cengage Learning

If you choose to, you could then calculate the inventory turns for any of the basic subclassifications within the products classification, such as dandruff shampoo, color treated shampoo, volumizing shampoo, curly hair shampoo, etc. You would just repeat the process of recording the subclassification sales per month and dividing that amount by the average inventory for that product subclassification. This would further refine the turnover goals by a more specific classification detail. For some of the key items that comprise the top 20 sellers, you may choose to carry out this exercise to the level of individual items.

As far as turnover is concerned, salon and spa retail operations fall into the same range as the average apparel and accessory specialty stores, which turn their inventory, on average, 3.5 times per year. General merchandise stores (such as Target) turn the inventory 4.7 times, while grocery stores turn their inventory an average of 12.7 times per year—more than once a month.

You should set a goal of turning your inventory three to four times per year. In practical terms, that means that you should have 12 to 16 weeks of supply for an item or class level.

Example:
One inventory turn per year = 1 month of product
(4 weeks)
Three inventory turns per year = 3 months of product
(12 weeks)
Four inventory turns per year = 4 months of product
(16 weeks)

What might that level of inventory look like? The Urban Salon and Spa has its own signature line and sells ten 8 oz. bottles of body lotion in an average week. Multiplying that by 12 to 16 weeks, the salon and spa's **par stock** will be between 120 and 160 bottles. That may sound like a lot to many managers, but consider this. With lead times for ordering, shipping, receiving, marking, and reviewing the sales and inventory to initiate the order process, it is entirely possible for eight weeks to elapse. Assuming this is a "key item" for the salon and spa, they would want to have merchandise for display and presentation, which could use another 20 bottles. That accounts for 100 units. Add to that number 20 to 60 units for backup for groups, special

**par stock.** The ideal number of items to carry based upon average sales and planned inventory turns. This may change due to seasonality. Par stock is hotel/ resort terminology; model stock is retail terminology.

## At the Level 42 Spa...
## Stocking Up Means Saving Money

Level 42 is a hip, full-service salon in an upscale area of San Francisco, CA. They carry three product lines and maintain the full array of products for each. The stylists are very strong in retail and they consistently recommend products to their clients. Because key products in each line tend to sell through quickly, the team always finds that they are running out of popular items. Maria, the owner, learned quickly that repeatedly selling out of key products sent a negative message to her clients, and at times, forced them to shop elsewhere.

"I tried to use a 'just–in–time' approach to my inventory, not stocking reserves, and ordering when levels got close to depletion so I could keep my money free," Maria said, "But making frequent small orders for these products created huge shipping costs each month, meant more work, and made for impatient customers and staff. My vendor suggested I start to order larger quantities of these items. It was a bit intimidating at first, but she showed me how I can take advantage of case prices and save on shipping because I can order once every two months instead of three times each month. Now I save on shipping and I don't have to worry about running out of my top sellers."

events, gifts, and unexpected multiple sales above the average, and that amount barely covers what is needed to avoid a stock-out situation.

### Determining Correct Inventory Levels

Salon and spa managers often ask, "How much retail inventory should I have?" The inventory turnover goal process will help establish the proper inventory values. Inventory turnover goals are typically established annually when you are planning your retail operation for the following year. If your salon or spa is in a seasonal market, it is appropriate to adjust the inventory amounts in the various seasons. For example, if your salon or spa were in a beach area, you would carry a higher inventory during the high season, in the spring and summer months, so you would

© Ilin Sergey/www.Shutterstock.com

not miss sales as a result of being out of popular items. During the slower months in fall and winter, you could scale back on re-stock orders, thus reducing the overall inventory amount.

Determining retail inventory for a new retail operation can be a particular challenge, because of the lack of a sales history. Chapter 9, Salon and Spa Retail Opening, covers this procedure in detail.

## Advanced Replenishment Strategies: Open to Buy

**Open to buy (OTB)** is a purchasing budget by classification that helps you determine the amount of money (in retail dollars) you have available or "open" to spend on vendor purchases to achieve your sales plan for a given month. Knowing your budgeted amount to spend will help you to achieve your sales forecast by classification for a given month. OTB allows you to achieve your desired inventory turns and cash management objectives by classification for your retail operations. This is a high-level budgeting process that is *not* broken down by item level (skin care cream X, skin care cream Y, etc.), The goal of OTB is to maintain a balance, so that you divide your overall available purchasing budget by classification effectively. This process, if done properly and followed consistently, will not allow over purchasing or under purchasing, or imbalances by classification. This is important to ultimately avoid unplanned markdowns, resulting in profit erosion or losses.

**open to buy.** A budgeting calculation stating the amount of stock in retail dollars that the buyer is open to receiving into stock during a certain period.

**Step 1: Calculate the end of month inventory forecast**
- Determine the beginning of the month inventory at retail
- Break down the classification sales plan/forecast by month so the sum of the sales by class equal the total expected retail sales for that month.
- Calculate the planned markdowns.
- Decide the amount of planned purchases.

    Beginning of the month inventory − Sales forecast − Markdowns + Planned purchases = End of month inventory forecast

**Step 2: Calculate the open to buy amount**
- Determine the planned end of month inventory by breaking down the inventory plan by classification for each month.
- Compare the end of month inventory forecast with the planned end of month inventory.

Planned end of month inventory – End of month inventory forecast = Open to buy

Example:

The Urban Salon and Spa has a planned inventory for their signature line of $10,000 (at retail) per month for June. They keep a 12-week supply of product on hand. The sales forecast by classification for June is $4,000 for the signature line. There are planned reductions. There is a week-long promotion during which the manager runs a "buy one, get one free" promotion on its signature line of shampoo and conditioner, for which they will take $1,000 (retail) in markdowns. Based upon min/max levels, there is a planned purchase of $3,000 at retail ($1,500 at cost with a 100 percent markup) based on last month's sales and comparison to min/max levels.

Figure 4-3 shows calculations for OTB for June and July. Note: End of month planned inventory minus end of month forecast equals open to buy, or purchase dollars available to spend in *retail* value.

Again, this dollar figure is at retail, so the buyer needs to order an additional $2,000 for delivery during June and $1500 for July. Since the line is carried at 100 percent markup, the order to the vendor will be $1,000 at cost. It is important for the salon and spa professionals to know the difference between buying at retail dollars versus at cost. If, by mistake, the buyer ordered $2,000

Figure 4-3
OTB for June and July

| | June | July | |
|---|---|---|---|
| Planned Inventory | $10,000 | $10,000 | |
| Sales Forecast | $4,000 | $3,000 | |
| – Planned Reductions | $1,000 | $500 | Step 1 |
| + Planned Purchase | $3,000 | $3,500 | |
| = End of Month Forecast | $8,000 | $10,000 | |
| Planned End of Month | | | |
| Inventory | $10,000 | $10,000 | |
| – Forecast Inventory | $8,000 | $10,000 | Step 2 |
| = Open to Buy | $2,000 | $0 | |

worth of products from a vendor and markup is 100 percent, the spa would have $4,000 of merchandise at retail—far more than their OTB would allow!

## Advanced Replenishment Strategies: Min/Max Levels

Most retailers have a par stock system on the items they will consistently carry—these will include key items and basic items like signature line products. At the Urban Salon and Spa, they know that the 8 oz. signature body lotion is one of their top 20 sellers and they can sell anywhere from 40 to 80 units per month.

They would like to turn their inventory four times per year so they like to use a 12-week supply of their key items, like this 8 oz. body lotion. So if the weekly sales could be from 10 to 20 units (depending on the time of year, promotional efforts, etc.), they consider 120 units (12 weeks × 10 per week) their minimum inventory. Whenever they fall below this number, they initiate a reorder.

Since they can sell as many as 20 bottles of body lotion per week, they also have looked at an inventory level of 240 units (12 weeks × 20 per week) as reasonable during higher-volume selling and use 240 units as their maximum level. If inventory goes beyond 240 units, they typically will not reorder, unless special circumstances, such as a special event/promotion or group sale, dictate more. The Urban Salon and Spa now has a min/max on this item of 120/240 units and Reuben has delegated to the lead retail person the authority to reorder when the product falls below 120 and to alert him if the inventory gets over 240 units.

## How Much to Order?

How do you know whether to go to min or max levels? This depends on seasonality, the reordering process, vendor turnaround time, and special promotions.

For example, let's look at body lotion. In January/February/March this product is in season, and they order to the max of 240 units. They know that reorders can take four to eight weeks from the time they check their inventory, contact the vendor, get the order processed, and receive the order. They also realize that even when the vendor ships the order, there is still a week or more for shipping and then additional time needed to receive and mark the merchandise.

Special promotions influence sales. The Urban Salon and Spa will sell additional lotion in that time period because of a sales contest on body lotion and due to training the staff on suggestive selling. The manager will want to add additional inventory to account for the special promotion.

During the off season, the Urban Salon and Spa will change to the minimum order level. The retail manager looks at inventory and places their July order based on the fact that in September/October/November when they are out of season, they want to be at the minimum, or 120 units of lotion. This could result in no order being placed in July if the minimum level of stock is on hand.

In the case of the signature line of products, their vendor has a minimum order of 120, so the retail staff has worked with their vendor to run the necessary minimum, but then hold it for them to draw from as needed. Even if this arrangement costs a little more, you may want to examine it and consider whether it will be beneficial to your retail operation.

## HERE'S A TIP

You should address markdowns consistently every month and not wait until the end of the year or end of the season to take them all on at once.

## Taking Markdowns

Many salon and spa professionals are confused about when to take markdowns and how much to mark down items. In an open to buy system, you should create a monthly markdown budget for each classification. In certain months of the year, this budget will be higher, and in other months it will be lower. It depends on the seasonality of your business and the merchandise classification; for example, markdown sales after the holiday season will likely be higher.

There is a better chance of selling something while it is newer and in its season at the first markdown, rather than holding it until after the season and needing to reduce it substantially more. For example, a spa in Florida may bring in some sweaters for fall selling in September. If the sell through goal is not met, the spa has a better chance to sell at first markdown in October or November, rather than hanging on until the following February or March when the weather is warming up and the tourist season is ending. By then, a markdown substantially below cost might be needed to even get a passing glance from the consumer.

Occasionally, you may wonder about the possibility of boxing up inventory and bringing it back on the floor the next year for that product's selling cycle. A good retail practice is to *never* leave your money tied up in inventory for a long period of time.

It is far more practical to liquidate the inventory and reinvest in the best sellers.

But what about a basic product that is not making the sell through goal of 5 percent, but is a key product and is planned as an ongoing part of your retail operation? There are a couple of factors for you to consider when not meeting your sell through goal, and these are discussed next.

### Initial Investment in Inventory

Perhaps the sell through goal is not being met because the initial investment was too high due to minimum requirements from the vendor or other issues related to start up. In this case, many retailers would "wait out" the imbalance through the reorder process and establish min/max levels for future months.

Another option is for you to work with your vendor partners in advance to see what flexibility they have with lower minimums. Sometimes higher prices for smaller quantities are a good idea. Good retailers never buy more than they feel they can sell in three to four months. Special "deals" (such as discounts, free freight, etc.) many times turn out not to be a good deal for the business. Sometimes you can run promotions such as 20 percent off or "buy one, get something else at a special price" to try to accelerate sales and balance inventory.

### Business Transitions

Perhaps the sell through is not being met because of a transition in your business, such as changing lines, changing demographics, changing your image, going through remodeling, new construction, etc. In this case, keep a close eye on the sales trend to see if it is moving in the right direction and ensure that staff is being trained and supported to make the transition a success.

## How Much to Mark Down?

A study by the Cotton Council asked women shoppers how much something would have to be marked down to get their attention. The number one answer was 25 to 30 percent.

One suggested pricing and markdown cycle is as follows:

- First markdown of 25 to 30 percent off regular price
- Second markdown of 40 to 50 percent off original price (30 days later)
- Third markdown of 60 to 75 percent off original price (30 days after second markdown)

## At the Urban Salon and Spa...

Oh, yes, Mrs. Avery. Of course we have the ginger root conditioner in stock. I know it's your favorite. Would you like one or two bottles? Reuben breathed a sigh of relief that he wouldn't have to disappoint one of the salon and spa's best customers. The days were over when they were out of its popular facial mask as often as it was in stock. Ever since Reuben was able to fill a special order for her daughter's bridal shower, Ms. Avery always asked for him personally, even though his retail manager was perfectly capable of assisting her.

He thought back to when he started at the Urban Salon and Spa and the conditioner was never in stock. It had taken some digging to discover why the boutique never seemed to have the conditioner and also why the cost of goods sold was always so high on the monthly financial statements. The answer was simple, but frustrating: shampoo assistants were coming into the retail area and grabbing bottles of the conditioner off the shelves whenever they ran out, which was often. The previous director had never enforced a policy of having employees fill out a transfer form when they moved merchandise from retail to professional product. That was one of the first changes Reuben had made as salon and spa director.

It had taken a couple of months, but eventually all of the employees had gotten into the habit of using the transfer forms, and everyone was much happier. Based on the information he had learned, Reuben was able to increase his professional order of the conditioner so the assistants had what they needed to do their treatments. Once he did that, the retail stock stopped disappearing, which made his customers—and him—happy.

Reuben's reverie ended as he approached the shelf where the conditioner that Mrs. Avery wanted was displayed. There were only three left! "How could that be?" he wondered. It was nowhere near the end of the month—there should be several more bottles in the display. As he reached for the two bottles he needed, another hand also reached into the shelf. He turned to see Patty, a recently-hired assistant, grabbing the last bottle. The look on his face must have startled her, because she began to stammer an excuse as she darted back to her treatment area.

"Sorry, we ran out. Very popular, you know. This is the third time this week I've had to borrow from the boutique," said Patty. "You know, you really should think about increasing our order for professional product. Gotta run—I have a client waiting."

After Reuben finished taking care of Mrs. Avery, he went behind the retail counter and glanced over that month's transfer form. Sure enough, there were transfers recorded by several employees—but Patty's name was nowhere on the list.

By consistently moving from first to second to third markdowns, you can effectively clear the merchandise and in the long term, be much more liquid (able to reinvest inventory dollars in new merchandise) than retailers that are inconsistent and have inventory imbalances they deal with only when in trouble.

There is still the question of what to do with any merchandise that is still left after three markdowns. Many retailers have successfully "price pointed" their leftover clearance merchandise, moving it from areas designated with signs indicating (for example) $29.99, then $19.99, then $9.99, then $4.99 (and even $1.99 in some cases). Retailers move this merchandise every 30 days to the next lower price category. How prominent this merchandise is on the selling floor is up to you and the salon and spa's philosophy on sale/clearance. Typically, using this technique to clear out sale merchandise will happen on holiday weekends such as Memorial Day, Labor Day, or the Fourth of July.

If there is still something left after all of this effort to liquidate, you may consider donating to a local charity, or giving it to deserving staff or other individuals with whom the salon and spa would like good will.

# MANUAL RECORDKEEPING

An important step in monitoring the retail plan requires posting to the planning spreadsheet each month's actual sales, markdowns, and other activity. To accomplish this, salon and spa professionals need to maintain appropriate records. Ideally, the salon and spa retail operation has a computerized data collection and reporting system. If such a system is not in place, the data must be recorded manually. The data outlined in this section must be produced by your recordkeeping system in order to accurately monitor your retail operations.

The following section discusses the procedures for salon and spa professionals who are using a manual recordkeeping method to manage their inventory. However, the information is a foundation that everyone should understand—even if their recordkeeping is fully automated.

## Recording Markdowns

A general definition of a markdown is any reduction in a retail price, regardless of the amount or reason. Markdowns must be tracked and may occur for the following reasons:

1. Clearance items: Clearance items are any merchandise marked with permanent price reductions. You may monitor your merchandise and implement a "markdown cycle" on items identified as slow movers. (Slow movers can be defined as any item that has gone for 90 days with only a 20 percent sell through.) In addition to the markdown cycle suggested previously, the following variation is common: 33 percent (⅓) off the first month; 50 percent (½) off the second month; 75 percent (¾) off the third month; and marked out-of-stock on the fourth month. You will need to decide what kind of markdown cycle works best for your inventory management needs.

2. Point-of-sale reductions for:
   - Damaged or shopworn merchandise
   - Employee/member discounts
   - Merchandise removed from stock for professional use
   - Donations or given as a VIP gift—if recorded at cost
   - Merchandise damaged due to a fire or a natural disaster, after it is first processed as an insurance claim prior to marking down or marking out

3. Temporary price reductions: The process for recording markdowns remains essentially the same regardless of the size of the salon and spa retail operation. If you are using a manual system, it is important to complete a markdown record by developing a form (see Figure 4-4). Since the price reduction

Figure 4-4
Markup/Markdown Record

| Markup and Markdown Record | | | | | Sub Classification—Nail Polish | | | |
|---|---|---|---|---|---|---|---|---|
| Date | Sku/Item | Reason | Old Price | New Price | Unit Change | Total Units | Total Markdown | Total Markup |
| 3/3 | 002-432 | Slow color | 8.50 | 4.25 | 4.25 | 5 | 21.25 | |
| 3/10 | 002-433 | Weekly special | 8.50 | 6.50 | 2.00 | 10 | 20.00 | |
| 3/15 | 002-532 | Damaged | 8.50 | 0.00 | 8.50 | 1 | 8.50 | |
| 3/21 | 002-327 | Employee discount | 8.50 | 6.80 | 1.70 | 2 | 3.40 | |
| March Total | | | | | | | 53.15 | 0.00 |

will have an effect on the retail cost of goods sold, this can be useful in researching variances at the end of the month. The form should include the following:

1. List the regular selling price of the item or items in the first column, and in the second column list the lower or marked-down selling price.
2. Subtract the markdown price from the original price to indicate the amount of markdown dollars per item and write that in the third column.
3. Multiply the markdown dollars by the number of units or items to find the total markdown dollars.
4. Enter these totals on the markdown record form in the last column.

If you have computer point-of-sale software, the markdowns may all be recorded on the sales receipts and also summarized on a management report, depending on the specific software used.

## Temporary Price Reduction

Merchandise temporarily reduced for a special event (for example, all nail polish is 20 percent off Friday and Saturday only) can be handled in one of two ways:

1. Treat as a point-of-sale markdown in accordance with specific software.
2. Take a physical inventory of the merchandise to be reduced immediately before the sale or special event, and another inventory immediately after the close of the sale. Record a markdown for the items sold at the reduced price on the markdown record form. Ensure that all sales staff know the correct selling prices in effect for any special event, so they can support the special and correctly close the sales transactions.

## Markups

A markup is any increase in a retail price, regardless of the amount or reason. Markups are handled in the same manner as markdowns on your markdown/markup form. Markups may be necessary for a couple of reasons:

1. Incorrect ticketing (or pricing) discovered after the merchandise has already been received into the inventory records. For instance, a bottle of shampoo is marked with the price at cost rather than the retail price.

2. Price increases on reorders. If reorders are billed at a cost higher than the cost of previous shipments, an increase in retail price is probably warranted. Any identical merchandise remaining in stock from previous orders should be increased to the new retail price.

## Merchandise Received

Upon receiving merchandise, check it over carefully, using the invoice and purchase order as a reference.

- Check the merchandise to be sure it agrees with the order, as well as the invoice.
- Check the cost billed on the invoice against the quoted price on the order.
- Enter the retail selling price next to the cost price on the invoice. This will show whether the goods received on this invoice were landed at an acceptable, profitable markup.
- Price all merchandise showing the correct classification letters or numbers.
- Be sure to record the merchandise received on the correct category and/or classification page. Be doubly sure that the extended totals pertain only to items in one classification or subclassification. Do not intermix classifications or subclassifications when posting to records.

To assure your retail operation is a success, make it a daily practice to post the merchandise received totals to your merchandise received form (see Figure 4-5) showing both cost and retail. If merchandise shipped against a canceled order is accepted at point of delivery, it must be received and posted in the records as "merchandise received." Then follow your procedures for chargebacks, as we will discuss next.

For ease of recordkeeping, many salon and spa professionals decide to keep track of retail inventory by the four basic classifications of products, apparel, gifts and accessories, and other. This provides valuable information that will help you in retail planning. To manage the inventory on a more detailed basis, the classifications can be broken down into specific subclassifications in order to provide more targeted information. Also, if sales within a specific subclassification are significant, it is a good practice to manage that inventory on a more detailed level.

Figure 4-5
Merchandise Received Form

# MERCHANDISE RECEIVED

## Classification _____

| Date | Manufacturer | Invoice Number | Received Total Retail | Received Total Cost | Vender Returns Retail | Transfer In Retail | Transfer Out Retail |
|------|--------------|----------------|-----------------------|---------------------|-----------------------|--------------------|---------------------|
|      |              |                |                       |                     |                       |                    |                     |
|      |              |                |                       |                     |                       |                    |                     |
|      |              |                |                       |                     |                       |                    |                     |
|      |              |                |                       |                     |                       |                    |                     |
|      |              |                |                       |                     |                       |                    |                     |
|      |              |                |                       |                     |                       |                    |                     |
|      |              |                |                       |                     |                       |                    |                     |
|      |              |                |                       |                     |                       |                    |                     |
|      |              |                |                       |                     |                       |                    |                     |
|      |              |                |                       |                     |                       |                    |                     |
|      |              |                |                       |                     |                       |                    |                     |
|      |              |                |                       |                     |                       |                    |                     |
|      |              |                |                       |                     |                       |                    |                     |
|      |              |                |                       |                     |                       |                    |                     |
|      |              |                |                       |                     |                       |                    |                     |
|      |              |                |                       |                     |                       |                    |                     |
|      |              |                |                       |                     |                       |                    |                     |
|      |              |                |                       |                     |                       |                    |                     |
|      |              |                |                       |                     |                       |                    |                     |
|      |              |                |                       |                     |                       |                    |                     |
|      |              |                |                       |                     |                       |                    |                     |
|      |              |                |                       |                     |                       |                    |                     |
|      |              |                |                       |                     |                       |                    |                     |
|      |              |                |                       |                     |                       |                    |                     |
|      |              |                |                       |                     |                       |                    |                     |
|      |              |                |                       |                     |                       |                    |                     |
|      |              |                |                       |                     |                       |                    |                     |
|      |              |                |                       |                     |                       |                    |                     |

## Chargebacks

A chargeback (return to vendor) is the term used to describe merchandise that is returned to the manufacturer. Merchandise can be returned for a variety of reasons: defective goods discovered at the time of receipt (or later on the selling floor), erroneous shipments, or a prior agreement with the vendor.

It is important to document all correspondence with the vendor regarding any discrepancies, and to verify their return policy. You should contact the vendor by e-mail or telephone (making note of the call in a written log) to request a return authorization (RA) number. Return the merchandise by traceable methods and maintain a shipping log or copy of the RA numbers or call tags, in the event that proof of delivery is requested from the vendor.

The returned shipment *must be recorded at the retail price* on the merchandise received record form to ensure that the book inventory figure will be properly reduced by the return.

If damaged or defective goods, over-shipments, or unwanted substitutions are discovered at time of receipt, two entries must be made on the merchandise received form:

1. Record the cost and retail amount of the shipment as received.
2. Record the retail amount of the chargeback.

The above two entries also apply to canceled goods that were erroneously accepted and must be returned.

## Transfers

Transfers are a common problem in a salon and spa retail operation for several reasons, including the use of retail product for services, having the same retail sold in multiple areas, and product being used gratis for gifting.

### The Need for Professional Use Products

Quite often, professional product (back bar) and the retail product are the same. The practice of therapists and technicians pulling product from the retail shelves to use on clients can be a significant retail challenge for your operations. How often does an esthetician grab a retail product off the shelf to use in a treatment because she is out of her professional product, or a stylist goes over to the retail display and takes a can of hairspray because he is out? There are salons and spas that have a cost of goods sold that's five to 10 percent higher than the budget or plan because they do not have a system to track the movement of merchandise from retail to professional use.

To keep your cost of goods sold and inventory accurate, you need to decide as part of your recordkeeping how you will handle transfers from retail inventory to professional usage products. Unless appropriately recorded on a transfer log, the cost of the product may not get charged to the professional products category and instead, it ends up inflating the retail cost of goods sold.

With respect to a transfer from retail to professional products, the log should indicate the product, retail price, number of units, an explanation as to why the product was transferred, and an authorization signature. If this record is not maintained, the cost of goods sold will be overstated and the cost of professional products understated. More importantly, no one will realize that they need to order additional professional products and the staff will pull product from the retail shelf again. Or worse, a guest will want to buy the retail product and none will be left on the shelf.

## Retail Sold in Multiple Areas

Transfers may also happen in venues where the gift shop on site also sells the same salon and spa merchandise. In this case, the movement of merchandise from the salon and spa retail space to another shop must be recorded. It is also common for day spas with multiple properties to transfer merchandise from one location to another.

## Gifting/Gratis

There is also a potential issue with VIP gifts, where the manager or staff member will simply walk into the retail area and pull some merchandise to give to a VIP guest. It is important to establish guidelines for how your department or another department will be charged for the merchandise, and whether it will be at retail or at cost (see your accountant for guidelines regarding tax deductions). That transfer must also be recorded.

Tracking the movement of merchandise from one usage to another, one store to another, or from one classification to another is extremely important. All transfers are recorded on the merchandise received form. It is important to remember that when a "transfer out" entry is made, a corresponding "transfer in" must be posted to the record of the receiving store or classification. Both entries must appear on the same month end report to ensure accurate book inventories for planning purposes.

# SHRINKAGE

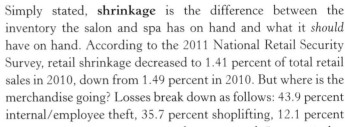

**shrinkage.** The difference between the actual inventory count on hand and what the records state.

Simply stated, **shrinkage** is the difference between the inventory the salon and spa has on hand and what it *should* have on hand. According to the 2011 National Retail Security Survey, retail shrinkage decreased to 1.41 percent of total retail sales in 2010, down from 1.49 percent in 2010. But where is the merchandise going? Losses break down as follows: 43.9 percent internal/employee theft, 35.7 percent shoplifting, 12.1 percent paperwork errors, and 5 percent due to vendor fraud. The cause of the remaining shrink is undetermined.

© Steve Lovegrove/www.Shutterstock.com

## Calculating Shrinkage

Any difference between the salon and spa's physical inventory, taken at retail, and the book (or calculated) inventory, also recorded at retail, is shrinkage. The recordkeeping processes outlined above allow the salon and spa to maintain a book (or calculated) inventory each month. The book inventory is calculated as follows:

Starting with physical inventory (actual count) at retail, subtract the following:

- Sales
- Markdowns
- Chargebacks
- Merchandise transferred out of the salon and spa to another location

Determine a subtotal, then *add* to that:

- Additional markups on merchandise
- Merchandise received at retail
- Merchandise transferred in from another location

After calculating shrinkage, the balance is the new book inventory at retail value. The ability to keep track of these figures easily and to compare them against the physical inventory is one of the benefits of using the retail method of accounting.

This accounting is done monthly. At the end of any month during the year or at the end of the last month of the year, a physical inventory is taken at retail. Theoretically, the amount of merchandise on hand at retail and the book inventory should be the same. They rarely are. The difference, expressed in a percentage, is shrinkage.

Where did the difference go? Some may have gone out the door with shoplifters, but this may not be the major loss. Much shrinkage comes from markdowns that were taken but not recorded. Some of it is probably in bookkeeping errors since the salon and spa last took a physical inventory. There may be errors in the physical inventory, either in the current counting or the previous physical inventory. Unfortunately, sometimes the losses are internal problems.

Shrinkage is a direct reflection of how well you control the inventory, from recordkeeping to security. Each year the amount of the shrinkage is measured against retail sales for the year. Anything more than 1 percent of net sales is cause for concern. An increase in the percentage of shrinkage from one year to the next warrants an investigation into the reasons for the shrinkage and tighter controls in the salon and spa's retail procedures.

## Paperwork Errors

Recording errors can result in shrinkage—at least on paper. Bookkeeping errors that result in shrinkage may include unrecorded markdowns, transfers, damaged goods, misreading or recording errors in sales and/or receipt invoices, or other inaccurate recording of information.

One major cause of inventory losses in paperwork is not checking the invoice or packing slip against a physical count when the merchandise is received and taking action to correct any errors. Assuming that "it's all there" or that testers weren't charged as retail product, or that special pricing was correct, can result in shortages or margin erosion. Always assure paperwork is accurate and packing slips and invoices are checked accurately. Managers who spend extra time training employees to properly handle receiving can have a noticeable payback on their investment.

While this inventory isn't physically missing, the difference between the book inventory and the physical inventory can have a costly effect on retail planning. Not knowing what is actually in inventory may cause you to over- or under-buy. OTB numbers may also be distorted.

## Pilferage

Losses not attributable to poor recordkeeping are probably the result of pilferage, or stealing. This can either be external—shoplifting, or internal—employee theft. Both of these can be controlled with simple measures that don't necessarily involve the purchase of expensive surveillance equipment or magnetic tagging of merchandise.

## Store Layout

The way that merchandise is displayed can deter would-be shoplifters. Your staff should be able to easily spot items that are missing from displays, which should be checked and straightened frequently. Uncluttered displays and adequate lighting also make it more difficult for shoplifters to succeed.

Placing valuable merchandise in a locked display case or close to the receptionist, where it can be monitored, is another good idea, although the risks and benefits of this tactic must be weighed. Locking up merchandise or putting it behind the counter can decrease sales, as many customers will not ask the staff to show them those items, perceiving them as too expensive or too much trouble. However, there are times when securing merchandise in that manner is warranted. Develop a consistent policy so staff will know what merchandise should be secured— for instance, jewelry over $100, leather/suede garments, or eye creams or serums above a certain price. It is also important to train staff on key control for counters and locks.

## Spot Checks

If a review of merchandise reveals that certain items are pilfered more frequently than others, you can initiate spot checks of those items—for instance, counting $250 moisturizing creams daily. Some merchandise may even warrant both morning and evening counts. Not only will this process enable you to monitor whether items are being shoplifted by customers, it will also serve as a deterrent to employee theft. When staff members know that merchandise is being counted daily, they may be less likely to try to steal it. The twice-daily inventories of high-loss items can also help identify when the loss is taking place and whether it might be pilferage from contract cleaning staff.

## Employee Education

You can solicit ideas from staff about how to keep merchandise from walking out of the doors. Then let them know the salon and spa's goals for reducing pilferage and offer training on how to identify potential shoplifters. Many local police departments will be happy to help with this kind of training.

Customer service training can also help to deter theft. A shoplifter may not necessarily be a hardened criminal, but just someone who sees an opportunity that is too good to pass up. The opportunity may arise from inadequate or inattentive staff, or poorly placed products. When employees acknowledge customers, check in on guests in fitting rooms, or offer help while guests are browsing shelves, those customers are less likely to steal.

## Inventory Storage and Control Procedures

Removing temptation is a strong deterrent to internal theft. Retail inventory that is stored with the professional product or in areas with high employee traffic, such as the break room, is more likely to be stolen than inventory that is properly stored. By having an organized and secure space in which to keep back stock and merchandise being received, your business is much less likely to have losses. It is essential to limit access to inventory stock areas and to separate storage from bulk or professional product. It is also a good idea to have a policy of not allowing merchandise to be removed until an order has been completely received.

Disciplined inventory control procedures—such as sign-out sheets and transfer forms for when employees remove stock from the selling area—also help to deter internal pilferage. When you communicate through words and actions that inventory is protected and counted, employees will also pick up on the importance of these procedures and will realize that it won't be easy to get away with pilfering merchandise.

# CHAPTER SUMMARY

- Using a disciplined approach to retail inventory management will lead to less frustration, stronger retail performance, better sell through, fewer markdowns, and greater profitability.
- A good turnover rate assures fresh inventory and the opportunity to change the product mix. A good turnover rate is between 3 and 4.
- A good sales-to-stock ratio will keep the proper amount of inventory on hand. The idea is to keep 3 to 4 months of product on hand.
- Setting and monitoring min/max levels of each item assures you reorder before you run out of product and do not overstock your inventory.

- The best retailers make a practice of a weekly review of top sellers and slow movers, then take action accordingly.
- By keeping track of inventory aging at 30, 60, and 90 days, you will know when to mark down items that have low sell through.
- Turnover is the major key to generating spendable retail dollars to support overall salon and spa operational expenses.
- Open to buy is a purchasing budget by classification that helps you to determine the amount of money in retail dollars you have available to spend on inventory replenishment.
- Always record inventory movement. Not recording between department transfers and gratis will skew the amount of cost of goods sold.

# LEARNING ACTIVITIES

## Learning Activity 4-1: Hustling the Slowpokes

Review your salon or spa's retail inventory and identify three to five items that are slow movers. Investigate why these items might be slow movers. Some causes might include:

- Presentation. Could a change of display position the item more effectively?
- Seasonal issues. Has an unusually warm autumn kept customers from buying sweaters? Has a particularly rainy summer decreased the market for sun care products?
- Merchandise quality. Are there issues with formulations, specifications, fabric, sewing, or color flaws? Is it difficult to match (accessories)? Is there too much or too little fragrance?
- Training in product knowledge. Does the staff understand the product's features and benefits? Are they actively promoting the product?

After identifying the reasons why the items you chose are slow movers, develop a plan to increase their sell through. If there does not seem to be a way to increase their sell through, develop a plan for clearing out that merchandise.

## Learning Activity 4-2: Stop That Shoplifter!

Conduct a training session about pilferage and shoplifting. Teach your staff how to identify potential shoplifters and how to act to prevent shoplifting. Your local police department may have training resources for your staff. Following the training session, monitor your losses from pilferage to determine if the training was effective.

# REVIEW QUESTIONS

1. Inventory management techniques include all of the following, EXCEPT:
   a. Min/max
   b. Top sellers/slow movers
   c. Chargebacks
   d. Inventory aging

2. Which of the following formulas calculate turnover?
   a. Total retail sales divided by the sum of average inventory at retail
   b. Sales divided by beginning inventory
   c. Beginning of month inventory minus retail reductions plus planned inventory increases
   d. Cost of goods sold divided by retail revenue

3. Lydia is setting min/max levels for one of her salon and spa's top sellers, a citrus-almond foot scrub. Which of the following factors should she keep in mind when setting her reorder point?
   a. The retail price of the item
   b. The length of time between ordering the product and its delivery to the salon and spa
   c. How long the salon and spa has carried the product
   d. Where the product will be displayed

4. The longer a product remains on the shelf, the greater the likelihood that it will not sell at regular price. This best describes the concept of:
   a. Stock-to-sales ratio
   b. Markdowns
   c. Turnover
   d. Inventory aging

5. Reuben analyzes the following numbers for the month of April.
   Beginning inventory: $9,000
   Sales: $3,500
   Markdowns: $750
   Purchases: $4,000
   Planned end of month inventory: $11,000
   Based on these figures, what is his open to buy?
   a. $1,750
   b. $2,250
   c. $1,125
   d. $4,500

6. Standard markup at the Urban Salon and Spa is 100 percent. Using the open to buy figure from Question 5, what will be the amount of Reuben's vendor order at cost?
   a. $2,250
   b. $ 875
   c. $4,500
   d. $1,125

7. The Urban Salon and Spa has been experiencing pilferage of its $150 moisturizers. Reuben decides to move the moisturizers to a display shelf behind the reception desk that can only be accessed by an employee. This represents what method of deterrent?
   a. Employee education
   b. Store layout
   c. Inventory storage
   d. Spot check

8. The Seasons Salon and Spa has an inventory of heavy wool caps that have been slow movers all season. As the weather warms up, Jazmine knows that the caps will be nearly impossible to sell. Which of the following solutions would be the LEAST desirable for her inventory problem?
   a. Box up the caps until fall, when customers will be looking for wool caps again.
   b. Donate the caps to a local charity and take a tax write-off.
   c. Begin a markdown cycle of 33 percent, then 50 percent, then 75 percent until the caps are sold.
   d. Develop a "free product with purchase" promotion, in which the wool caps are the free product.

9. To calculate shrinkage, you must know which of the following numbers:
    a. Turnover
    b. Stock-to-sales ratio
    c. Book inventory
    d. Min/max levels

10. The inventory planning process begins with:
    a. Placing orders with vendors
    b. Determining inventory levels for each classification
    c. Determining the inventory turnover the salon and spa would like to achieve
    d. Determining the retail calendar for the year

# Evaluating Financial Performance

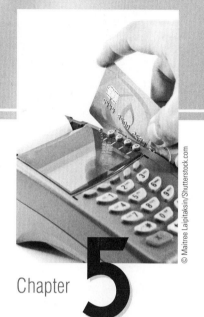

## INTRODUCTION

There are many key business indicators for retail. As you can see from the example in the Salon and Spa Snapshot 5.1, just one measure is not enough. There are eight measurements that provide the most important information for you. These are indicators that you will want to watch closely to get the information you need for good management decision making. These are key evaluators that will help you maximize the profit in the retail department.

They are also indicators that will help the salon and spa industry as a whole. Research surveys into these indicators can help identify retail trends and set industry benchmarks. The key business indicators are:

- Retail Sales Percentage of Total Salon and Spa Revenue
- Retail Sales Contribution by Merchandise Classification
- Retail Sales per Ticket
- Retail Sales by Service Provider
- Retail Markdown Percentage
- Retail Sales per Square Foot
- Cost of Sales Percentage

## KEY BUSINESS INDICATORS IN SALON AND SPA RETAIL OPERATIONS

Before we discuss the most common key indicators, it will be helpful to familiarize yourself with some common accounting terms. Some common definitions of terms used in this section are defined later within this chapter. These definitions will be used and expanded upon

Chapter **5**

© Maitree Laipitaksin/Shutterstock.com

## LEARNING OBJECTIVES

After successfully completing this chapter, the reader will be able to:

- Calculate retail sales as a percentage of total revenue.

- Calculate the retail sales contribution by merchandise classification.

- Calculate retail sales by ticket (average retail sales per visit).

- Explain why salons and spas track retail sales by service provider.

- Identify the importance inventory has on measuring financial performance.

## At the Urban Salon and Spa...

Reuben decided he needed to examine his preliminary financial statements more closely. He arranged to have a morning meeting with Mae, and the two of them began combing over the financial statements.

"Let's start with the retail revenue as reported in the March Statement of Income," Mae said.

"We were right on target!" Reuben said. "Look, we have a retail revenue of $10,000, with total salon and spa revenue of $78,000. The $10,000 in retail revenue is exactly what we had planned for, 12.8 percent of the total salon and spa revenue."

"That's true," agreed Mae. "And that number would have been good if the salon and spa had done the business that it had forecasted, or even great if it had had 10 percent fewer guests than we planned. Do you remember anything out of the ordinary that month?"

Reuben thought for a moment and then said, "Was that the month we got the last-minute bridal shower of 50 ladies because the spa downtown wouldn't offer them a private reception room for before the services? That was quite the coup for us."

Mae nodded. "It must have been. It probably partially explains why our overall treatments were up by 20 percent over what had been forecast. The forecast for the month of total salon and spa revenue was only $65,000. So total salon and spa revenue was up, but the retail revenue stayed flat. If the revenue had been at forecast, then the salon and spa retail would have been at 15.4 percent of total sales. As it was, it was at only 12.8 percent of spa revenue."

"But isn't it a good thing that total revenue was up?" asked Reuben.

"Yes, but I think what Fiona feels is that since revenue exceeded the forecast and we were giving more treatments, the retail should have been up a like amount—especially since the bride did register here at the salon and spa and many of her guests made purchases."

**total retail revenue.**
The sum total of retail revenue from each product classification. Sales tax is not included in this figure.

**revenue adjustments.**
Adjustments to revenue, which may include employee discounts, merchandise returns, overages, and undercharges.

as we move through the material. For more detailed definitions and information, reference the International SPA Association Foundation's *Uniform System of Financial Reporting for Spas.*

- **Total retail revenue:** Total retail revenue is the sum total of retail revenue from each product classification. Sales tax is not included in this figure.
- **Revenue adjustments:** These adjustments might include employee discounts, merchandise returns, and allowances.
- **Net retail revenue:** Net retail revenue is calculated by subtracting the total retail revenue adjustments from total retail revenue.

- **Cost of goods sold:** Cost of goods sold is the direct cost, including freight, of merchandise purchased for resale. This number is typically expressed as a dollar amount, but converted to a percentage to become the cost of sales.
- **Cost of sales:** The cost of goods sold converted into a percentage. The cost of goods sold dollar amount is divided by the total retail revenue.

## Retail Sales Percentage of Total Salon and Spa Revenue

One way to understand how well your retail is performing is to determine the **retail sales percentage** of total salon and spa revenue. As in the example in the Salon and Spa Snapshot 5.1, the retail accounted for 12.8 percent of the total salon and spa revenue. This is a straightforward calculation, taking the net retail revenue and dividing it by the total salon and spa revenue.

In the example using the Urban Salon and Spa, the net retail revenue was $10,000 and the total salon and spa revenue was $78,000, therefore, $10,000 \div 78,000 = 12.8\%$.

This result allows you to get a snapshot regarding how your retail operation impacts the total sales of the salon and spa, yet it does not tell you how the sales were distributed across your product classifications, or which department contributed the most sales, or even if each service provider contributed to sales. These measures are very important, and we will look more closely at them in the following sections.

## Retail Sales Contribution by Merchandise Classification

If your salon or spa has significant retail revenue, you will want to monitor retail sales by classification as compared to plan. This information is valuable as it can aid you in:

- Making adjustments to the salon and spa's inventory levels of the various classifications
- Considering the addition of new merchandise in a product classification
- Reducing emphasis on slower selling classifications

Retail sales are broken down into basic classifications such as shampoo, styling products, bath/products, makeup products, and so on, along with several subclassifications of each. Chapter 2 goes into more detail about classifications and subclassifications.

**net retail revenue.** Subtracting the total retail adjustments (employee discounts, merchandise returns, and allowances such as overcharges or undercharges) from the total retail revenue.

**cost of goods sold.** The direct cost, including freight, of merchandise purchased for resale. This number is typically expressed as a dollar amount but is converted to a percentage to become the cost of sales.

**cost of sales.** The profitability of retail sales expressed as a percentage.

**retail sales percentage.** A calculation used to evaluate the impact of retail sales on the total salon and spa revenue.

**FYI**

One way you can get an overall sense of the impact of your retail operation is to determine how much the retail sales contribute to the total salon and spa revenue.

**retail sales contribution by classification.** A calculation used to evaluate the impact of a particular product classification on the total retail sales.

**retail per ticket.** A calculation used to compare average retail sales to the number of tickets.

**retail per service ticket.** A calculation used to evaluate the average amount of merchandise sold per customers receiving services, allowing the retail per service provider to be tracked.

**HERE'S A TIP**

Another way to evaluate the retail sales of your salon and spa operation is to compare retail sales to the number of tickets posted during the month.

The **retail sales contribution by classification** (also called mix of sales) is calculated for each classification by dividing the total sales in a classification by total retail sales (total retail sales in a classification ÷ total retail sales = classification sales percentage).

For example, if the Urban Salon and Spa did $10,000 in total retail revenue, and $2,800 was in product sales, the product classification contribution would be 28 percent ($2,800 ÷ $10,000).

## Retail Sales per Ticket

Measuring by ticket allows you to factor in those guests who have multiple treatments on one ticket. It expresses how much on average the customers who come to the salon and spa for services are also purchasing in retail at each visit.

**Retail per ticket** can give more useful data than retail per service.

Example:
The Urban Salon and Spa had 695 tickets in the month. Retail was $10,000. What was the average retail per ticket?
Total retail sales ÷ Total number of tickets =
Retail per ticket
$10,000 ÷ 695 = $14.38 average retail per ticket

Measuring by ticket can be further broken down to retail sales that appear on *service tickets* versus sales that have only retail sales on them. Measuring by service ticket also helps you determine whether your service providers are selling retail. Many salons and spas are in an environment where customers will visit for the sole purpose of buying retail. These retail-only customers can distort the retail performance of your business. Measuring **retail per service ticket** tracks the retail performance of service providers. We will discuss the importance of this measure in the next section.

Example:
The three nail technicians at the Urban Salon and Spa sold $749 in retail in a month. There were 325 guest tickets in the month. What is the average retail per service ticket for the month?

Total revenue from retail on service tickets ÷ Number of
service tickets = Retail per service ticket
$749 ÷ 325 = $2.30 average retail per ticket

**FYI**

The most common measurement of
salon and spa retail is retail sales
per treatment by service provider.

## Retail Sales by Service Provider

While this text is not a "how to train your therapists to sell
more retail" program, it is about the business of retail and it is
appropriate to monitor the sales by individual staff members.

There are dozens of ways you can track retail sales by service provider, whether they receive a flat commission or a tiered commission. Some salons and spas recognize that an esthetician with many retail subcategories (covering various skin types and treatments, for example) will sell more retail in dollars than a nail technician or massage therapist with just a few subcategories. Therefore, you will need to have goals for each service provider depending on their department. You may track daily, weekly, or by pay period for your sales results by service provider. Tracking individual sales is important because retail sales are such a critical component of your salon and spa's financial sustainability. Measuring the fact that Mary generated $1,200 in retail sales and Sue only generated $400 during the past month is not a meaningful comparison. For example, Mary may be an esthetician who works full time and Sue may be a nail technician only working one or two days a week. What is important to track is Mary and Sue's retail sales per treatment performed by each. That is a statistic that can be used to reward employees and to provide additional training or counseling for others.

Although you may be tracking sales by individual, it is still a common mindset that service providers feel uncomfortable selling or do not see it as a part of their job. To assure that your service providers are aware of their role in recommending products, you

© Yuri Arcurs/www.Shutterstock.com

## At the Savvy Salon...
## Retail Goals for Team Growth

The Savvy Salon in Redondo Beach, California, has measures in place to assure all staff is serving their customer through retail. Each service provider has an average retail sales per ticket goal and a personal retail sales goal. These goals are evaluated monthly and team performance is acknowledged at the monthly meeting. Stephanie, the owner, knows the importance of each stylist being an advocate for the products, so she assures product knowledge and sampling is part of the program. "I can't expect my team to recommend home care products if they are not using the products during the service or if they don't have a solid knowledge base. I ask the vendor to supply the team with products to take home and try. This has made a huge impact on the success of my retail operation."

can include "retail sales" as a position responsibility on their job description. For further employee development opportunities, there are several wonderful programs, workshops, articles, and other resources at milady.cengage.com that focus on this subject.

### Retail Markdown Percentage

Retail markdowns are made to move merchandise that has a low sell through or to increase retail revenue by a special promotion. You will want to know what the markdown percentage is because it is a measurement of how successful purchasing, marketing, training, and other factors are. For example, the point-of-sale system needs to be set up to track retail markdowns and discounts separately. You will always need to be able to track the effect of discounts on the cost of sales in order to communicate that effect to management. For while both retail markdowns and discounts increase the cost of sales percentage, the managerial response to each is different.

It is a good idea to conduct a monthly review of sales, and use that time as an opportunity to study special promotional programs that occurred during the month. Examples would include a special holiday sales program, a gift with purchase program, or a clearance sale. Since these promotions affect sales, they are important information for planning future retail promotions. You can note the results of the special retail programs and attach them to the monthly statements for planning the same month in the following year.

In the salon and spa industry, markdowns and coupons are used heavily to stimulate service and retail sales. Without careful analysis and frequent review, markdowns and coupons can skew retail profitability comparisons from one month to another. An average retail markdown ratio can provide managers and owners the opportunity to monitor how revenue is affected by these promotions.

The **average retail markdown** rate is calculated by dividing the total retail markdowns taken by the total retail revenue. For example, the Urban Salon and Spa had total retail revenue of $15,000 for the month and had $1,400 in total retail markdowns taken:

**average retail markdown.**
A calculation used to evaluate the impact of coupons and discounts taken on the total retail revenue.

10 face creams at 20% off retail = $240
19 anti-aging serums at 20% off retail = $550
12 conditioners at 100% off retail (free with a shampoo) = $280
11 robes at 30% off retail (end-of-season sale) = $330

Total retail markdowns ÷ Total retail revenue = $1,400 ÷ $15,000 = 9.3%

The markdown percentage equals the sum of sales of all retail reductions to price whether markdown had been taken on item price sticker or at point-of-sale. The total markdown amount is divided by the total retail revenue.

Look at your average markdown compared with the average markdown for your industry and similar industries. Are you buying too much? Are you buying the right items for your customers? While on the surface it may seem like the right strategy is to minimize your markdown rate, some view it as a sign of stagnation. Too low a markdown rate can mean that you are avoiding "clearing out" older inventory (over 90–120 days in inventory). It might also be a sign that too few new trends are being introduced into the merchandise assortment, as this is typically riskier merchandise that sometimes requires a higher markdown rate. We will discuss the markdowns as they relate to the cost of sales later on in this section.

**FYI**

The average apparel retailer runs a 20 percent markdown rate on average. When you know where you stand compared to your peers or in similar industries, you can tell how you are doing at buying.

## Retail Sales per Square Foot

In the classic retail environment, revenue is monitored on a **retail sales per square foot** basis that is calculated annually. This calculation is done by dividing total retail revenue by the square

**retail sales per square foot.**
A calculation to monitor retail revenue contribution within the salon and spa retail space.

© MaiDix/www.Shutterstock.com

footage of the retail space. For example, if retail sales were $300,000 for the year at the Seasons Salon and Spa, and the retail space measures 20 feet by 40 feet, or 800 square feet (20 × 40 = 800), then the retail sales per square foot would be $375 ($300,000 ÷ 800 square feet = $375).

There is a wide degree of variance in comparing retail operations in the salon and spa industry, such as differences in location and size. Most resort/hotel salons and spas have sales per square foot in the $500 to $1,000 range with anything over $1,000 per square foot suggesting that they could use more space devoted to retail.

This statistic is less meaningful to salons and spas that display their retail merchandise in the reception area or scattered throughout various areas, as it becomes more difficult to calculate the square footage devoted to retail sales. However, it is still a useful statistic because it gets you thinking of the retail operations in terms of what is generated in each small square foot of potential sales space. Visual display is still important—you don't boost sales by jamming merchandise into the space, but by thinking of your display space as a valuable asset that contributes to the salon and spa's overall retail profitability.

For example, a salon and spa may have a display of high-end blow dryers and impressive travel cases that it sells only a few of each month. Although the display looks appealing, the display occupies several square feet of space and produces little revenue. Then there is a small rack with home fragrances and candles that occupies only two square feet, but which generates hundreds of dollars in retail sales each month.

The key to maximizing your retail space is to utilize the basic principles of retail space planning and visual merchandising. For more information on these topics, please see *Retail Analysis and Coaching Tools for the Salon and Spa* offered by Milady, a part of Cengage Learning.

SALON AND SPA SNAPSHOT 5.3

## At the Urban Salon and Spa…

Reuben hung up the phone in frustration. Fiona Matthews, the owner of the Urban Salon and Spa, was demanding that Reuben explain why the cost of sales percentage in April was 56.5 percent when it was budgeted to be 50 percent.

It simply didn't make sense to Reuben. A month ago they were not only on track, they were doing great. The March cost of sales was only 47.5 percent. He was thrilled when he saw that number as it let him focus on marketing the recent changes in the services menu and take his attention off of the retail operations.

"What could cause such a drastic change and why didn't I have any warning?" Reuben thought as he punched in the phone number of Mae, the staff accountant. He rushed through the pleasantries and then asked, "Mae, I've got a problem. Can you tell me what's up with my retail cost of sales? Why did it spike so high in one month when we didn't have any markdowns during April and everything seemed to be on target in March?"

"Actually, Reuben, they weren't on target," answered Mae. "But I didn't know that because no one turned in the invoice for the March 17 extra skin care order of $225 until April 5. If I'd had that in March, your actual cost of sales would have been 52 percent, not 47.5 percent. I had to apply it to your April sales, which then inflated the cost percentage even further for that month."

# COST OF GOODS SOLD/COST OF SALES PERCENTAGE

Retail planning, purchasing, and inventory management are only the beginning of the story for salon and spa professionals. Those three tasks lay the groundwork for the day-to-day success of a retail operation. Once those tasks are complete, salon and spa professionals monitor their daily business reports and monthly financial statements and evaluate their operation continually.

There is a natural tendency for managers to glance quickly at the monthly financial statement and check the key numbers. At a glance to determine whether revenue met the forecast for the month, whether the cost of sales percentage is low, whether retail payroll is in line, and whether other expenses were controlled.

If no red flags pop up, they pat themselves on the back and move along to the other issues of the day. But, as shown in the Urban Salon and Spa story above, these summary numbers are the result of layers of individual entries. There could well be a condition called **compensating errors** that caused the positive results.

While all of the financial entries for the month are recorded by account in the general ledger, it isn't necessary that managers examine every entry. That could take all day or even several days for a large operation. But there are key business indicators that can be monitored monthly to measure the success of the retail department. As Reuben found out, sometimes when financial news is too good to be true, it really *is* too good to be true. The role of a proactive salon and spa retail manager is to react when financial news is bad and to be suspicious when the results are better than their instincts say they should be.

## Cost of Goods Sold

How much does it cost you to sell a bottle of shampoo or body cream (or any goods) to your customers? You may purchase a single unit of merchandise for $16.25, but there is a direct cost to associate with that, such as freight or even insurance. These direct costs need to be considered when you consider your profit from your retail operation.

The reduction of inventory and retail sales is then recorded at the point of sale, causing the revenue and related expense to be recorded at the same time. So the cost of goods sold can also be calculated as the difference between opening inventory plus purchases at cost and the closing inventory at cost. "Freight in" is normally added to purchases at cost. The cost of goods sold is always expressed in a dollar amount, then used in a formula to calculate the cost of sales percentage. We will look at this calculation in this section.

Several factors can increase your cost of goods sold, or decrease it. As you saw in the example with the Urban Salon and Spa, a delay in processing the paperwork on an incoming order artificially lowered Ruben's cost of goods sold. How? He had extra inventory on hand that was not recorded by accounting, making his inventory value inaccurate. The cost of goods sold is calculated using the cost of actual items (with no markup) as follows:

> Inventory at beginning of period
> + Purchases or additions during the period
> − Inventory at end of period
> = Cost of goods sold (dollar amount)

Example:

Body moisturizer costs $16.50 each (including freight). There are 10 on hand at the beginning of the month, with 25 purchased during the month. There are 7 units available at the end of the month. What was the cost of goods sold for the month for body moisturizer?

Inventory at cost, beginning of month = $165.00

(10 units on hand)

Purchases @ cost + freight during month = $412.50

(purchased 25 units)

Total available ($165.00 + $412.50) = $577.50

Inventory on hand, end of month @ cost = $115.50 (7 units)

Cost of goods sold ($577.50 − $115.50) = $462.00

Cost of goods sold (28 units sold at a cost of $16.50 ea.)

The cost of sales measures the profitability of retail sales. It is a ratio between the cost of the goods sold and the net revenue. It is always expressed as a percentage of net revenue, never as a specific dollar amount. It is the largest expense within a salon and spa retail department and merits study on a monthly basis. The cost of sales is the percentage expression of the cost of goods sold compared to the total retail revenue.

You will sometimes hear the cost of sales percentage called the cost of goods sold. Here the cost of goods sold and the cost of sales are used interchangeably. The cost of sales is the cost of goods sold ÷ net retail revenue = cost of sales percentage.

To calculate the cost of sales percentage, you will need to know the following:

- Cost of goods sold
- Total retail revenue
- Net retail revenue, which is your total retail revenue, minus any **revenue adjustments**

**HERE'S A TIP**

Freight can add a large expense if you are ordering frequently to replenish inventory. Take advantage of case pricing and stretch your ordering frequency by ordering popular items in bulk.

Example (as above, continued):

The cost of goods sold for the 28 units of body moisturizer is $462.00, the product retailed at $40.00, the net retail revenue is $1,080 (total revenue of $1,120.00 − $40.00 for a returned bottle). What is the cost of sales percentage for the body moisturizer?

Cost of goods sold ÷ Net retail revenue = Cost of sales percentage
$462 ÷ $1,080 = 43%, cost of sales percentage

## Things That Make the Cost of Sales Percentage High

Look at these eight areas to see what's making your cost of sales higher than you might expect:

1. Markdowns: Consider markdowns taken during the month to move old merchandise. Although you want to clear out old inventory to reduce stagnation, evaluate your quantities to assure you are not buying too much. We will talk more about markdowns later on in this section.

2. Pilferage: Loss of inventory due to internal or external theft. Take additional measures to reduce opportunities for theft. Take a physical count of high-dollar items daily.

3. Transfers: Products transferred from retail to professional areas that were not recorded. Assure stock is not taken from the front for professional use and then not recorded.

4. Discounts: It is customary to offer employee discounts and perhaps member discounts on retail merchandise. If a significant amount of merchandise is sold at a discount, it will increase the cost of goods sold/cost of sales. We will explore discounts later on in this section.

5. Discount promotions: Some markdown promotions may be so successful that they increase the overall cost of sales percentage. For example, a candle that is a "gift with purchase" offer has a real cost associated with it and will be included in the cost of goods sold. Special promotions like this must each be evaluated for what the profit contribution was from the promotion (net revenue). Did the promotion increase not only revenue from the main item, but also dollars put into the bank?

6. Incorrect physical inventory count: For example, the purchase price of a night cream is $100 and there are 10 units counted in the inventory. The value of the inventory is recorded as $1,000. However, if the cost

© mmaaxr/www.Shutterstock.com

is mistakenly recorded as $10 per unit, the value of the inventory would be $100, making the value of the inventory understated and the reported cost of sales too high.

7. Delays in recordkeeping: Sometimes merchandise has been received, but the invoice has not been given to the accountant. When this happens, it is not recorded in the general ledger as an addition to inventory, causing the cost of sales percentage to be understated one month and overstated in the next month—or whenever the invoice is given to the accountant. Remember how the cost of sales was inflated by 4.5 percent for the Urban Salon and Spa because a purchase invoice was not accounted for?

8. Uncounted inventory: If merchandise has been received and the accounting staff has processed the invoice, but the box is still sitting in the manager's office and not counted, it will cause inventory to be understated (the cost of goods sold inaccurate) and increase the cost of sales percentage.

## Things That Make the Cost of Sales Percentage Low

1. Increased sales of merchandise with a higher margin. Your initial markup will have the most impact on the cost of goods sold and the cost of sales percentage. There is further discussion on calculating the initial markup later on in this section.

2. Less sales at a discount.

3. High sales of items at a higher markup. For example, a special closeout merchandise item from a vendor at a higher markup.

4. Incorrect physical inventory count. For example, if the night cream from the previous example was purchased for $10, and again 10 units were counted in the inventory but mistakenly reported at $100 rather than $10, it will overstate the inventory value and reduce the cost of goods sold.

5. Merchandise received but the invoice not recorded. If merchandise has been received but the invoice is not recorded by the accounting staff, the inventory has been overstated, thus reducing the cost of goods sold and

cost of sales percentage. This is the result of the delay in paperwork, and will cause the cost of sales to be higher the next month. (See item 7, "Delays in recordkeeping".)

Too often, you will analyze the problem when the cost of sales percentage is too high, and just accept the good news if the cost is significantly lower than planned. While this sounds acceptable, it might be allowing an error to go undetected that causes a cost of sales percentage higher than planned during the following month. When this happens, the salon and spa ends up going three months without reporting a true financial picture of the retail department, making the budgeting and planning process much harder when it comes time to plan for the following year.

For example, you see that your cost of sales dropped by 7 percent from the previous month. As you analyze the revenue adjustments and compare these with the previous month, you find the lower revenue adjustments were due to the "buy one, get one free" promotion that was not part of the current month. By understanding how these promotions impact your numbers, you can evaluate the impact of the promotion on profits.

The cost of goods sold value is a reflection of the inventory count in dollars. It is important to remember that cost of goods sold is not affected by purchases or by orders that are received during the month, unless they are unrecorded. A salon and spa does not expense purchase orders when merchandise is ordered or received. The retail inventory appears on the balance sheet as an asset just like cash or credit card receivables or the furniture in the facility. Merchandise is only expensed as it is sold. Points to remember:

- The cost of goods sold is an inventory value at cost in dollars, with no retail markup.
- The cost of sales percentage is the retail revenue generated once these goods are sold.

If the cost of goods sold dollar amount is inaccurate (too high or too low) the cost of sales percentage will be affected in the opposite way.

## What Affects Cost of Goods Sold/Cost of Sales Percentage?

The cost of goods sold is calculated with a formula reflecting the change in inventory value for the month, and ends up being an account of what has happened each month and for the year to date. It becomes one of many tools to plan sales and inventories so that the retail operation provides a good gross profit.

As mentioned previously, there are several significant influencers that affect the cost of goods sold and cost of sales percentage. They include the five following factors, all important, and which we will explore a bit further: initial markups, markdowns, invoice discounts and freight, merchandise movement, and physical inventories.

## Initial Markups

Initial markup has the greatest effect on total revenue and the cost of sales percentage. The higher the markup, the lower the cost of sales percentage, unless that initial markup is eroded by excessive markdowns. At the same time, there is a limit to how high the markup can be and still have the salon and spa be perceived by the guest as having a reasonable price/value relationship.

Typical initial markup in the industry is to simply double the cost of the retail item (keystone markup), and take the cost of the purchase price and multiply by two to get the retail price. However, most vendors will supply salons and spas with suggested retail prices. These prices are important to consider as today's consumers are knowledgeable and likely to be familiar with the current market. If one salon and spa has an exfoliate for $30 and the salon and spa down the street has the same brand and same item for $25, the customer is likely to go with the salon and spa that has the lower price, unless the pricier salon and spa has established a strong point of difference in some other way. This can be done, for example, through their rich customer service experience or by their "100% satisfaction guaranteed" return policy.

There are two methods for achieving higher markup:
1. Raising the retail price
2. Lowering the cost price, either through vendor negotiation or by increasing quantities ordered

Factors to consider in establishing markup include:
- Manufacturer's suggested retail price
- Competition and availability of merchandise in your market
- Exclusivity, such as items with the salon and spa's logo
- Operating expenses
- Expected turnover
- Customer acceptance

**CAUTION**

Raising prices too high can price merchandise out of the competitive range and therefore decrease its salability.

The following is a quick way to establish the correct retail price when you set an initial markup goal for merchandise:

Cost price (including freight) ÷ **Cost complement** of markup goal = Retail price

The cost complement = 100% − the markup %. For example: markup of 55 percent has a cost complement of 45 percent (100 − 55 = 45).

Example:

A box of body moisturizers has been received at the Seasons Salon and Spa from the vendor at a cost of $16.50 each, including freight. The salon and spa's markup goal for that type of product is 58 percent. *The cost complement of 58 percent is 42 percent (100 − 58).* Divide $16.50 by the cost complement of 42 percent. (0.42) = $39.29. Since $39.29 would be a strange price for the merchandise, and the Seasons Salon and Spa's policy is to price merchandise at the even dollar, the retail price becomes $40.00. When Seasons applies the initial markup percentage formula, it has:

$40.00 − $16.50 = $23.50 (gross profit from markup)
$23.50 ÷ $40.00 = 58.8%

We will continue with this example later in this section when we discuss maintained markup.

## Markdowns

**Markdowns** result in decreased total retail revenue and a higher cost of sales percentage. As a manager or buyer, you have a responsibility to learn to plan properly so that you can control excessive markdowns. The better the planning that goes into purchasing, the less likely it is that markdowns will be necessary.

Any incentive to stimulate sales—including special offerings, packages of discounted products linked to treatment, loyalty cards, and/or preferred programs—can result in a higher cost of sales and a lower **margin.** The planning process should allow for expected markdowns. We will look at markdowns and discounts as they relate to the inventory planning process later in this section.

## Invoice Discounts/Freight

Depending on accounting practices, invoice discounts on freight will affect the cost of goods sold. The cost of shipping is typically added to the cost of the product.

## Merchandise Movement

Pilferage, transfer of retail products to treatments or professional use, damaged merchandise, and using live retail product for sampling, all have an effect on the cost of sales percentage. These adjustments affect the total revenue and inventory count. Specifically, they reduce the inventory count, used to calculate the cost of goods sold. You will want to carefully document movement via transfers, inventory reduction forms, return-to-vendor forms, etc.

## Physical Inventory

Incorrect inventory counts can incorrectly state the cost of goods sold. It is important to develop a methodical system to take an accurate physical inventory. Salons and spas differ on how often they take inventory. Monthly inventories provide the most useful information and reduce incorrect counts. However, some salons and spas will take inventories only every three months, six months, or perhaps only annually.

Salons and spas that cannot take a full physical inventory every month often use cycle counts as a way of organizing their inventories and keeping their counts up to date. With cycle counts, a single classification is counted on a set frequency schedule. Within each cycle, the entire inventory is physically counted. If a particular classification is experiencing higher than usual variances, it might get counted more frequently until the problem can be identified. Markdowns are any reduction in retail price after merchandise has been received in stock. Discounts to employees or members may be recorded separately from markdowns of merchandise in stock, but the effect of those discounts is exactly the same as that of markdowns.

© Darko1981/www.Shutterstock.com

While excessive markdowns are typically to be avoided—and one of the goals of planning is to minimize the need for markdowns—you usually end up marking down products in the following instances:

- Overbuying or incorrect buying
- Product does not match customers' needs or buying habits
- Recession or downturn in local economy affects sales unexpectedly
- Increased competition the salon and spa must meet
- Damaged merchandise (flood, tornado, hurricane, or just shopworn)
- Late deliveries with inadequate selling time remaining in the season (sun products, slimming products, summer apparel collection received too late)
- Products getting close to expiration date
- Repackaging or discontinued items

**FYI**

Markdowns are expressed as a percentage of net sales, just like any other expense. This provides a measurement of the profitability of sales activity and is an essential part of the planning process.

Example:

A group of suntan lotions were initially priced at $20.00. These lotions are not selling well and a markdown is necessary to accelerate the sales and clear the lotions from stock before the winter products arrive. The lotions are sold for 20 percent off. In determining the effect of the markdown on profit, this is not referred to as a 20 percent markdown in the merchandising records. It is a 25 percent markdown.

Explanation:

Original retail for each lotion was $20.00. The price at 20 percent off is $16.00. This is a $4 markdown. The markdown of $4 is measured against the net sale of $16.

$$\$4.00 \div \$16.00 = 0.25, \text{ or } 25\%$$

As another example, consider this: Total sales for the month in hair conditioner was $2,500. This figure includes both regular price merchandise and any marked down hair conditioner. If the total dollar markdown on the reduced hair conditioner was $250, the total markdown percentage for hair conditioner would be 10 percent. ($250.00 is 10 percent of $2,500.) Understanding this relationship will be helpful in working with sales and inventory projecting.

## Gross Margin

One of the measurements of profitability from year to year is gross margin. Gross margin is calculated by subtracting the cost of sales percentage from 100 percent. Gross margin is expressed as a percentage of sales. Professional merchandisers work to achieve gross margin goals by understanding their market and buying correctly.

## Maintained Markup

The amount above cost at which goods are sold establishes the **maintained markup,** which is the gross margin ÷ net sales.

**maintained markup.** The consistent amount above cost at which goods are sold.

Example:

Initial markup and maintained markup are computed using this information:

| Total buy: | 100 body moisturizers |
|---|---|
| Cost: | $16.50 |
| Retail: | $40.00 |
| Sell through: | 90 body moisturizers at $40.00 |
| | 10 body moisturizers at $30.00 (marked down as winter is coming and sales of body treatments will slow down) |

First calculate the initial markup in dollars. In this example, we will also calculate the markup after discounting the moisturizer.

Initial Markup:

| **Retail** | − | **Cost** | = | **Initial Markup** |
|---|---|---|---|---|
| $40.00 | − | $16.50 | = | $23.50 |
| $30.00 | − | $16.50 | = | $13.50 discounted items |

Next, convert the initial markup dollars into a percentage.

Initial Markup Percentage:

| **Initial Markup** | ÷ | **Retail Price** | = | **Initial Markup** |
|---|---|---|---|---|
| $23.50 | ÷ | $40.00 | = | 58.8% |
| $13.50 | ÷ | $30.00 | = | 45.0% discounted items |

Then, calculate the gross margin in dollars (total net sales − cost of goods sold).

Maintained Markup:

|  | Units |  | Dollars |  | Extension | Markup |
|---|---|---|---|---|---|---|
| Sales at retail | 90 | × | $40.00 | = | $3,600 | 58.8% |
| Markdown sales | 10 | × | $30.00 | = | $300 | 45.0% |
| Total net sales |  |  |  |  | $3,900 |  |
| Total cost | 100 | × | $16.50 | = | $1,650 |  |
| Gross margin |  |  |  | = | $2,250 (total net sales − cost of goods sold) |  |

| Net Sales | − | Cost | = Gross Margin |
|---|---|---|---|
| $3,900 |  | $1,650 | $2,250 |

Now, take the gross margin dollars and divide it by the net sales for the maintained markup.

| Gross Margin | ÷ | Net Sales | = Maintained Markup |
|---|---|---|---|
| $2,250 |  | $3,900 | 57.7% |

Summary:
Net sales after markdown: $3,900
Cost of goods sold (COGS) = $1,650 (Initial inventory + Purchases − End inventory)
Gross margin = Net sales − COGS = $3,900 − $1,650 = $2,250
Maintained markup = Gross margin ÷ Net sales

© patpitchaya/www.Shutterstock.com

# INVENTORY TURNOVER

While inventory has been thoroughly covered in a previous chapter, some of the concepts apply directly to evaluating performance and maximizing a salon and spa's profits.

## Inventory Counts

In traditional retail, it is customary to conduct full physical inventories of retail merchandise annually, semi-annually, or quarterly. In the salon and spa industry, it is the

## At the Urban Salon and Spa...

Mae poured herself a cup of tea and watched as Reuben flipped through the sales figures and thought about what they had been discussing. She winced slightly as she saw his shoulders and neck tighten up.

"Mae," he said finally, "I feel like I'm in a no-win situation here. Remember that bridal shower? Nearly all of them wanted to purchase the ginger root facial mask. Only half of them were able to because we ran out of inventory. It's one of our most popular items and I've wanted to increase how much we carry in the past. However, you keep telling me that there aren't enough inventory dollars available to increase our purchases."

Mae sipped her tea and nodded. "That's true, Reuben. For those answers, you're going to have to look beyond the statement of income summary. Take a look at the retail inventory report on the balance sheet in the blue folder." She paused as he opened up the folder.

"Remember," she continued, "there is only a 10 percent chance that merchandise that is 90 days old will sell for full price. Let's look at your inventory. In the fall, you purchased some pumpkin body cream for the holiday season. Here we are in spring and we have dozens of these creams in the back stock room collecting dust. Our inventory is way too high and we've got dollars tied up in items that aren't selling. If you want those to move, you're going to have to discount them."

"But if I discount them," Reuben objected, "I'm going to increase my cost of goods sold even further."

"That's true," Mae agreed. "At least until those items are moved out. However, until you do you also won't be able to buy those ginger root masks you need, which would ultimately improve the overall profitability of the salon and spa's retail."

practice to conduct complete physical inventories on a monthly basis. This is particularly true for resort spas that align with the hospitality industry, which requires monthly inventories to control costs.

From an evaluation perspective, the more frequently inventories are counted, the better the information available for management decision making. For example, perhaps your retail department takes a physical inventory only once a quarter. You may use the cost of sales percentage for the previous months or year to date and book that amount as the expense for the month. If there is a budgeted cost of sales percentage, you may choose to use that number instead. Then when the physical inventory is taken, the

© Korn/www.Shutterstock.com

amount reported on the balance sheet will be adjusted to the actual inventory value, which may cause a significant swing in cost of sales reported for that month. It is now far more difficult to research the cause of any problems because the number of transactions that have occurred is so much larger.

If the cost of sales percentage has remained very consistent over a long period of time, you may be able to conduct physical inventories infrequently and rely on cycle counts as a way to monitor inventory accuracy. However, if you have experienced significant swings in the reported cost of sales—any swing greater than 3 percent—you will want to conduct physical inventories more frequently.

## Days of Inventory on Hand

Inventory turnover, as discussed in the inventory management chapter, is an important statistic in running a profitable retail operation. However, sometimes it is easier to think in terms of how many days of inventory is on hand. This is a method the automotive industry commonly uses. For example, automobile manufacturers will sometimes report that they have 83 days of cars in inventory and will thus begin reducing manufacturing hours or reducing plant production.

Days of inventory on hand is calculated by taking the value of the inventory and dividing it by the average daily retail sales.

Below is an example of the Seasons Salon and Spa and how to calculate its days of inventory on hand.

Example:
The Seasons Salon and Spa has annual retail revenue of $300,000, with an average inventory value of $50,000, which is 6 turns per year ($300,000 ÷ $50,000 = 6 turns). The average daily sales (assuming the salon and spa is open 365 days a year) is $821.92.

There are two ways to calculate the days of inventory on hand using the information above.

**Method 1:**

Divide the number of days the salon and spa is open by the number of turns: $365 \div 6 = 60.83$.

**Method 2:**

Divide the average inventory value by the average daily sales: $\$50,000 \div \$821.92 = 60.83$.

# SALON AND SPA RETAIL BUDGETING

Salon and spa professionals prepare the retail department annual budget at the same time that they prepare the budget for the entire salon and spa operation. For the budget to be most useful and accurate, it is necessary to prepare a forecast of retail activities, as this represents the road map of the retail operation.

If you are the manager or owner, you will lead this process or work with your accountant. Once created, the operating budget itself serves as a measure of how well the salon and spa retail department is achieving its goals during the budget period. Deviations from the budget can signal a need for prompt corrective action to achieve the overall financial results of the retail department.

A salon and spa retail budget forecasts specified retail activities for a definite period of time. Its essential elements are sales or revenue, gross margin, payroll, other operating expenses, and net profit. Revenue and expenses are planned on a monthly basis.

**FYI**

The process of creating a retail budget requires you to plan for the financial results you expect or desire over the coming year.

## Forecasting Revenue

The starting point for creating the retail department budget is the salon and spa's forecasted number of treatments for the following year. This chapter has discussed the importance of monitoring the retail sales whether it is by guest, by treatment, or by ticket, and the importance of measuring the retail revenue against a measure of overall salon and spa activity. Benchmark numbers in budgets will help you verify your revenue assumptions. These benchmark assumptions will help you determine what your annual forecasted revenue will be. For example, if the Urban Salon and Spa is projecting 833 tickets for the month of June next year and the benchmark retail revenue is $12.50 per ticket, the budgeted revenue would be $10,412.50.

Your overall revenue forecast and the monthly retail sales plan should contain many of the same assumptions. The

**HERE'S A TIP**

Consider the addition of new services, products, advertising, marketing promotions, and staff additions when forecasting your revenue. These factors will influence your overall business.

documents should support one another and draw upon each other's forecasts.

While this mathematical extension is simple, considerable thought and planning go into the determination of the per ticket revenue number. Some of the influences would include:

- Are there seasonal variances in the per ticket retail average?
- Will you introduce a new product line or additions to the current product lines?
- Is the treatment menu being revised to include new services with associated products that present additional retail revenue opportunities?
- Has the salon and spa established a strong mail order business that should continue to build as additional loyal product users are added to the mail order client base?
- Are there new facilities opening in the area with similar products that will represent competition to the salon and spa's retail sales?
- How well did the retail promotions and special offers work during the previous year and what is planned for the coming year?
- Is the salon and spa adding additional treatment rooms, work stations, or expanding the retail space?
- What is the anticipated walk-in retail traffic?

Likewise, there are many other external factors for you to consider. A resort/hotel salon and spa will want to work closely with the resort staff to find out its occupancy forecasts. A day spa may want to determine whether there are any local events that will affect business.

Revenue forecasting requires an intimate knowledge of the salon and spa's business cycles. It is not enough to simply pick a day in a month, look at the retail revenue for that day, and multiply that by the number of days in the month. In most salons and spas, Saturdays are busier than Tuesdays. An important holiday like Easter will fall in different months and Valentine's Day may have different productivity depending on the day of the week it occurs. You have to carefully review the days of the week from one year to the next when preparing the revenue projection.

Many salons and spas build their overall revenue forecast by department (massage, skin care, hair and nails, etc.). This breakdown makes it easier to forecast revenue by service type and classification of merchandise. It also assists in the accuracy of retail sales forecasting.

Once the overall retail revenue has been determined for the budget period, you can further dissect the overall number into the merchandise classifications enabling you to monitor sales trends throughout the coming year. This is done by reviewing the historical makeup of the overall classification revenue distribution. For example, if the forecast for total retail sales at the Seasons Salon and Spa for a given month is $40,000, the revenue would be distributed as follows based upon historical experience:

| | | |
|---|---|---|
| Styling products | 30% | $12,000 |
| Fashion accessories | 15% | $6,000 |
| Skincare | 50% | $20,000 |
| Jewelry | 5% | $2,000 |

If the retail history further provides breakdown by subclassification, you would further distribute the revenue forecast into the appropriate subclassifications. For example, the Seasons Salon and Spa's $20,000 for the skincare category could be distributed as follows:

| | | |
|---|---|---|
| Face serum | 30% | $6,000 |
| Masks | 8% | $1,600 |
| Sunscreen | 3% | $600 |
| Eye cream | 6% | $1,200 |
| Face cream | 53% | $10,600 |

At the Savvy Salon...
Personal Accountability

SALON AND SPA SNAPSHOT 5.5

Stephanie, owner of the Savvy Salon in Redondo Beach, California, takes forecasting to a deeper level so the overall salon retail goals are met. "I know that the salon retail goals are dependent upon the efforts of the team. So I ask each staff member to forecast their own goals for a quarterly period. These goals are by ticket average and total sales for the quarter. Biweekly reviews assure the team gains feedback and can adjust their performance as needed."

## Revenue Adjustments

As mentioned previously in the section discussing the cost of sales percentage, another part of the revenue budgeting process includes making adjustments to revenue that are recorded on the retail department schedule. These adjustments might include:

- Employee discounts: Discounts given on merchandise sold to employees at a discounted price.
- Merchandise returns: Goods returned by customers. These are recorded, as the merchandise returned can be placed back in stock and resold.
- Allowances: This account includes refunds and overcharges of sales not known at the time of the sale but adjusted at a later date.

## Budgeting the Cost of Sales Percentage

The cost of sales is unlikely to change from year to year unless there are significant operational changes in the salon and spa. Even though the percentage will probably stay approximately the same, it is a good practice to review the current year history, by month, to see whether there were any significant occurrences that influenced the cost of sales.

For example, Reuben at the Urban Salon and Spa may have discovered that the salon and spa was not recording product transfers from retail to professional treatment. He worked with Mae, the accountant, during the year to correct this problem. When he reviews the previous year, he'll want to note that the cause of the increased cost of sales for that particular month has been fixed. Another example that can skew the cost of sales is a costly gift with purchase program. If the salon and spa has discontinued that program for the upcoming year, that will factor into the forecasts for next year.

Once the cost of sales percentage has been settled on, it is a simple mathematical calculation to budget the cost of sales for the upcoming year.

For example, the salon and spa settles on a 50 percent cost of sales benchmark. For the month of March the budget is forecasting $40,000 in net retail sales. That makes the budgeted cost of goods $20,000 ($40,000 × 0.50 = $20,000).

## Payroll Expense

The payroll expense in the retail department is generally constant as there are very few employees (sometimes just one) except in very large salon and spa retail operations. Many salon and spas have their guest receptionists or front desk agents handle retail sales transactions.

Some salon and spas will charge some of the reception payroll to the retail department, which is acceptable if the owner/operator feels this is a more accurate reflection of the business. On the other hand, it can be an artificial allocation of payroll expense if the number of front desk receptionists and the hours worked would remain the same regardless of whether they handle retail transactions.

The budget for retail salaries and wages includes salaried compensation for a retail manager and all regular pay, overtime pay, vacation pay, severance pay, holiday pay, and bonuses for employees of the retail department, including those of a working supervisor.

Commissions is an account that includes compensation to employees in the form of commissions paid on retail sales or other retail incentives regardless of the employee's department. Retail commissions paid to therapists or any other employees on the retail sales they generate are not a payroll expense of the service department, but are an expense of the retail department. These commissions can represent a significant expense to the retail operation. If, for example, a hair designer sells $1,200 in products during the course of the month and receives a 10 percent commission on the retail products, that $120 is not a cost of performing the service, but a cost of selling retail just as if he or she was standing in the retail area suggesting products to the guest.

Benefits include payroll taxes, payroll-related insurance expenses, retirement, and other payroll-related expenses applicable to the retail department. The customary taxes and benefits would include:

- FICA (Social Security and Medicare)
- FUTA (Federal Unemployment Tax)
- SUTA (State Unemployment Tax)
- Worker's Compensation Insurance
- Health and Life Insurance
- Retirement plans such as a 401(k)

Generally a benefit expense percentage will be established for the overall salon and spa operation and the same benefit percentage will be applied to the retail department payroll.

## Other Expenses

Other expenses represent a relatively small portion of total retail revenue—usually less than 5 percent. Salon and spa professionals have found it a good practice to monitor the overall "other expense" percentage to ensure that it remains consistent—while understanding that larger expenses for things like buying trips occur infrequently, and those expenses should be budgeted in the month they are expected to take place. When this happens, it will distort the other expense percentages for that month.

## Buying Trips

This account includes all of the costs associated with the retail buyer's travel expenses and registration fees to attend merchandise markets or shows for the purpose of selecting merchandise for the retail department. This includes any trips to individual suppliers to view new lines. Expense should be budgeted based on actual trips planned for the upcoming year and the expense should be shown in those months.

## Contract Service

This account includes any expenses associated with an activity that is normally charged to the retail department, but is now outsourced. Examples would include window washing, carpet cleaning, inventory analysis services, and point-of-sale service contracts. As a contract has a specific dollar expense associated with it, the budget should reflect the actual contracted expense for each month when the service is anticipated to be performed.

## Dues and Subscriptions

This account includes the cost of memberships, and subscriptions to newspapers and magazines for use by employees in the retail department. If the retail manager is a member of the National Retailers Association and the salon and spa pays for the dues for that organization, those dues would be recorded in this account during the month they are paid. If the retail department subscribes to retail trade publications, the cost of those publications would be recorded in this account.

## Equipment Rental

The cost of equipment rented for use in the retail department should be charged to this account. Generally an equipment rental will have a fixed expense each month, which is the number to be budgeted in this account.

## Gift Wrap
This account includes the cost of shopping bags, wrapping paper, tissue, ribbon, and packaging supplies used in the retail department. It also includes any costs associated with the development of any private label packaging such as design fees or printing. The best way to budget this expense is as a percent of total revenue. For example, if the expense has been running 0.7 percent of total retail revenue, that percentage is applied to the budgeted revenue by month.

## Licenses and Fees
This account includes the costs of all federal, state, and municipal licenses for the retail facilities of the salon and spa. These are generally paid once a year and should be budgeted in the months when the renewals are paid.

## Merchandise Displays and Accessories
This account is for all non-capitalized specialty displays or accessories used to enhance the visual appeal of the shop merchandise. Examples would include seasonal or holiday accessories or minor artifacts used on the store fixtures to increase interest.

## Merchandise Tags
This account includes the costs associated with pricing retail merchandise.

## Operating Supplies
This account includes the cost of cleaning supplies, paper supplies (other than gift wrap or packaging materials), and similar operating expenses applicable to the retail department. This account should be budgeted based on the historical percentage of retail revenue. For example, if they are running 0.3 percent of sales, that amount would be applied to each month's revenue.

## Packaging and Freight
This account is used for any costs associated with shipping retail products to guests, including the costs of packaging materials and mail or shipping charges. Again, this is budgeted as a percentage of retail revenue with adjustments for significant shipping expense that may occur during a holiday month (for example).

### Professional Development

This account includes costs, other than time, associated with training retail employees. Examples include the costs of training materials, supplies, instructor's fees, and outside seminars and conferences. This cost is expensed during the month or months for which the training is scheduled.

### Telecommunications

Any telephone expenditures that can be directly related to the retail department should be charged to this account. An example would include a specific retail toll-free line for mail order sales. If identified separately on the salon and spa phone bills, the retail budget can be created using actual history.

### Uniforms

This account includes the cost or rental of uniforms for the employees of the retail department. This account also includes the cost of cleaning and repairing uniforms of employees. The cost of the care of retail employee uniforms should be budgeted on an average amount each month. Any purchases of additional uniforms should be budgeted during the month in which the new uniforms are expected to be purchased.

### Other Retail Expense

This account includes other expenses applicable to the retail department that do not apply to accounts listed above. This also should be budgeted based on the historical percentage of retail revenue. Figure 5-1 shows a sample budget planner form.

## Departmental Income or Loss

The retail department income is important as an overall contribution to the success of the salon and spa. For example, if the departmental income from the retail department has been running 23 percent for the past several months and suddenly it is only 16 percent in one month, you need to immediately research variances—line item by line item. Invariably, this will uncover several issues that require management attention.

A standard method of reporting the retail department's income or loss is with a profit and loss statement. It might be prepared by the accountant or the accounting department of a resort/hotel salon and spa.

**FYI**

In the final analysis, it is the retail department income, or contribution to the overall salon and spa, that is the most important measure of the retail success.

Figure 5-1
Sample Budget Planner Form

| | January | February | March | Total 1st qtr |
|---|---|---|---|---|
| **Revenue-Budget** | $ 36,000 | $ 40,000 | $ 35,000 | $ 111,000 |
| Apparel | | | | |
| Footwear | $ 1,200 | $ 1,480 | $ 1,160 | $ 3,840 |
| Men's Unisex | $ 1,800 | $ 1,900 | $ 1,600 | $ 5,300 |
| Robes and Terry | $ 1,400 | $ 1,800 | $ 1,360 | $ 4,560 |
| Women's | $ 4,600 | $ 4,980 | $ 4,200 | $ 13,780 |
| **Total Apparel** | **$ 9,000** | **$ 10,160** | **$ 8,320** | **$ 27,480** |
| Gifts and Accessories | | | | |
| Books and Media | $ 1,200 | $ 1,500 | $ 1,250 | $ 3,950 |
| Fashion Accessories | $ 2,800 | $ 2,920 | $ 2,640 | $ 8,360 |
| Home | $ 900 | $ 980 | $ 850 | $ 2,730 |
| **Total Gifts and Accessories** | **$ 4,900** | **$ 5,400** | **$ 4,740** | **$ 15,040** |
| Products | | | | |
| Bath and Body Products | $ 2,400 | $ 3,460 | $ 2,590 | $ 8,450 |
| Hair Products | $ 1,400 | $ 1,340 | $ 1,200 | $ 3,940 |
| Makeup Products | $ 1,500 | $ 1,460 | $ 1,220 | $ 4,180 |
| Nail Products | $ 1,000 | $ 980 | $ 1,000 | $ 2,980 |
| Private Label Products | $ 2,600 | $ 2,730 | $ 2,450 | $ 7,780 |
| Skin Care Products | $ 12,000 | $ 13,300 | $ 12,400 | $ 37,700 |
| **Total Products** | **$ 20,900** | **$ 23,270** | **$ 20,860** | **$ 65,030** |
| Other Retail | | | | |
| Snacks and Beverages | $ 600 | $ 580 | $ 450 | $ 1,630 |
| Sundries | $ 250 | $ 320 | $ 290 | $ 860 |
| Other | $ 350 | $ 270 | $ 340 | $ 960 |
| **Total Other Retail** | **$ 1,200** | **$ 1,170** | **$ 1,080** | **$ 3,450** |
| **Total Revenue** | **$ 36,000** | **$ 40,000** | **$ 35,000** | **$ 111,000** |
| **Revenue Adjustments** | | | | |
| Employee Discounts | $ 500 | $ 980 | $ 600 | $ 2,080 |
| Merchandise Returns | $ 700 | $ 1,200 | $ 800 | $ 2,700 |
| Allowances | $ - | $ 48 | $ 32 | $ 80 |
| **Total Revenue Adjustments** | **$ 1,200** | **$ 2,228** | **$ 1,432** | **$ 4,860** |
| **Net Revenue** | **$ 34,800** | **$ 37,772** | **$ 33,568** | **$ 106,140** |
| **Cost of Goods Sold** | **$ 17,650** | **$ 19,400** | **$ 17,100** | **$ 54,150** |
| **Gross Margin** | **$ 17,150** | **$ 18,372** | **$ 16,468** | **$ 51,990** |

*(Continued)*

Figure 5-1
Sample Budget Planner Form (cont.)

| | January | February | March | Total 1st qtr |
|---|---|---|---|---|
| **Direct Expenses** | | | | |
| Payroll and Related Expenses | | | | |
| Salaries and Wages | $ 4,000 | $ 4,460 | $ 4,200 | $ 12,660 |
| Commissions | $ 1,200 | $ 1,490 | $ 1,320 | $ 4,010 |
| Payroll Taxes and Employee Benefits | $ 1,000 | $ 1,265 | $ 1,145 | $ 3,410 |
| **Total Payroll and Related Expenses** | $ **6,200** | $ **7,215** | $ **6,665** | $ **20,080** |
| Other Expenses | | | | |
| Buying Trips | $ 300 | $ 240 | $ 965 | $ 1,505 |
| Contract Services | $ 500 | $ 500 | $ 500 | $ 1,500 |
| Dues and Subscriptions | $ 30 | $ 30 | $ 260 | $ 320 |
| Equipment Rental | $ - | $ 80 | $ - | $ 80 |
| Gift Wrap and Packaging | $ 300 | $ 560 | $ 420 | $ 1,280 |
| Licenses and Fees | $ 60 | $ 60 | $ 60 | $ 180 |
| Merchandise Displays and Accessories | $ 400 | $ 600 | $ 500 | $ 1,500 |
| Merchandise Tags | $ 40 | $ 50 | $ 40 | $ 130 |
| Operating Supplies | $ 280 | $ 450 | $ 340 | $ 1,070 |
| Packaging and Freight | $ 200 | $ 680 | $ 320 | $ 1,200 |
| Professional Development | $ 50 | $ 50 | $ 150 | $ 250 |
| Telecommunications | $ 240 | $ 280 | $ 260 | $ 780 |
| Uniforms | $ 120 | $ 200 | $ 180 | $ 500 |
| Other Retail Expenses | $ 130 | $ 160 | $ 140 | $ 430 |
| **Total Other Expenses** | $ **2,650** | $ **3,940** | $ **4,135** | $ **10,725** |
| **Total Direct Expenses** | $ **8,850** | $ **11,155** | $ **10,800** | $ **30,805** |
| **Departmental Income (Loss)** | $ **8,300** | $ **7,217** | $ **5,668** | $ **21,185** |
| **% to Sales Revenue** | **23.9%** | **19.1%** | **16.9%** | **20.0%** |

Included on a profit and loss statement are the total sales, cost of goods sold, gross profit from sales, operating expenses, and the departmental net profit before income taxes. Retail cash flow management is a different issue. If receiving, markdowns, turnover, and other areas of the retail operation are well controlled, these dollars generated should be in the bank. However, if there has been over-buying, these dollars might be tied up in paying for excess inventory.

# Variances

If your salon and spa retail operation has a supervisor or manager, it is advisable to have that person complete a variance report on a monthly basis, which will keep the supervisor focused on the business of retail. It also provides owners, or the salon and spa director, with key insights for management decision making. Just knowing that they are required to report on variances will likely make them more mindful of expenses and strategies to maximize profitability resulting in better retail department operating results.

Variances are the way in which the actual income and expense figures differ from the budgeted income and expense figures. Each variance will require analysis to determine its cause. All of the detailed variances will support the net income/loss variance.

Below are common variances in a salon and spa budget:

- Sales differences: Sales differences are found by analyzing variables such as the number of services, tickets, promotions, special events, and discounts.
- Payroll variables: To understand payroll variances, research includes time cards and scheduling sheets. Retail payroll is typically over budget or under budget due to poor budgeting, lack of management and pre-planning, and unexpected business changes such as an increase or decrease in sales.
- Expense variations in the other expense category: These variations may demonstrate planning errors or business problems not anticipated in the budgeting process. In some cases, items planned for a particular activity, such as a buying trip that was planned for one month and actually occurred in another, may cause the retail area to be under budget one month and over budget the next.

Other things to watch out for when researching variances include:

- Coding error: When you analyze the entries of an account, you may discover items posted to the wrong account, causing a variance in two accounts.
- Vendor price changes: Inflation will affect a budget and cannot always be anticipated. If a salon and spa's budget assumptions did not allow for price increases and vendors are now charging higher rates, then that explanation can be included in any variance report prepared.

- Timing of expenses: Some expenses are budgeted in one month but are booked in another month.
- Unbudgeted expense: Occasionally an expense comes up that was not in the salon and spa's budget.

There are times when re-forecasting or budget revisions are necessary due to significant variances from the initial plan. Typically, this is a result of swift economic changes, such as natural or economic disasters, that suddenly affect business. Generally, revenue must be re-forecasted and line item revisions are necessary, as opposed to a complete rewrite of the total budget.

# CHAPTER SUMMARY

- The retail sales percentage of total salon and spa revenue calculation will provide an indication of the impact your retail operation has on total revenue.
- If your business has significant retail revenue, you will want to monitor retail sales by product classification.
- Determine the level of retail activity of your staff by calculating retail sales by provider and service ticket.
- Markdowns and discounts affect retail profitability. Are you buying too much? Are you buying the right items for your customers?
- Every square foot of retail space is valuable. The retail sales per square foot calculation will tell you how much revenue each square foot contributes. Utilize the most space for high sell through items.
- The cost of goods sold calculation indicates the profitability of your retail operation. Freight, markdowns, pilferage, promotions, and incorrect inventory affect your COGS.
- Your margin will indicate profit derived from sales after all deductions are made.
- Spa retail budgeting will allow you to forecast your retail activities and the goals (sales, revenue, margin, payroll, operating expenses, etc.) you expect over the coming year.
- An important component in reaching your retail goals is retail forecasting, achieved by studying past sales trends, seasonality, promotions, marketing activity, etc., and then forecasting future retail performance.
- Variances in the budget contribute to the eventual net income or loss. Variances can be key indicators of areas for improvement

- Wise salon and spa professionals use good financial tools to manage their retail. By keeping track of what happens financially in the salon and spa from day to day and month to month, they are able to identify their challenges and capitalize on their strengths.

# LEARNING ACTIVITIES

## Learning Activity 5-1: Out of Sync

Get a copy of your salon and spa's retail budget for the year. Look at the budget for the month just completed. Pull copies of the financial reports and prepare a variance report. Provide an explanation for each variance—positive or negative.

## Learning Activity 5-2: Keeping Track of Sales

Examine the figures below. Calculate the following ratios for the Urban Salon and Spa for the month of August:

Total spa Revenue: $58,000

Retail Revenue:

> Hair products: $2,500
> Thinning Hair/regrowth treatments: $950
> Skincare: $6,440
> Cosmetics: $2,200
> Number of Retail Tickets: 150
> Number of Retail Tickets with Service: 132
> Retail Markdown Taken: $1,100
> Square Feet of Retail Space: 20 feet by 30 feet
> Opening Inventory: $30,000
> Purchases at Cost: $2,000
> Closing Inventory at Cost: $21,800

1. Retail sales percentage of total salon and spa revenue
2. Retail sales contribution by merchandise classification
3. Retail sales per ticket
4. Retail markdown percentage
5. Retail per square foot
6. Cost of sales
7. Gross margin

# REVIEW QUESTIONS

1. Which of the following is NOT a key indicator of salon and spa retail business success?
    a. Retail sales per ticket
    b. Cost of sales percentage
    c. Labor cost per treatment room
    d. Retail sales per square foot

2. Which of the following formulas calculates the retail sales percentage of total salon and spa revenue?
    a. Net retail revenue ÷ total salon and spa revenue
    b. Total labor expense ÷ total salon and spa revenue
    c. Cost of goods sold ÷ retail revenue
    d. Total revenue ÷ number of employees

3. The Seasons Salon and Spa had 1,500 tickets during the month of August. The retail revenue for that month was $48,500. What was the retail sales per ticket?
    a. $3.23
    b. $30
    c. $30.92
    d. $32.33

4. What information is needed to calculate the retail discount percentage?
    a. Total number of treatments and total retail discounts
    b. Total retail discounts and total retail revenue
    c. Average retail discounts and average number of treatments
    d. Average retail discounts and average retail revenue

5. In a classic retail environment, what is the most common way to monitor revenue?
    a. Retail sales per employee
    b. Return on equity
    c. Return on assets
    d. Retail sales per square foot

6. In which account would a salon and spa professional record refunds and overcharges of sales that are adjusted later?
    a. Employee discounts
    b. Merchandise returns
    c. Allowances
    d. Sundries

7. Which of the following does NOT affect the cost of sales percentage?
    a. Fewer sales at the discounted rate
    b. Pilferage
    c. Recorded purchases received during a month
    d. Markdowns

8. What measurement is determined when you divide the value of inventory by the cost of average daily retail sales?
    a. Days of inventory on hand
    b. Retail revenue contribution to overall revenue
    c. Retail cost of sales percentage
    d. Average revenue per ticket

9. The Urban Salon and Spa recently received a shipment of 24 pairs of lounge pants with the salon and spa's logo. The purchase price is $42, but it is mistakenly put into the POS system as $24. How does this affect the cost of goods sold?
    a. It makes the reported cost of goods sold too low.
    b. It makes the reported cost of goods sold too high.
    c. It evens out the cost of goods sold with previous months.
    d. It has no effect on the cost of goods sold.

10. Jazmine, the salon and spa director for the Seasons Salon and Spa, will be attending two buying shows next year to look at new skin care and body care products. When creating her annual budget, in which account should she budget for these expenses?
    a. Contract services
    b. Dues and subscriptions
    c. Salaries and wages
    d. Buying trips

# Sales and Service

© Gemenacom/Shutterstock.com

Chapter **6**

## INTRODUCTION

**M**any beauty and wellness professionals carry existing beliefs and fears that become barriers to selling. Technicians often feel they are being pushy by selling, that they are not natural salespeople, or selling is not a part of their job. Technicians often do not make the connection that clients come to them to fulfill many emotional needs and to solve challenges. By not offering suggestions in the form of products and services, they are doing a disservice to the client.

Salon and spa guests are motivated to seek services not only to enhance their appearance, but to enhance the way they feel about themselves. So what can you do as a manager to enhance the attitudes of your staff to suggest products to your guests? As a manager, you can educate each technician and create a shift in their thinking, from "selling" to "serving," thus eliminating these beliefs that are barriers to selling. You can do this by helping the team connect with the notion that their clients rely on them as trusted advisors. The act of advising clients is giving a gift of information and making a difference in the lives of others.

## A UNIQUE OPPORTUNITY

As the technician is carrying out the service, they are demonstrating and educating clients about the products used for skin care, hair care, and body care. Service providers are able to build rapport through experience and education. It is the responsibility of the service provider to recommend the appropriate products so guests can

## LEARNING OBJECTIVES

After successfully completing this chapter, the reader will be able to:

- Describe the synergy between sales and service.

- Identify the retail challenges and opportunities for salon and spa managers, front desk staff, service providers, and sales specialists, and determine ways to overcome them.

- Distinguish between education and training, and understand how each contributes to more effective sales.

- Describe ways to add value to a customer's purchasing experience.

SALON AND SPA SNAPSHOT 6.1

## At the Seasons Salon and Spa...

Mrs. Huddleston turned around in front of the mirror, feeling her hair after Sonya, the hair designer, completed her style. "I love the results. I am so hard on my hair because of the color and the chlorine."

Sonya smiled and removed the styling cape, then gestured for Mrs. Huddleston to step out of the chair. "I know, the products and the cut really brought your hair to life."

"The only time my hair feels like anything but straw is when I come in and see you. I feel so much better like this," Mrs. Huddleston said, as she ran her fingers through her hair.

Sonya escorted Mrs. Huddleston to the changing room. "Let's get you changed and I will meet you in the front. I'll have Margie pull some conditioner for you to use in between time."

In a rush to stay on schedule, Sonya went to the desk. "Margie, can you pull some conditioner for color-treated hair from the shelf and have it ready for my client?"

"Which one do you want?" Margie asked. "We have several."

"She will freak if I try to get her to buy the system she really needs. It's $65.00. Let me have the one there on the second shelf," Sonya said, pointing to the blue bottle of conditioner.

Margie placed the bottle next to Mrs. Huddleston's ticket. Sonya went to the reception area and greeted her next client.

Mrs. Huddleston approached the front desk and began examining the shelves. "Margie," she called out over her shoulder. "I think Sonya used a styling cream, but it was the shampoo and conditioner Sonya used that really transformed my hair. Do you sell it?"

Margie bit her lip. She knew there were several types of products at the back bar, but had no clue what was what.

"She left this bottle here for you, so I think this is it," Margie said, holding up the bottle of conditioner. She was relieved that Sonya had pulled something from the shelf.

As Sonya walked her next client to the shampoo area, she glanced to the front desk, where Margie was settling her ticket.

"Thank you for coming in Mrs. Huddleston. I will see you in six weeks," Sonya called out while giving a hearty wave good-bye.

recreate their results, whether through a hair color, straightening, style make-over, or facial treatment. There is also an opportunity for guests to "take home" their total experience by exposing them to apparel, books, and relaxation CDs that are sold in the gift shop. The salon and spa's services are unique opportunities to connect with guests in a nontraditional sales manner.

In fact, many traditional retailers would groan with envy over the opportunities that salon and spa professionals have. For example, a hair designer or therapist spends often more than an hour with a client performing a service. They get all that one-on-one time that traditional retailers simply don't have. In addition, retail salespeople do not perform fee-based services for clients, whereas salon and spa professionals generate income in two ways; by providing a service, and through suggesting products.

Past studies reported from ISPA (the International SPA Association) stated that most of the people who purchased spa products did so because they had a good experience with the product on their visit, or the spa therapist recommended it. Since salon and spa services are high-touch in nature and the service provider is looked upon as a credible expert, these results can be generalized to your salon clients as well. Although sales techniques in the salon and spa are not within the scope of this text you can find specific strategies for salon and spa professionals at milady.cengage.com.

© Brian A Jackson/www.Shutterstock.com

# MAXIMIZING THE TOTAL ENVIRONMENT

The salon and spa setting in itself provides an ideal sales opportunity through the delivery of services. However, the influence that the salon and spa visit has on the purchase of products cannot be overstated. Carol Phillips, a well-known spa industry marketing authority, has identified several sales mistakes service professionals often make in their service encounter. Spa environments in particular, simply by the focus on providing a relaxing environment, often have a negative effect on retail sales. The following points are potential challenge areas in the salon and spa environment.

## DID YOU KNOW?

In the beauty and wellness industry, clients are motivated to visit not just for practical needs, such as to get a facial, a new haircut, or a fresh coat of polish on their nails; they are looking for emotional enhancement and to feel uplifted and more confident.

- Inadequate time: The treatment may not provide enough consultation time to discuss products, as there is not enough time built in to do so. In a spa situation, the treatment itself may cause the client to feel overexposed and vulnerable, so the technician may dispense with any product consultation and go right into the service.
- Relaxation music: Music should enhance the experience, not put the guests to sleep. Sometimes the client may want to interact, and is looking for a connection with other people. Clients who express a sincere interest in the products being used during the service are a signal for multiple services and product sales.

- The visual experience: Salons and spas can give shoppers something to look at—reminders of "What do I need to recreate the experience at home?" They can have retail products/impulse buy items peppered throughout the environment, rather than just in the lobby or retail area.
- Lighting: Lighting also plays a key role in the retail environment. Does the lighting make the clients feel good about themselves? You can evaluate how the spa lighting is affecting your guests by taking a mirror throughout the space and seeing how the change in lighting affects your own looks or self-esteem. It also helps to remember that older clients may not see as well in a very dim environment.
- Sales leadership: Spas and salons alike can have challenges in the area of sales leadership. Quite often, there is no set sales process in place. For example, who is responsible for your sales and marketing? Is there someone responsible for creating promotions? For changing displays? Does every member of your team, from the service providers to the front desk, feel that recommending products is a part of their job? These questions are important to consider, as they directly influence the experience our customers have with your products.
- Follow-up: Once the sale is generated and your client leaves, what process do you have in place for follow-up? It is easier to keep a customer than to find a new one. So it is worthwhile to invest care in gaining feedback from your current customers regarding their service experience. How can your team follow up with clients? The front desk might make a follow-up call to the guest within 72 hours. The front desk might offer a management survey that lets the client know the salon and spa cares about what they have to say. The salon and spa could also offer an auto-delivery program that gives the client a chance to automatically order a product at set intervals. A good rule of thumb is for clients to hear from your salon or spa at least every 90 days. Contact can come in the form of new customer cards, thank-you cards, or "haven't seen you in a while" cards.
- Training: Finally, what many salon and spa managers often overlook is the training component for your salon and spa staff. The staff needs to have extensive product knowledge and people skills. You may even want to offer graciousness

or etiquette training. The entire salon and spa staff also needs selling skills that can be honed through ongoing retail training. After all, "Everyone in the company sells the company." We will discuss training on product knowledge later in this section.

## SEIZE THE SALE

As mentioned earlier, salons and spas have a unique advantage over traditional retailers; talented service providers deliver services using products that are then available for guests to purchase and use in their homes. Given that service providers establish a connection before and after the treatment, the sell through becomes a natural progression—part of the service model. Although the bulk of the responsibility lies within the hands of the service provider, everyone in the salon and spa facilitates the sale.

There are four main groups of individuals who are responsible for facilitating sales within the retail environment:

1. Retail managers or salon and spa managers/directors
2. Front desk and other staff who may have a broad range of responsibilities within the salon and spa
3. Technicians who provide services to the guest and offer retail as an extension of their service
4. Retail consultants, whose sole purpose is to generate sales within the retail environment

© FWStupidio/www.Shutterstock.com

## RETAIL CHALLENGES FOR THE SALON AND SPA MANAGER

As a salon and spa manager, there is pressure applied from a lot of different angles. You will have therapists and technicians who resist being salespeople, yet they have the responsibility to recommend products to their clients. In many instances, you may have commissioned employees, salaried employees, and renters. Each of these members of the team need be accountable for the sales process. Depending on the size of the business, you may also have owners, general managers, and upper management who push retail sales to increase the profitability of the salon and spa and provide it with financial sustainability.

Motivating the team, assuring they maintain accountability for their results, and knowing the business well yourself are all core responsibilities of a retail manager. How can you balance the need to lead and motivate your team and assure they are accountable for their retail results?

## Overcoming Common Challenges

Establishing a sense of responsibility and pride in your team members is the key to motivating them to take a larger role in the retail operation. You can accomplish this in two ways. First, by taking on several key behaviors yourself that will contribute to a more successful retail operation. Second, by leveraging the knowledge of your team by creating a brand ambassador program. We will discuss the key behaviors of successful retail managers first.

Successful behaviors of retail managers:
1. Maintain good communication with vendors and staff.
2. Know the brands you carry. Know each brand's features, especially advantages and benefits.
3. Motivate and reward everyone in the sales process: service providers, renters, and front desk.
4. Project a positive attitude that will motivate the team.
5. Stay connected in the industry. Read professional articles, attend trade shows, and research trends.
6. Communicate information and hold monthly meetings.
7. Hold your team accountable.
8. Develop your staff through coaching and mentoring.
9. Assure resources are available for learning about products.
10. Set retail sales goals for your team, create a reward structure, and then celebrate their success!

## A Brand Ambassador Program

**brand ambassador.**
A member of the staff who serves as the subject matter expert and educator of a particular product line.

Many salons and spas see retail sales flourish when there are in-house mentors or **brand ambassadors**, who are service providers that drive the sales of any given product line. The brand ambassadors can be linked to the in-house educational strategy of the salon and spa, and can partner with the vendor to develop their job descriptions. A brand ambassador role can become a coveted spot earned by your service team, or if the operation is small, each service provider can take the responsibility for one or more products. Ideally, each service provider should be responsible for representing a single line of products.

Below is a list of responsibilities a brand ambassador will commonly have. Many of these tasks are shared with the retail manager, so consistent communication between each brand ambassador and the retail manager is recommended:

- Know the brand and become an expert resource for the salon and spa.
- Maintain good communication with the vendor of the product line. Assure the vendor is apprised of customer feedback, educational needs of the salon and spa staff, product samples required, and collateral to support sell through such as sell sheets and signage.
- Know the features, advantages, and benefits of their product line. Share selling tips with the rest of the staff.
- Coordinate product retail information; assure testers and product samples are maintained.
- Project a positive attitude and encourage sales within their given brand.

## FYI

Brand ambassadors become extremely important to retail success, especially when a salon and spa carries a vast number of product lines.

# RETAIL CHALLENGES FOR FRONT DESK AND OTHER SALON AND SPA STAFF

Sometimes the goals of the retail operation are at odds with the skills of the staff. Front desk and other salon and spa staff are, in many cases, the dominant inhabitants of the retail area of the salon and spa. The front desk staff sets the tone for the entire experience and can make or break a guest's overall opinion of the visit. The front desk is much like the host station at a restaurant. If the guest is greeted with enthusiasm, checked in with

© Sakala/www.Shutterstock.com

attention to detail, and treated with respect, the guest will start their visit off with a positive attitude. After the visit, the host or hostess is also the last stop before the guest leaves the front doors.

This is the same pathway that a guest in your salon and spa will travel. In most salon and spas, the front desk staff is the pivotal point at which a retail opportunity is either seized or missed. In most situations, the service provider will consult with the client and recommend products during the visit, then the front desk will pull the products and close the sale. In other situations, customers will come in specifically for retail, and not have a service. In this case, the front desk person will recommend the products.

In many salons and spas, the front desk staff person is someone who was hired with the major responsibility of answering the phone and cashing out the client. Yet this may be the person responsible for the single act that most directly contributes to the salon and spa's profitability. Unfortunately, the front desk person is not usually hired as a salesperson, yet it is a responsibility that is often overlooked and a task that the employee is not necessarily fond of doing.

It is unlikely that the block is a dislike for interacting with the public, because even though there are numerous misconceptions about what it is like to work at the front desk, the need for public interaction is pretty obvious. So, what could be interfering with their selling success? Education and training in the sales process may be the answer.

Here is a list of just a few of the objections front desk personnel frequently raise as to why they are not able to actively retail:

### Retail knowledge and skills
- "I don't understand the products."
- "I don't really like the products," or "I have never tried the products."
- "I can't afford the products and so I feel uncomfortable selling them to others."
- "I don't really know how to speak about the products effectively."

### Requirements and incentives
- "It was not initially explained to me that selling was part of the job description."
- "There is no financial or other type of incentive for me to sell."

### Obstacles and constraints
- "I rarely have time to step away from the desk."
- "I often find the product that I would recommend is out of stock, so I have become frustrated and discouraged."

**FYI**

In thinking of the actual sequence of events affecting the guest's experience and any retail sales, the front desk role is much more than that of receptionist. The front desk person is often key in closing a sale.

Before giving too much credence to the impression that front desk personnel are complaining staff members, consider this: Although this is a list of why the front desk personnel might not be pulling their weight as salespeople, the obligation for recognizing and initiating change lies within your role as the retail manager.

## Overcoming Common Front Desk Challenges

- Retail knowledge and skills: Objections related to not knowing or understanding the products, not liking them, and similar objections, all indicate the need for training to develop the basic selling skills of front desk or guest reception employees. Training can help to overcome some of the common obstacles to making a sale. Likewise, education will instill in staff an appreciation for the products. One of the great benefits of allowing vendors to conduct regular product knowledge sessions is that they generally provide testers, samples, or the opportunity to make direct, limited purchases at a discount or at wholesale. These are great opportunities for your staff to experience the products at little or no cost to the salon and spa. If there is a brand ambassador in place, coordinate with this person to obtain the vendor training and resources.

- Requirements and incentives: If your staff objects that selling is not a part of the job or that they have no incentive to sell, then there's a need to clarify job responsibilities or provide incentives. Ideally, this should occur when an individual is hired. But, if a staff is inherited, then you may need to institute new guidelines and have the staff sign off on them. Providing rewards and recognition for good performance helps motivate and inspire your staff. There are many ways to reward staff with non-cash incentives, which can be as simple as a sincere thank you. And there are also many ways to create a fun environment that makes the staff person's sales-related job responsibilities fun. An example might be creating games for product education, or perhaps rewarding correct answers to product education trivia with $1 to $5. If you have a brand ambassador in place, you will want to get that person involved in tracking sales performance or creating the product education game.

- Obstacles and constraints: Time or product shortages indicate the need to revisit the retailing strategy. For example, if retail sales are an important job for the front desk, then the list of duties should be focused on activities that drive sales, such as closing sales at the cash wrap for the service technicians, merchandising, assisting guests, expanding product knowledge, etc.

Retail inventory should be kept stocked using the min/max levels. There should be a regular evaluation of the shelves to assure stock is maintained.

# RETAIL CHALLENGES FOR SERVICE PROVIDERS

**FYI**

Running out of stock sends a negative message to the staff and guests that providing full service is not an integral part of the salon and spa's philosophy.

Service providers must understand how to build trust, establish credibility, and build a relationship with their clients. The process of conducting the consultation and understanding the client in terms of their concerns, goals, and maintenance requirements are part of the client intake process. Once the client's needs are discovered, the service provider can begin to recommend solutions in the form of products. In order to recommend the appropriate solutions, service providers must have a deep level of product knowledge.

It is a common challenge for technicians to resist prescribing retail products for their clients. They may not feel confident or they may feel pushy when it comes to the general act of selling. Many technicians are resistant to selling products, and will have various beliefs about their role in sales. It is a common belief that some services are naturally designed to sell retail and some are not. For example, a massage therapist may see their role as a "healer" and they may perceive sales as taking away from the benefits of the service they provide (Figure 6-1).

It is possible to overcome almost all of the obstacles posed by your service staff. If training sessions supply the right kind of information, even massage therapists and body technicians can become passionate about sharing information about the products. That should, in part, be the focus of retail training and education at every turn. When educating this group, bear in mind that the therapists will never get on board with retailing unless they clearly understand the *goal* of a product application and the *reason* that it works to the benefit of their client.

## At the Seasons Salon and Spa

Fiorello handed the menus back to the server with a smile and sipped his iced tea, enjoying the pleasant atmosphere at the café down the street from the Seasons Salon and Spa where both he and Azhara, his dining companion, worked.

"You've been bursting with some sort of news," he said to Azhara. "Did your day go well?"

"It did!" Azhara answered. "I had a great facial with Mrs. Santana. She bought a series of three facials and had her second one today. I remember her because she had terrible skin. That was the month that we were having the special incentive program to sell the revitalizing serum and cream . Do you remember?"

Fiorello rolled his eyes. "No—it was just one in a long line of programs that Jazmine developed to push us into foisting useless products on gullible guests. I try not to remember those."

"But, Fiorello, that's what I'm so excited about. The product wasn't useless at all," Azhara said. "When I saw her today, I noticed how smooth her skin looked, especially under her eyes. She said it was because of the cream I recommended. I almost didn't recognize Mrs. Santana. Her skin couldn't have looked any more different if she'd had a transplant. She wasn't even wearing foundation anymore and her face looked beautiful."

"Oh?" said Fiorello, raising his eyebrows. "I guess the cream worked."

"She told me that she had been faithfully using the skin-care regimen that she and I had set up together. She told me she'd never in her life had such beautiful skin and that she now took pleasure out of looking in the mirror every morning. She told me that I'd changed her life—that she'd been getting facials for years, but that I was the first esthetician who ever gave her the tools she needed to take care of her own face."

The conversation paused as the server set cranberry-walnut salads in front of each of them. Azhara began eating enthusiastically, but Fiorello just picked at his for a few moments. Finally he said, "That's all well and good for you, but it's different for me. I can see that it makes sense for estheticians to sell skin care products. But I still don't think that massage therapists should be asked to do so. I can't sell my touch and it is my touch that helps to heal my guests."

Azhara put her fork down with a huff. "Haven't you been listening to me, Fiorello? Have you heard anything that I just said? Why do you think that what you and I do is so different? My touch heals my guests too—it isn't just the product I put on their faces."

"It certainly makes it easier to sell product when you use product," Fiorello replied.

"So use that creativity you're always bragging about!" Azhara came back in frustration. "Are you telling me that you never see clients with dry skin? Do you not have clients whose lives would be better if they used a balm as a spot treatment at home? What about your clients with really tight muscles that take forever to relax? Why couldn't you suggest a re-mineralizing salt treatment in the bath water for them? Instead of resisting every attempt at selling product, why don't you look at our store from the client's perspective? Maybe you could make your healing last for longer than the 60 minutes that they're lying on your table."

SALON AND SPA SNAPSHOT 6.2

Figure 6-1
Challenges to Selling

| Perceived Challenges in Selling | Commitment to Retail |
|---|---|
| Service providers are focused more on the treatment itself, not on home care. | The right homecare products can be an extension of the same treatment. |
| Service providers have not experienced the products. | service providers understand the products and have first hand knowledge so they can recommend them as credible experts. |
| They do not understand the relevance of the products as they relate to the treatment. | They have education and experience with the products and can relate the benefits of the products to the treatment. |
| They have become accustomed to their services not leading to a sale, so they have ceased to anticipate the possibility. | They feel comfortable with the process of recommending products as a part of the total service experience. To eliminate expert product recommendations is not serving the client well. |
| Service providers may not clearly understand the needs of their clients. | Through the consultation, service providers understand the needs of the client and are communicating effectively |
| They are not passionate about the products' potential. | Service providers have a clear understanding of the product benefits and how they support the treatment and help the client experience more improvements at home. |
| They feel that their job is demanding enough without having to shift gears mentally to generate a sale. | Recommending products is part of being a credible expert and helping the client an opportunity to extend the benefits/maintain the results of the service through home care. |
| It is often not made clear to the service providers that retailing is not an optional activity. | All service providers understand their role as an expert consultant and have goals to measure their success. |
| They assign their attitude about the products to the client. | Service providers see the value of the products and represent each in an unbiased way. |
| They view themselves as "healers" or "artists" and selling as mercenary. | They can connect the fact that recommending products that support the healing process and allow clients to recreate their results at home is part of their role. |
| They have not been trained to sell. | All service providers understand the process of relationship selling and consultative selling so they can effectively recommend products. |

Service providers can ask some of the toughest, most realistic questions about products because they are in the trenches. In the treatment rooms and on the floor, they respond to client questions and hear firsthand feedback about the products that clients use or might have seen. Your service staff is in a position to be a valuable resource to the person making purchasing decisions for the salon and spa.

# MASSAGE THERAPISTS AND RETAIL

Massage therapists may pose an additional challenge in selling retail for several reasons. For example, their treatments are very silent in nature, and focused on relaxation, often not allowing the time for

SALON AND SPA SNAPSHOT 6.3

## At International Skin & Body Care... It's Not Selling, It's Service

Mimi Barre, of International Skin & Body Care, Redlands, CA, has a solid strategy in gaining support in retail from her massage therapists. "Our massage therapists do well with take-home products. It is all in the training. Massage therapists are never asked, urged, or required to sell. We don't even talk about sales. I give classes in customer service and on 'Putting More Money in Your Pocket.' These classes talk about making the guests happy. Massage therapists want everybody to be happy, feel well, and come back in four weeks. This is accomplished by showing the guests ways that they can extend their visit by having a spa at home."

"Every treatment has a selected group of take-home items that the guest is shown. Every time that the guest uses one of our products at home she thinks about the wonderful massage therapist who recommended it to her. It etches that therapist on the guest's mind. When the products are almost gone, the guest needs to return to take home more products. Retail is a great hook for getting the guest back in. It is a constant reminder as it sits on her vanity."

"We stock lots of items that our massage therapists are eager for the guests to take home: muscle heat cream, Dead Sea salts, unscented bath salts, massage tools, Happy Wraps (heated neck wraps), body scrubs, scrubby gloves, dry brush brushes, mud, lotions, foot cream, relaxation CDs, candles, children's and men's gift items, all in addition to skin care.

Each therapist fills out a recommendation slip, pulls the items, puts them in a basket, and leaves. The receptionist does the close."

much dialogue. There are ways you can encourage your massage therapists to sell by spending one-on-one time with them and making creative suggestions for them. For example, massage therapists can use hydration as a selling point—they could prescribe teas for healing and wellness. You can encourage them to make recommendations on body problem areas instead of directly mentioning product first.

Other ideas for massage therapists include:

- Having products that your staff can sell that relate to the service, such as CDs, teas, and books.
- Adjust commission based on whether they meet sales quotas.
- Ask what the client needs at home to maintain the same level of relaxation after treatment. Is it candles? Music? Body products?
- Find areas of opportunity where they already succeed. If the therapist is successful at selling

service packages, the spa professional can have him or her include products in the package.

- Offer continuing education units (CEUs) as incentives. If they sell "x" amount of product, the spa will pay for CEUs.
- Offer a sampling program so therapists can experience product firsthand.

## Why Some Service Areas Sell Well

Are the estheticians and hair designers retail magicians? Well, not exactly. They are, however, in a more advantageous position because they act as subliminal treatment tour guides. For example, even if an esthetician takes the less-is-more approach when delivering information throughout her facial, she will still comment gently and briefly on the highlights of the experience. "I am now applying our enzymatic exfoliant that removes dead surface cells," or "This mask will calm and soothe your sensitive skin," etc. Often without realizing it, the client emerges having been delicately indoctrinated to appreciate and replicate the ideal home care regimen. The retailing process that follows is then simply a reinforcement of that experience.

Hair designers have a great advantage by nature of their work environment. In a salon, the stylist work station offers a great opportunity to promote products in an interactive way. For example, a hair designer works in front of a mirror and can make eye contact, show how products are used, and actually have the client hold the product container. The nature of the entire service is interactive and visual, and the results of the products are immediate, as in the case of a root boosting hair volumizer or straightening iron.

Nail technicians also share many of the same advantages that estheticians and hair designers do. Just as hair designers can prescribe regimens for their customers based on what they have experienced with their hair, nail technicians can prescribe products and routines based on what they have experienced with their customers nails. If the customer's hair is dry, the stylist might recommend a conditioning regimen. They can also take the time to explain the advantages that salon shampoos and hair products have over the cheap dollar shampoos that can be found in supermarkets. Likewise, a nail technician can suggest a repair regimen for the customer who has dry and calloused feet or a nail polish for brittle nails.

A parallel can be drawn by using an example that many service providers use: the biannual visit to the dentist. A person's teeth never look and feel as good as they do when leaving the office after a professional cleaning. If the dental hygienist told her patient that he could purchase all of the same products he just used to continue his home care, he would undoubtedly be interested, even if the cost were well above what he normally paid for toothpaste and mouthwash. After all, people purchase those products anyway, so it would be money well spent to buy the ones that produce a superior result. This results in a compelling argument for both the purchase of a complete home care program as well as the scheduling of regular appointments.

# RETAIL CHALLENGES FOR RETAIL CONSULTANTS IN SPA ENVIRONMENTS

In a spa environment, the front desk or receptionist serves as an assistant to sales. Although they must be apprised of the product offerings, they may not have the level of expertise to go in depth with clients regarding product recommendations. For this reason, many traditional spas offer a separate retail boutique with specialized salespeople. This is especially the case in a resort setting.

Given the importance of retail to the spa's bottom line, it isn't surprising to see the advent of sales specialists or retail consultants on the spa's staff. Retail sales consultants have unique opportunities to complete the guest experience. Often their interactions with guests will determine whether guests want to return to the spa and whether they will recommend it to their friends and families.

Retail consultants can convey a sense of professionalism and efficiency while giving guests the personal touch that they have come to expect from spas. Figure 6-2 provides a sample retail consultants job description from ISPA's Standard Operating Procedures Manual.

When guests visit the spa, they are subject to many first impressions. Each of those impressions is collected and stored in their minds. By the end of the guest's time with the spa, these impressions have compounded into their overall experience. Retail consultants are often the last person guests have contact with. Their impression of the retail consultant will conclude their overall spa experience evaluation.

Retail consultants often see the guest directly after a service and are an extension of that experience. For this reason, retail

Figure 6-2
Retail Consultant Job Description

## RETAIL CONSULTANT JOB DESCRIPTION

Reports to:                «INSERT HERE»

Department:               «INSERT HERE»

### Job Summary:

The Spa Retail Consultant is responsible for the sale and service of all retail products to guests. They are responsible for maintaining the retail area of the spa in a clean and orderly manner. The Retail Consultant should be knowledgeable of the features and benefits of all retail offerings, product sales and promotions. He or she must understand how to effectively recommend products to meet the needs of our guests.

### Duties and Responsibilities:

- Be on time for shift.
- Properly open and close retail area each day according to standard operating procedures.
- Acknowledge and greet everyone who enters and leaves the retail area.
- Actively promote and provide detailed descriptions of retail products, sales, and special promotions.
- Assist guests with appropriate retail selections.
- Handle product inquiries and returns professionally and courteously, ensuring complete guest satisfaction.
- Utilize spa retail sales system with skill and proficiency.
- Maintain a retail bank.
- Regularly cross-check physical inventory with computer inventory to manage/ avoid shrinkage and to ensure appropriate inventories are available.
- Regularly create and change product displays to promote various products, seasons, and holidays.
- Meet monthly/quarterly sales goals as outlined by management.
- Actively promote the spa, treatments, services, sessions, and retail, as well as programs, promotions, and/or discounts available.
- Maintain eye contact when addressing external and internal guests.
- Handle guests' questions and concerns professionally and courteously.
- Provide accurate, appropriate, and immediate responses to all requests by guests.
- Maintain a clean, safe, fully stocked, and well-organized work area.
- Ability to work without direct supervision and remain at assigned post for extended periods of time.
- Maintain a positive attitude and contribute toward a quality work environment.
- Regularly attend, participate in, and support training and staff meetings for the spa.
- Assist in all areas of spa operation as requested by management.

### Position Requirements:

- Ability to be efficient and productive in a fast-paced environment
- Must be detail and multi-task oriented
- Must have enthusiasm and possess excellent customer service skills
- Must possess basic math and money handling skills
- Enjoy working with people and possess a friendly and outgoing personality
- Excellent communication, listening, and computer skills
- Must be a team player

(Continues)

Figure 6-2
Retail Consultant Job Description (cont.)

---

### Education and Experience Requirements:

- Minimum of «INSERT YOUR SPA'S EXPERIENCE REQUIREMENTS HERE»

- «INSERT ANY OTHER REQUIREMENTS HERE»

*Note* All duties and requirements stated are essential job functions. This job description in no way states or implies that these are the only duties to be performed by the staff occupying this position. Staff members may be required to perform other job-related duties by their supervisor.

I have thoroughly reviewed and understand the responsibilities and expectations of this job description

Staff Signature: _____    Date: _____

---

International SPA Association Foundation/International SPA Association Standard Operating Procedures Manual.

consultants should be notified of any product recommendations made by the technician or therapist. They are familiar with the types of products that technicians recommend so they help the guest recall what the technician said.

For retail-only guests, it is also the retail consultant's job to learn, understand, and meet the beauty needs and desires of guests. They can uncover hidden beauty needs, and effectively inform and educate the guest. Many guests are not educated about a spa's product offerings. A spa specialist can assist them by being able to explain each product's features and benefits and by differentiating between similar products.

Because many spa products for the face and body are treatment-oriented, the retail consultant must take several things into account when making recommendations. In some cases, retail consultants combine common sense with the knowledge of the guest's needs to determine the product that is best suited to them. If they are in doubt, they can consult an esthetician or massage therapist before making the sale. Other guidelines include:

- When recommending home care products containing essential oils, they ensure that the guest does not have allergies or sensitivities to any of the essential oils. When applicable, they use product testers to help the guest determine by smell and feel if the product is suitable.
- They recommend sunscreens to help protect the skin after treatments such as waxing, facials, or body exfoliation.
- They are always educated on the products that the spa offers. Depending on the process used, some products

containing seaweeds may not be appropriate for guests with iodine sensitivities or shellfish allergies.

- If not currently available at their spa, they obtain product contraindications for face and body treatment lines from the product vendors.

- When recommending face and/or body treatment products to pregnant guests, they inform them that due to the many physiological and hormonal changes that occur in the body, some products may not be appropriate for use until after they are finished breastfeeding. They are aware of any products that have special considerations for a pregnant woman, and when in doubt, they recommend that she check with her physician first.

- If, at the time of a product return, a guest is experiencing any skin reactions to a treatment product, the retail consultant sees whether an esthetician or massage therapist is available to talk with the guest. If not, the consultant asks the appropriate technician to provide a follow up call to ensure the comfort of the guest. The consultant obtains as much information about the reaction as possible to assist the technician in this process.

# EDUCATION AND TRAINING FOR EFFECTIVE SELLING

Anyone in the position of clarifying why an individual would possibly be compelled to give money in exchange for goods or services—is a salesperson. Think about selling in one of its subtlest forms for just a moment. When guests sit down at a lovely restaurant they expect to be informed of the daily specials. The server will describe, often with mouthwatering detail, the edible treasures available on the menu. Better still, the server might deliver a firsthand account of the delicious flavors that each dish imparts, describing exactly how the food tasted when he or she tried it. This type of presentation often sways the hungry patron to

© Valerie Potapova/www.Shutterstock.com

choose the special over other items. Who could possibly say "no" to every single delicacy that was offered? After all, the guests did come to dine, didn't they?

Why then, is the assumption that a salon and spa guest *will* purchase so often disregarded? Just like the dining guests, your guests have selected to be with you. Simply by their presence, they have given your staff permission to present them with a few specials, in services and in products that might appeal to their senses.

To return to the example of the dining guests: They would be perplexed indeed by a server who did not know *if* there were any entrées worth mentioning, *how* the entrées might be prepared, or *what* the food actually tasted like (because he or she had never tried it). But, it is not uncommon to find many salon and spa staffers who are unfamiliar with the selection of products or the range of services. They have never been trained on the proper approach to retailing, or attended product knowledge classes, or sampled the salon and spa's products or services.

A comprehensive approach to training and education can remedy all of these shortcomings. When coupled with a commission structure that provides an appropriate level of incentives, the result is a skilled and supportive retailing team.

The following sections discuss the basic structure of retail training vs. retail education and how to begin to assemble an in-house program that will meet the needs of the staff and the goals of the facility.

All of the following concepts can be applied to the marketing of salon and spa services as well as retail products. The section below focuses on the selling of merchandise.

## Training vs. Education

Training and education are different things. By definition, **training** is defined as an interactive process that aims to improve knowledge, skills, attitudes, and/or behaviors in a person to accomplish a specific job, task, or goal. Training is often *task focused,* showing you *how* to do something, and is driven by time-critical business skills and knowledge; its goal is often to improve performance. **Education** is defined as the act or process of acquiring particular knowledge or skills for thinking, reasoning, and using judgment. Education is *knowledge focused* and is about why you do something. It is not specifically aligned with a particular task. These broad concepts are different both in theory and in application for salon and spa retail operations.

**training.** A process that aims to improve knowledge, skills, attitudes, and/or behaviors in a person to accomplish a specific job task or goal.

**education.** A learning process that builds up over time as knowledge is acquired, skills are developed, thought processes are changed, and lessons are learned through experience.

When referring to the *training* of the salon and spa's retail staff, the focus is on familiarizing employees with the methodology or systems through which they are to function or abide by within the retail environment. For example, Pat will attend a seminar on how to apply the five-step sales process. *Education,* on the other hand, is what takes place when these individuals are introduced to the information they will impart concerning the features and benefits of the actual products to the client in order to achieve a sale. For example, Pat learned what motivates salon and spa guests and why they buy from you. Now he has the ability to build instant rapport because he can appeal to another's motivations. In short, training is the "how" while education is the "why."

## Training in the Salon and Spa

Training is the communication of the facility's retail protocol and includes such things as how to greet the guests and how to perform basic housekeeping and merchandising in the retail area. Training covers how to perform one's assigned role within the day-to-day workings of the retail space. Training involves information, or formats or structures used, that are, for the most part, not negotiable.

For example, the front desk staff needs to be trained to acknowledge or greet each guest who enters the space. Often, the exact verbiage to be used is part of the training process so that it is consistent with the philosophy of the salon and spa. Many salons and spas that strive for consistency with regard to their sales approach use sales scripts as part of their training method. This ensures that the staff is consistently engaging the guest in what is known as open-ended conversation, such as: "I see that you are looking at the Relaxing Bath Crystals. Would you like to experience their new fragrance?"—as opposed to "May I help you?" So, what do managers do when, for whatever the reason, they don't have a staff of natural born salespeople? They take the initiative to develop an in-house sales training program. The program that best suits a salon and spa's needs and staff may depend on a number of factors, such as:

- Your salon and spa's retailing philosophy
- The size of your retail operation
- The various levels of sales experience within the existing staff

If the salon and spa views retailing as an integral part of the business then, just as sales support is part of the description of responsibilities for the staff, formal sales technique instruction should be a mandatory part of the training program they receive. If the retail operation is part of a resort that already has a hospitality and service training program in place, the manager may be able to rely on that program for some basic instruction. If the retail operation is small and staffed by only the front desk person, and mainly driven by the recommendations of seasoned technicians, then the manager can turn to vendors for periodic refresher courses and role-playing.

Sales training is important because product knowledge alone doesn't guarantee sell through. Service providers need to know how to link the product information with their services. Many salons and spas will write scripts for therapists and have them practice those scripts so that they sound natural and not forced.

The scope of this text is designed to discuss retail management, and to touch on the importance of training. Figure 6-3 provides tips to increase your sales training. For training resources for your salon and spa, consult milady.cengage.com for a suite of sales training resources to strengthen your sales results.

## HERE'S A TIP

Utilize your brand ambassador or star salesperson in the training delivery, even if it is just for a quick 5-minute spotlight. By giving these contributors a chance to shine in front of the team, it will build their feelings of importance.

Figure 6-3
Jump Start Your Sales Training

| Training Tips | Take Training a Step Further |
|---|---|
| Visit vendor learning resources such as DVD's, webinars online tutorials, or product sheets. | If no formal training is available, ask for a volunteer (or the brand ambassador) to review vendor websites for product information. Make a note of the areas on each website that contain key information. Create a worksheet or guide for the staff to use as they explore the website to learn about the products. |
| Create a learning library of resources so there is consistency in the training and products change or new staff is added | Manage the training process so product training is a part of the new employee orientation process. Assure refresher training is given on products with low sell through. |
| Have a sampling program in place so the entire staff gains experience with the products. | At a team meeting, have staff members report their experience with the products. This will give everyone real-life results to share with guests. |
| Create training games using client scenario cards so service staff can increase their consultation skills for appropriate product recommendations. | Role play the technician/client interaction so the technician can practice consultative selling skills. |
| Hold "mini" trainings during non-peek hours in the retail area with small groups or one-on-one to maximize every training opportunity. | Give incentives to your staff for attending training. Create a team leader role for the service provider that is the most engaged in the training/selling activities. Rotate the role quarterly based upon performance. |

## Education

Knowing the details about the products selected for retail is essential to supporting their sale. But as with any achievement of excellence, this mastery cannot be achieved instantaneously. Salon and spa staff must "begin to learn how to learn." As with any discipline, there is a required period of study, the gradual absorption of detail that eventually leads to an integrated understanding of the information. It is that integrated understanding and change in thought, judgment, reasoning, and behavior that is the result of **education.** Education can be defined as a learning process that builds up over time as knowledge is acquired, skills are developed, thought processes change, and lessons are learned through experience.

This education can be too time-consuming a mission for you, if you are largely consumed with the day-to-day needs of the business. Expecting the staff to be responsible for their own sales development activities and product knowledge expertise may be equally unrealistic. After all, to educate there must be an educator to *lead* those who would learn in the right direction. That is why most salon and spa professionals in the United States rely on their vendor representatives for this type of informational programming. In many large operations, there is often an educational director or educator on staff who is responsible for initial and ongoing training of all treatments offered in the salon and spa. This person is also responsible for the continuing education and development of the service team.

Whether you are part of a large salon and spa with an educational staff or a smaller salon and spa with a smaller structure, you will want to utilize the training resources from your vendors. Most of the competitive brands in the salon and spa market are well aware of the need to provide education at all levels for their clients. Many cite education as one of the selling points when the vendor first begins a relationship with a salon and spa. However, busy schedules, poor attendance at provided sessions, and the need to compensate attendees all take a toll on good intentions to redouble a salon and spa's commitment to building a solid educational program.

In Chapter 3, it was stated that one of the criteria for selecting a vendor should be the provision of product education. If a vendor is unable or unwilling to provide some type of initial, as well as ongoing, education for the salon and spa's main merchandise lines, then you would be advised to continue shopping for another line. While some merchandise, such as t-shirts and candles, might require only minimal education and support, a hair color line, straightening system, or skin care line will require regular education sessions to hone the knowledge base of the staff.

Some facilities can rely on vendors entirely for their education needs, but if staff turnover is high, or if staff is seasonal, you may also want to consider appointing an in-house educator to close the knowledge gaps. If that option makes the most sense for your operation, it would be good to have the vendor's representative work closely with the in-house educator to assist in preparing a program. The vendor's representative will either have, or may be able to develop, a whole range of materials to support the educational efforts, such as manuals, consumer brochures, samples, and testers.

The real-life perspective provided by the Seasons Salon and Spa can help highlight the difference between training and education:

## At the Seasons Salon and Spa...

Holly is a recently re-trained twenty-something front desk receptionist. With great effort, she overcomes her persistent tendency of lingering behind the counter and steps out to speak to a guest near the retail display of body creams.

The dreaded pop quiz begins as the guest gratefully looks up at Holly's approach. "What would you recommend for dehydrated skin?"

*"Hmmm,"* thinks Holly. *"I think that means she has sensitive skin, but which body cream is the one that has sunscreen? It must be the one with the blue stripe on the package—I think."*

After Holly directs the guest to a sample of the body cream, the guest moves on to the next question: "Does this product address flaky skin or would I need a scrub?"

*"I don't have a clue about the scrubs,"* thinks Holly, but then she recommends one of the scrubs in the hope that the guest will purchase both the body cream and the scrub—then she'll get a higher commission, and the guest will walk away happy.

"Does it have an SPF and if so, what is it?" the guest asks.

*"Geez, lady,"* Holly thinks to herself, *"I'm just part-time. Thank goodness the phone is ringing. I'll just give her a brochure and excuse myself."*

"Oh, huh? You don't mind waiting?! Oh, okay," Holly says as she scurries to the desk to pick up the phone. *"Rats, well maybe I can find a technician to help her,"* she thinks as she picks up the phone.

SALON AND SPA SNAPSHOT 6.4

No one likes to be put in the position of revealing the areas in which they lack expertise. It helps to remind staffers that every day millions of consumers make a purchase with little, or no solid information about the ingredients, features, benefits, and, perhaps most importantly, the contraindications of the products they are buying. With a modest amount of time and effort, any individual capable of performing basic customer service tasks can also understand the product lines to the degree that is necessary to sell them with confidence. What they may be lacking, however, is:

Education + Experience = Enlightenment

The basic components of retail education are relatively simple. The only way for retail staffers to convey the value of the goods on the shelves is by providing every staff member the opportunity to receive an *education* about the products and *experience* the products firsthand. It is then, and only then, that they can reasonably *enlighten* the client with the features and benefits of a given product.

One of the reasons that salon and spa staff needs to be well educated on products is because consumers also really want education. With the vast amount of information available on the Internet, such as online magazines, message boards, blogs, and videos, sometimes consumers are more up-to-date on the latest trends and information than the salon and spa staff. They will come in and ask very specific questions—such as why a product is a particular color or how it reacts with other products. These customers will expect answers when they interface with your staff.

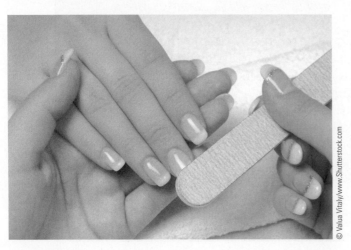

© Valua Vitaly/www.Shutterstock.com

## Understanding the Guest's Experience

Imagine you are visiting a fine dining restaurant in a trendy part of town. It is Saturday night, the restaurant is well-known for its gourmet menu and reservations are booked two weeks in advance. You chose the restaurant because you are celebrating a special occasion and the venue is known for its five-star service. After a long wait, the busboy comes to your table in a rush; pen in hand, and after a hasty greeting, he asks you what you want to order for dinner. You and your guest are taken by surprise. Since when does the busboy take your order? That is quite an inappropriate service style for a fine dining restaurant.

This scenario shows a realistic example of how important it is to think of your retail operation from the guest's perspective. What kind of retail experience do you want each guest to have when they visit your retail space and come in contact with your products and your staff? It is important to keep in tune with your salon and spa philosophy when defining your retail guest protocol.

## Creating an Appropriate Retail Protocol

When developing your retail protocol, it is important to focus on the following four elements:

1. The customer
2. The initiator of the sale
3. The salon and spa philosophy
4. The financial goals of the retail operation

### The Customer

The most effective retail protocol is going to be the one that is best suited to the type of guest that is being approached. This will necessarily differ depending on the type of salon and spa and the location. Let's say that a salon is located in a traditional spa. The retail protocol for a salon client for hair and nail services is going to be vastly different from the retail protocol used to initiate conversation with a day spa guest who came into the retail space to simply browse after a relaxing massage treatment. The regular salon client may view a visit to the salon area of the spa as something no more special than a visit to the dry cleaners because it is part of his or her regular routine. For this customer, selling "the spa experience" may not be compelling. Just as in a traditional "standalone" salon, these regular clients may, however, show more of an interest in practical items or items that support their nail and hair care needs.

### The Initiator of the Sale

The most effective retail protocol is going to be the one that is best suited to the type of associate that is initiating the sale. For example, what transpires in an exchange with a therapist or technician who has just completed a service with the guest will differ significantly from the retail protocol for a front desk person or a retail consultant who has not established the same level of intimacy with the guest. For therapists and technicians, the level of connection that is established during a service will be the foundation for the conversation involving retail. After the service, it is not at all unusual to see the service provider continue to make gentle and appropriate physical contact as they discuss products with the client, reinforcing the bond, and thus reinforcing the sale. The front desk personnel and the retail consultant will not have that kind of connection, but they can make up for it by sharing the pulse of the retail area. They hear all the buzz about all the products and can relate that to the client as if sharing the inside scoop and off-label uses that go beyond the standard sales pitch. Usually, the retail consultant also benefits from having more time to chat with the client. This gives them the opportunity to share more in-depth product and ingredient information that the therapists may not have time to elaborate on.

### The Salon and Spa Philosophy

The most effective retail protocol is going to be the one that is best suited to the overall theme, brand concept, or philosophy that the salon and spa conveys. For example, a very Zen-like atmosphere would best be paired with a leisurely, but attentive style of service that allows the client plenty of time to browse and personally experience the products. A trendy salon appealing to busy executives will have a more upbeat, quick approach.

### The Financial Goals of the Retail Operation

The most effective retail protocol is going to be the one that is best suited to the overarching financial goals of the retail facility. A careful review of the operational budget will serve as a general guide to the importance of the retail operations in the overall success of the salon and spa. For example, a medical spa (a medi spa) that easily meets all of its financial goals through services may choose to limit or de-emphasize its retail component as opposed to a salon and spa that relies on 40 percent of its revenue to come from retail.

# VALUE-ADDED CUSTOMER SERVICE

Sometimes simple add-ons can make a difference to customers between buying a product at a salon or spa and buying it at a department store (or any other competing organization).

The following are some examples of low-cost, value-added services that can make customers' shopping experiences enjoyable, effortless, time-saving, and money-saving:

- Gift wrapping: Provide free gift wrapping year round.
- Delivery service: Offer free delivery service to customers' homes (if local) or free shipping if out-of-town.
- Special orders: If a customer likes a particular product and the salon and spa does not have the product in stock, offer to special order it.
- Wish list: Especially during the holidays, encourage customers to complete a "wish list" card. Telephone the spouse or friend indicated on the form about the wish and volunteer to gift wrap the item for pickup or mailing.

You can expand on the above list in other ways to add value. The relationship can be supported by:

- Short approach times
- Quick check outs
- Seating areas
- In-store events or after-hours shopping
- Layaway
- Good, clear signage
- Gift certificates
- Personal shoppers (phone orders)
- Longer hours during the holidays
- Personal notes

What is the measure of success for sales and service? There are various retail checkpoints and goals you can set for your salon and spa. These are good to create because they allow you to measure your success—and it doesn't just have to be on the salon and spa's financials.

Success is also seeing someone who has never before been in the retail section, seriously considering a product. It is having guests purchase something to take to their homes. It is having guests buy a gift for a friend so that they can share the experience they had at the salon and spa with someone they care about. Or it is the guest that sends the follow-up note or submits a review on a blog about how much they appreciated your helpful service staff. For your staff, it's the sense of pride felt when the client walks out with a product that brought him or her so much joy. Success can be measured not just in what a salon spa achieves, but in what a salon and spa is.

# CHAPTER SUMMARY

- Salon and spa guests are motivated to seek services not only to enhance their appearance, but to enhance the way they feel about themselves.
- As a manager, you can help your team connect with the notion that clients rely on them as a trusted advisor.
- The entire salon and spa team contributes to the sale, either directly or indirectly.
- There are creative ways for your staff to sell products to clients. As a manager, you can help make these suggestions so everyone feels involved in the retail operation.
- Simply by being present in your salon and spa, guests give your staff permission to suggest products and services to them.
- Your vendors will be an important resource in developing your training programs.
- The most effective sales protocol is one that is aligned with the salon and spa philosophy, the customer, the sales initiator, and the sales goals.
- Have service providers use products themselves so they can learn firsthand about the products results.
- Low-cost, value-added services such as gift wrapping can encourage guests to buy from you instead of from a department store.
- The staff needs to be well-versed on products, as guests seek education from their service providers.

# LEARNING ACTIVITIES

## Learning Activity 6-1: Quick Time Training

Select one of the products in your retail area in which the salon and spa has not done any training. Gather information about that product and then develop a 15-minute education session on it for your team. Work at making the session fun and interactive. Perhaps you will want to develop a game show format or compose a rhyme to help the technicians remember important benefits.

After you've developed the session, practice it and then present it to your team. At the end of it, ask them to fill out a brief evaluation of the education session and then use that information to improve your training skills

## Learning Activity 6-2: Focus for Success

Create a 30-day promotion using the product you trained the team on in Activity 1. Place the product in key areas of the salon, assure the team recommends the product to clients that would benefit from it. Create a special incentive for guests if they make a purchase. Track your sales results for the month and compare them to sales prior to providing the training. Lastly, provide feedback to the team regarding the impact of the promotion and reward employees for their efforts.

# REVIEW QUESTIONS

1. Which of the following statements about sales in a salon and spa is TRUE?
   a. A salon and spa has a much more challenging time making sales than a traditional retailer because of the extended time they spend with the guest.
   b. Most people who purchase salon and spa products do so at department stores after a salon and spa visit.
   c. The salon and spa's services are a unique opportunity to connect with guests about sales because therapists build rapport through touch.
   d. Salon and spa staff should use hard-sell techniques during a service because they have a captive audience.

2. During her performance evaluation, Rose, a front desk receptionist at the Seasons Salon and Spa, complains that she can't make retail sales. "I can't afford any of our products," she says, "and it just doesn't feel right to ask someone who has just spent $150 on a massage to spend more money on product." What category of objection has Rose raised?
   a. Retail knowledge and skills
   b. Incentives and requirements
   c. Obstacles and constraints
   d. Ethical and moral

3. The people responsible for the sales of retail in the salon and spa are:
   a. The service providers.
   b. The front desk, retail consultant, and the manager.
   c. The service providers, the front desk and/or retail consultant, and the manager.
   d. Everyone, with the exception of the massage therapists.

4. Jazmine is waiting for an in-depth product knowledge training class from the vendor. What can she do in the meantime to assure the staff can speak about the product?
   a. Visit the vendor website and download a product information sheet.
   b. Have her brand ambassador take the product home and use it for a week, then share her experience with the team.
   c. Nothing, just wait for the expert to provide the training and not display the product.
   d. None of the above.

5. When thinking about the customer experience in defining a sales protocol, it is best to:
   a. Consider the salon and spa philosophy.
   b. Always consider the potential for retail commission for your staff.
   c. Think about how it will suit the target customer.
   d. Think about objection prevention.

6. Sales as a part of service can be best described as:
   a. Offering suggestions in the form of products and services.
   b. Serving your client and being a trusted advisor.
   c. Making the difference in the lives of others by solving their challenges.
   d. All of the above.

7. Which of the following make the salon and spa environment a unique selling opportunity over a store?
   a. The guest can sample products and have dialogue with an expert.
   b. Full services are performed in a 1:1 setting.
   c. There is an appointment booked and a fee paid for services.
   d. Education is provided and connections are made in a nontraditional sales manner.

8. Jazmine has been building her retail product offerings and adding several new lines. She is worried about managing the ongoing product knowledge training for her growing retail space. What is the most effective action she can take to manage the product knowledge training?

    a. Establish brand ambassador roles.

    b. Rearrange her schedule to accommodate the extra responsibility.

    c. Place a computer in the break room so the staff can access online education.

    d. None of the above.

9. Which of the following statements refers to training?

    a. Introducing spa staff to information about a product

    b. Listing the features and benefits of a spa product

    c. Teaching employees the methodology of selling

    d. Allowing retail staff to experience the products firsthand

10. Patty, a massage therapist, is not engaged in selling retail. She feels like it is interfering with her role as a healer. To encourage her to recommend products you might:

    a. Help her understand the relevance of products as they relate to therapy.

    b. Help her think of products that will enable the client to maintain the same level of relaxation at home.

    c. Offer a sampling program so she can experience products firsthand.

    d. All of the above.

# Visual Merchandising

© Milady, a part of Cengage Learning.
Photography by Visual Recollection.

Chapter **7**

## INTRODUCTION

O nce you have purchased the salon and spa's retail products and learned how to hire and train a sales staff, you can spend some time working on the design of the actual retail space. If you are opening or building a new salon and spa, you will most likely work with an architect or interior designer to ensure the correct retail space is part of the initial design process. If the salon and spa is already in business and the plan is to expand the retail space, dedicated space must be carved out somewhere within the existing floor plan.

Most retail operations are a part of the salon and spa, many times as an area surrounding the reception desk or waiting area. In some larger resort properties, the retail boutique may be a totally separate space. There is no right or wrong; the key issue is that the retail area is its own entity, not an extension or afterthought of the reception area. It must have its own purpose, which is to suggest products to your customers that will extend the benefits of a treatment and remind them of the wonderful experience they had with you.

And, last but not least, the retail space must be staffed by employees who are trained on the benefits and features of each product line.

## BASIC STORE PLANNING AND FLOOR LAYOUT

Before beginning the design and floor layout of a salon and spa boutique, you will need to look at the bigger picture. You can start by looking at some of your competitors' boutiques within salons and spas,

## LEARNING OBJECTIVES

After successfully completing this chapter, the reader will be able to:

- Explain the purposes of visual merchandising as they relate to customer satisfaction and profitability.
- Describe areas of the salon and spa that can be focal points for visual display.
- Explain the role that lighting plays in visual merchandising.
- Prepare skin, body, hair, and other beauty products for display.
- Describe various types of written display materials and their purposes.
- Describe types of fixtures used to display merchandise and explain how each is used.

(continues)

© Kzenon/www.Shutterstock.com

resorts, and possibly even some local retail boutiques that are not part of a salon or spa. This should offer a general understanding of how a retail space can look. Points to look for, and make note of during a walk-through include areas that draw the customer in and easy-to-maneuver floor plans. It is a good idea to look at retail areas that are similar in size to the planned boutique. This will help you envision how much fixturing and merchandise can comfortably fit into the planned or current retail space. Going to look at how a department store merchandises its floor may be less beneficial, as its huge open space can be deceiving.

After reviewing other similar retail areas, you can return to your own business and analyze the retail space, looking both inside and outside, and making notes of retail focal points. Several areas are particularly important to consider:

- Storefront windows
- Entryway
- Floor plan
- Cash wrap counter
- Dressing rooms

## Storefront Windows

Are there windows in the front of the salon and spa that can house visual displays that will draw customers in? Most salons and spas will have the advantage of customers needing to walk in to get to the reception desk to check in for an appointment, thus pulling them through the retail area. But having great window displays will entice customers to shop while they are waiting for their service to begin. Likewise, there may be many people who walk by the salon and spa each day and could be drawn in by an attractive display. The goal of a window display is to get potential customers to cross the threshold of your business, and ultimately, to come into the retail area to shop.

Windows can be the most important location to make a good first impression. To make an interesting, eye-catching window, you can choose some key items from product inventory, focusing around a theme. In general, window displays should encompass as

SALON AND SPA SNAPSHOT 7.1

## At the Urban Salon and Spa ...

Reuben rounded the corner by the Urban Salon and Spa's cash/wrap counter and nearly collided with the nesting tables that held a display of Zen sand gardens and other relaxation products. He grabbed for the table to steady it before the contents of the sand garden ended up on the floor—again.

Picking up the tiny rake and smoothing the sand into soothing swirls, Reuben contemplated the display that Bree, his retail manager, had created earlier in the week. In addition to the sand garden, she had artfully arranged a selection of relaxation CDs, a couple of pillar candles in soft earth tones, and a book on Eastern meditation. Unfortunately, the placement of the display had caused more than a few customers—and staff members—to have a less-than-relaxing encounter with the nesting tables. Bree looked distressed when Reuben had jokingly suggested selling ice packs to soothe people's barked shins.

Reuben knew that Bree had figured placing the display near the cash/wrap counter would encourage customers to make impulse purchases of the items, but that didn't seem to be happening. Perhaps they were so embarrassed about knocking into the display that they couldn't bring themselves to pick up any of the products for purchase.

Visual merchandising in the salon and spa retail environment is about placing products consciously, and with the intention of creating the desired atmosphere. Studies have shown that customers perceive only about one-fourth of the store's environment as they walk through the doors. By frequently rearranging displays, salons and spas can create the impression that their merchandise is new and exciting. Layout and design can also guide customers through the retail space in patterns that will lead them past the greatest amount of merchandise. A carefully planned layout can serve as a powerful tool that generates interest and increases sales.

many different product categories as possible while still following a theme. A unique grouping of products is more likely to send a visual message and evoke feelings that might lure prospective customers into the salon and spa.

For example, a theme of *a fresh spring look* can be built around the message of renewal. You could have a special arrangement of items, including exfoliation for the face and body, a new makeup palate, and hair-brightening treatments such as highlights. The display could include baskets with colorful flowers and a mannequin with a colorful dress. A theme of *relaxation with an evening bath* might include a couple of mannequins displaying apparel items like a robe and some loungewear, and around their base might be some coordinating slippers. Worked into that same area might be some skin care and bath products related to cleansing and moisturizing before bed. There might be a few books that talk of relaxing away the tensions of the day, possibly some candles, or some caffeine-free tea products that encourage relaxation.

Window displays that are changed approximately every four to six weeks will keep regular customers from seeing the same display and skipping over it in boredom. Window displays can focus on a special promotion or event, acting as an advertisement for these specials. If the salon and spa doesn't have a special promotion or event, the display can focus on a trendy color palette that's hot for the season, or possibly feature items that relate to the season in general, such as summer's arrival, or spring, as in the example above.

It is important to note that merchandise displayed in a window is subject to fading from continued exposure to the sun. Store windows may be treated with some type of UV protection. If you have products in the window for a month and they are exposed to sunlight for several hours a day, chances are the sun will discolor them. Plan to mark these items "out of stock" due to sun damage.

## A Welcoming Entryway

What does the entry to the retail space look like? The entry should be inviting, and should follow the theme of the salon and spa. A sign above the door or somewhere in front is key to identifying the name of the boutique, if a separate name is applied. The first visual display is usually located just inside the entry door, almost as if it is welcoming customers to the retail area.

## What Makes a Floor Plan Flow?

Making the floor design flow well will guide customers through the retail space, and will visually encourage them to enjoy the experience of shopping. The goal is to entice them to purchase some items that will help them prolong the effects, and the memory, of their visit and the results of their service. Bumping into other customers or fixtures while trying to shop is not a relaxing experience. While you want to use all of your space to maximize retail profitability, be careful not to make it appear crowded. To prevent over-crowding of the floor space, retail designers realize that walls are key areas for merchandise, building in shelves, hanging bars, and cube or cubbyhole type fixtures. We will discuss fixtures later in the chapter.

To keep customers moving all the way to the back of the retail space, you can place enticing displays on the back wall, high enough for customers to see from a distance. Placing the cash/wrap area and the dressing rooms toward the back will also keep customers looking and shopping throughout the entire retail space.

## Cash Wrap Counter

Where will the cash register/wrap area be and what does it need to accomplish? If the retail space surrounds the salon and spa's appointment desk, will the two areas share the same desk? If it is to be shared, is it large enough? The counter should also look enough like a retail counter that passing shoppers are not intimidated by the idea that they may have to talk with the staff at the appointment desk if they just want to come in and browse. A cash/wrap station for retail needs space for a cash register, as well as storage for bags and tissue wrap for customers' purchases. For spas, the countertop space needs to be large enough to lay out and fold large items such as robes or blankets. The counter is an ideal place for impulse purchases such as travel-sized beauty products, lip balms, nail polishes, hair accessories, or small cards to accompany gift purchases. It may also require some storage space for small items such as paper clips, price tickets, vendor catalogs for reference, a booklet to keep track of special orders for customers, etc. If this space is properly planned, it will be easy to keep it neat and organized.

## Dressing Rooms

A dressing room is a good idea if the salon and spa sells apparel. Ideally this needs to be part of the retail store or very close by. A bathroom or an unused treatment room down the hall is not a good choice for a dressing room, as the customer may need assistance while trying on clothing. This will be challenging for both the customer and the retail consultant (or front desk) if they need to make repeated trips from the retail area to a far-away space. The overall size of the retail space and the amount of apparel carried will help determine how many dressing rooms are needed.

The dressing room space will typically be a minimum of 3 feet by 4 feet and will include the following items:

- A mirror—at least one-sided, but three-way mirrors are the best for seeing the back view
- Hooks to hang hangers or garments
- A chair or bench for placing personal items or to sit down if shoes need to be removed
- Good lighting
- A door, or opaque curtain, that covers the opening from side to side

Guests will appreciate finding a neat, clean dressing room—not one that holds garments tried on and rejected by the previous customer. The retail area staff must be trained to clean out a dressing room as soon as the customer is finished.

## Enhancing the Basic Space

Within each focal point of the retail space, and in fact, in the space as a whole, decisions about key elements such as décor and lighting will make a huge difference in the way customers perceive the salon and spa and its retail offerings.

### Overall Décor

© Milady, a part of Cengage Learning. Photography by Dino Petrocelli.

Color and décor are vital to the impression the salon and spa boutique or retail space will make on customers. Whether your retail is a separate store located within the salon and spa or a shelving area in the entrance, it needs to harmonize with the rest of the environment. If your area consists of a simple free-standing shelving unit within the reception area, be sure the unit ties in with the furniture and theme. For example, if your salon is modern, with chrome and black accents predominant throughout, assure the shelving unit blends in and is unobtrusive. If you have a separate boutique within the salon and spa, choose a similar color theme for the walls and similar flooring materials such as wood, carpet, or tile, but preferably not vinyl flooring as it may cheapen the appearance of the retail space. The environment should be a continuation of that experience in the treatment areas.

## Fixtures

Salon and spa fixtures are also selected for their ability to blend well together and with the environment. The décor will decide the direction of fixturing—for instance, light-colored wood versus dark wood, or black finishes on fixtures, or shiny chrome versus brushed aluminum metal finishes. You can collect brochures from fixture and display companies to help you make decisions. Some of your selected vendors may offer fixtures that complement their type of merchandise. However, they need to blend in with other fixtures in the space, otherwise they may not be desirable to use.

In the construction of a new salon and spa, the architect will work with you to build walls with a flexible system. The best system will allow the staff to change out shelves for hanging bars or cubed fixtures, depending on what product will be placed in a designated area. Flexibility is the key as the retail floor will change month after month, depending on product quantities and varieties. Doing your homework at the beginning of the process prevents you from being locked into something that isn't flexible enough to fit your needs.

## Sound and Scent

What customers hear while they shop is another consideration when thinking about the overall space. Music is an important element in any retail environment. Background music can create energy, excitement, and mood. It should coordinate with music played in the salon or spa, not be too loud, and should be available to purchase in the retail area. Never play a radio as background music, as the music is interrupted by advertisements and announcements.

Scent is another important element for association and helps bring back memories. It, too, should not be too strong or overwhelming. Scent can originate from an aromatherapy diffuser or scented candles; however, scents must not compete with one another. Again, the products scenting the retail area should be available for purchase.

## Lighting

In addition to the general lighting considerations discussed in the previous chapter, pay attention to specific lighting issues when reviewing your overall visual plan. Good lighting design will allow for the light beam from each fixture to slightly overlap the next with no dark spots in the store. Some displays might have a little brighter light, almost a spotlight effect, shining on them. Remember to light the merchandise on the walls (Figure 7-1). When using glass shelves or glass cases, the lighting should not be so bright that it bounces off the glass.

A key area in which to focus on getting the lighting perfect would be the makeup area. It must be correct if customers will be testing makeup colors on their skin. Another area in which to remember good lighting is the dressing rooms. A lighting designer can assist you with answering your lighting questions about these key areas, and other areas.

In the theater, good lighting generally goes unnoticed. If the designer gets it right, the performers and scenery are illuminated in a way that clearly reveals all of the subtle details the viewer needs to see to follow the actions and emotions as they unfold. If the lighting is too dark, unfocused, or simply inconsistent with the mood of the play, the overall experience will be compromised.

The same can also be said for lighting the retail "stage." This aspect should be an important part of the design process and not an afterthought. Lighting can prove disastrous if not thoroughly addressed with a comprehensive lighting design. Many beautiful, mood-evoking light fixtures can perform inadequately in casting light on the featured attraction—the products. These mood-setting lights are great for creating the desired ambiance, but may do little to directly encourage the buying experience. A good

Figure 7-1
In-depth understanding of how lighting works can improve the way the retail space looks.

© Milady, a part of Cengage Learning. Photography by Dino Petrocelli.

lighting strategy always counterbalances lighting placement designed to enhance ambiance, with brightly focused lighting that makes the packaging and signage easy to read.

Retail lighting must be designed to facilitate the tasks of buying and selling by attracting customers to the retail space, helping them evaluate the merchandise, and helping the salespeople complete each sale quickly and accurately. Research has shown that lighting installations that are carefully designed with these three factors in mind will actually increase retail sales.

When dealing with lighting that is problematic within an existing retail space, it would be best to consult a lighting designer who has extensive experience with retail environments. When selecting lighting for the retail area, consider several issues, as noted here:

- Color index: Choose lighting with a high color-rendering index (CRI). Retail areas need lamps that make colors appear as natural as possible. A CRI of 80 or above (on a scale of 1 to 100) will render colors most accurately. There are standard and halogen incandescent, fluorescent, and metal halide lamps that meet this CRI value.
- Glare: Lighting fixtures should limit glare. For customers to examine merchandise comfortably and employees to work without eyestrain, contractors choose lighting fixtures carefully and install them properly. For the retail area's general lighting, fixtures are chosen that limit the shopper's view of the lamp itself, such as louvers, baffles, and lenses. This cuts down on the glare of these fixtures. For accent lighting that is aimed directly at merchandise, lamps with narrow beams (often called spotlights) can be selected, as well as fixtures in which the lamp is recessed or set back from the fixture's opening. The contractor should ensure that this lighting is not aimed directly toward aisles or doorways, where it could shine directly into shoppers' eyes.
- Direction: Lighting for vertical surfaces, such as wall displays and shelving, requires adjustable fixtures that can be aimed where needed; these fixtures should direct some light to the sides rather than directly down. Lighting within display cases or shelving units can also provide needed illumination.
- The wrong lighting: Too many halogen reflector lamps used as spot lighting can create visual clutter and

Figure 7-2
Lighting can affect the shelf life and temperature of the product used in services.

confuse customers. The retail area needs both general lighting in areas where people need to walk and move, as well as accent lighting. It can be very effective to light important displays and sales counters to a higher level (sometimes as much as five times brighter) than the general areas of the retail space. If the contractor limits accent lighting to these two areas, it will be much more effective in catching a customer's attention than scattered accent lighting.

- Temperature: A particular concern in the salon and spa environment is the heat emitted by retail light fixtures. Salon and spa professionals need to ensure that cool lighting is used, because some spotlights can be too hot and can damage products with ingredients that are sensitive to temperature. The treatment areas require adequate balanced lighting (see Figure 7-2).

- Direct lighting on products: Retail lighting above product shelves will highlight products and make packaging visible (see Figure 7-3).

Figure 7-3
Décor and lighting make a huge difference in the way customers see the retail offerings.

# FLOOR LAYOUT AND PRODUCT POSITIONING

No matter what its physical appearance, the retail space needs to address the needs of its customers. It has to maintain, enhance, and provide the products designed to continue the benefits provided by the service.

The retail layout should entice customers to move around the retail environment to purchase more products than they intended to. If the layout is too cumbersome and disjointed, guests may find it difficult to locate the merchandise and decide just to walk out. The trade-off between ease of finding merchandise and providing a varied and interesting retail space is determined by the needs of the customers. For example, grocery store shoppers typically have specific items they want to buy, so these retailers need to place an emphasis on the ease of locating certain types of merchandise. On the other hand, department store or specialty store retailers can place more emphasis on exploration.

One method of encouraging customers to explore is to present a retail layout that facilitates a specific traffic pattern. Another method of assisting customer flow through the retail environment is to provide interesting design patterns.

Today's modern retailers use four general types of store layout design: grid, racetrack, free-form, and feature areas (see Figures 7-4 to 7-7).

After reviewing the big picture of what your salon and spa's retail area can be, and deciding on a basic layout concept, you can get down to the details of actually sketching out the layout and turning it into reality. If you are reconfiguring an existing space, you may be able to simply rearrange the moveable shelving and displays to achieve your goals. If you are designing a new space, it will likely require working with a design professional, using a computer program to lay out various spaces for consideration.

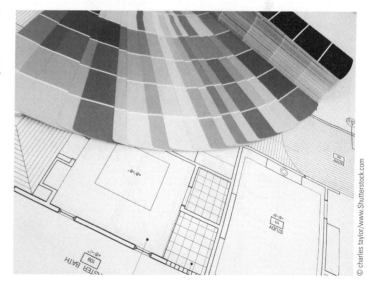

© charles taylor/www.Shutterstock.com

Figure 7-4
The grid retail design is used in most grocery stores.

Figure 7-5
The racetrack is also known as the "loop." Typically used by department stores, it entices the customer to visit various departments.

Figure 7-6
The free-form also known as the boutique layout. It is a relaxed environment, where customers feel they are strolling through someone's home.

Figure 7-7
Feature areas are areas within the retail environment designed to get the customer's attention. They include end caps, promotional aisles or areas, freestanding fixtures, and mannequins, windows, point-of-sale checkout, and walls.

Once that space is created, you can do your own redesigns by hand. Some basic supplies are necessary for layout and design:

- A copy of the original blueprint, focusing on the area designated for retail space
- A pad of tracing paper, large enough to cover the blueprint area
- Scotch tape
- A pencil
- An eraser
- A small ruler for sketching fixtures
- A retractable tape measure
- A large clipboard that will hold the blueprint copy
- A list of available fixture types for reference
- A list of the product classifications

The process starts by taping the blueprint copy onto a board with a firm backing and covering it with a sheet of tracing paper. Using a pencil, sketch out different options for floor plans, playing with various designs. Be creative, but always consider the feasibility of the plan. To help with accuracy, floor plan sketches should be done while standing in (or above) the actual retail space, not while sitting in an office.

Below are some general criteria to consider while sketching out floor plans:

- Key vendors and products should occupy the key positions in the store; the key hair care and skin care lines do not belong at the back of the room in the corner. You can, however, have secondary product display of these items in areas near treatment/service areas. For example, placing a new deep conditioner on the front shelf and near the hair styling station reminds stylists to use and discuss the product.
- Consider the profit potential of the merchandise and give more profitable items the appropriate space to spotlight them.
- The percentage of space occupied by a product classification should reflect the approximate percentage of its contribution to sales. For instance, if hair care is approximately 60 percent of the salon and spa's total sales plan, then 60 percent of the retail space will be devoted to hair care products.
- Visual merchandising is an art, not a science, so there is no right or wrong. Be open to experimenting and consider various ways of grouping merchandise, examining the

## HERE'S A TIP

When reviewing the design of the retail area, you need to walk the space from the entrance, all of the way through the display areas, to the cash wrap. When doing so, think of how customers will feel when they enter the space, how they will move through it, and how the layout will get them to walk through the entire retail area. In the end, think of the overall impression given of your salon and spa.

## FYI

Think of your retail space as real estate, with those areas having the best views and most foot traffic as prime. Carefully placing top sellers with the highest margin will increase your retail sales per square footage.

pros and cons of each. For instance, is it better to put all hair or skin care products together, or to spread them throughout the store, creating a layout that pulls the customer around the retail space? For apparel, should all the merchandise from one vendor be displayed together, or should displays be set by product subclassification, that is all robes together, all logo t-shirts together, etc.?

- Impulse merchandise displays are typically found on the cash/wrap counter. As mentioned earlier, these are usually made up of smaller items, such as a bowl of SPF lip balms, or travel-sized items. These little displays promote unplanned purchase decisions that occur while the customer is standing at the cash/wrap counter waiting to pay.

- Each product category needs some displays to catch the customer's eye. The stock of these items must be close by the display on the sales floor. Other than window displays, if there is a display in the retail area, the stock must be near it so that the customer doesn't struggle to find it, eventually losing interest. For example, a trio of skin care products on a riser will attract attention to the line. It is not the intention for customers to necessarily pull product from that display. Have the product stocked on the lower shelf so customers can easily select items for their purchase.

Throughout the planning process, ask yourself many questions as you sketch and erase various retail layouts. Where will you put hair care line A, hair care line B? Skin care line A, skin care line B? What areas are best suited for apparel? Wall layouts are less flexible, because they are semi-permanent. The floor layout can be adjusted more easily when the staff physically begins placing the fixtures in the space, but it all starts with a plan.

# PRESENTATION AND DISPLAY FOR SKIN, BODY, AND BEAUTY PRODUCTS

When creating retail displays, keep in mind that the majority of the shoppers who enter this retail space will be women. According to recent industry studies, men account for less than 30 percent of salon and spa visits in the United States. The biggest slice of the retail pie in nearly all merchandise arenas has always been women. The need to create an environment where women are comfortable browsing will be the top priority. In order to achieve this, one must consider *how* women shop. No one has distilled this information better than retail guru Paco Underhill in his book, *Why We Buy: The Science of Shopping.*

This uniquely female approach to the act of shopping should become the manicured hand that guides every design component of the space, and it translates into something quite simple. The retail space should be an experiential haven where shoppers can linger and easily absorb the information needed to process the decision to purchase. This retailer's mantra will indulge the shopping style of the salon and spa's female clientele while encouraging the "grab and go" males to browse at a more leisurely pace. For salons and spas to achieve this with hair, skin, and body care assortments, the goods must adhere to the standard guidelines for retail, which is to say that they need to be visible, inviting, and accessible.[1]

Research indicates that while the first two tenets (make it visible and inviting) are key to attracting shoppers, the last one (make it accessible) is critical for keeping them in the store. All shoppers, but women in particular, are sensitive to the proximity between their "personal space" and other objects (fixtures, other shoppers, etc.). Allowing that knowledge to influence each design decision will ensure that the space created is as practical and hospitable as it is beautiful and alluring.

While these goals can be achieved through a number of creative variations, they will invariably require the purchase or custom construction of some type, or several types, of fixtures to effectively and attractively house what will likely be the largest segment of the retail revenues.

---

[1]Underhill, P. (1999) Why we buy: the science of shopping. New York: Simon & Schuster.

## Fixtures and Shelving

In salons and spas across the world, products can be found displayed in every imaginable way, from antique hutches arranged with hair products to bundles of bath salts in decorative birdbaths. The choices for creative and enticing retail displays are limited only by the imagination, and perhaps by floor space. These unusual types of displays, however, fall more into the category of *temporary installments*. Temporary installments are like art exhibitions; they are unique and eye-catching but they are featured for a limited time. And while they provide a focal point to call attention to a specific product or collection, they generally do not provide a permanent home for the bulk of the retail products. Salons and spas need some sort of shelving to house the majority of the stock in skin care, body care, hair care, and cosmetics.

While shelving can be built of almost any material that is in keeping with the ambiance and philosophy of the salon and spa, most retailers opt for clear glass. Glass shelving provides some degree of flexibility in its setup, making it possible to space out the shelves according to the height of the products and create a configuration that is perfectly suited for the general dimensions of the products. Glass does have the disadvantage of showing dust and fingerprints, so it requires ongoing housekeeping. But its visual advantages far outweigh the inconveniences of its upkeep. The greatest argument for using glass shelving is that glass allows light to spill onto the products from all angles, which achieves the first, and perhaps the most important, goal of merchandising—that the product be visible.

## Prepping Products for Display

When goods arrive, the salon and spa staff should unpack them immediately. This will not only confirm that the order was correct, but if something was broken or began leaking during shipment, the damage can often be caught before neighboring products are also ruined. Most vendors take great pains to ensure that their merchandise arrives in pristine condition, but occasionally something goes awry. If a product arrives damaged, contact the vendor immediately. Vendors will usually replace the merchandise at no cost. If only the outer box sustained the damage, that, too, can be replaced to make the goods saleable. Product inventory is explained in more detail in Chapter 4.

Consistency is important when applying price stickers to the retail goods. If the price sticker appears on the back of some merchandise and on the bottom of other goods, a shopper can become frustrated at having to examine all sides of the box to locate the price. Pricing all products, including testers, also avoids the awkwardness of the customer having to ask.

Many salon and spa professionals have found that it is generally best to apply the stickers to the bottom or to the back of the package so that the front of the product lineup is visually uncluttered. Most vendors now offer UPC coded tags for their products, which can provide the salon and spa with professional-looking stickers that include the product name and suggested retail price point. These UPC coded tags can be used even if a UPC code reader is not going to be used. If UPC coded tags are not available, printing price tags through other methods can suffice.

For a large group of products all featured at the same price point, signage can take the place of stickers. But since signage needs to be limited, to present pleasant and uncluttered visual lines, this approach should be applied judiciously.

## Successful Display Techniques

Once the products have their price stickers, they are ready to be put on display. A good merchandise display will make the products look appealing to customers and invite them to take a closer look at what the product has to offer. Consumer surveys indicate that shoppers prefer to try skin care and cosmetic products, and are statistically more likely to purchase items that they have been able to experience. With this in mind, the majority of the product displays should be designed to encourage hands-on activity by the customer and to encourage learning through detailed product application cards. This "play station" interface allows the retail display unit to function as a self-led demonstration opportunity that will increase sales.

Generally, retail product displays follow one of two variations: showcasing or mass merchandising. When showcasing a product, a few examples are placed on the shelves and the remainder is kept in back stock. Mass merchandising, on the other hand, places as much product as possible on the shelves. While the showcasing method may make more sense when retail space is limited, most merchandisers follow the mass-merchandising method, because it cuts down on storage costs and allows clients to navigate their shopping experience independently—another aspect for which consumers have shown a decided preference. Also, studies have shown that the most important factor considered by the consumer when making a purchase is "availability of product." Clients should see at least three to six of each product on the shelf. It lets them know that the salon and spa has a selection to choose from.

With products neatly lined up, grouped according to usage, clearly labeled with their prices, and sprinkled with an occasional shelf talker to clarify each product's benefits, shoppers can navigate their way through the shelves and make an independent selection.

This arrangement is familiar and this familiarity imparts an immediate sense of comfort and confidence to the shopper's experience. It also deters theft, because when one product is missing from what is otherwise a full row, it calls attention to its absence. But most importantly perhaps, mass merchandising sends the message that the retailer strongly believes in the merchandise. Otherwise, why would so many pieces of that same item be stocked?

While rows of products lined up like little soldiers may seem rather limiting to those who envisioned a retail area inspired by a European fruit market with baskets of brightly colored bottles spilling onto the floor, bear in mind that the bulk of your merchandise needs to fulfill the previously stated goals:

## SALON AND SPA SNAPSHOT 7.2

### At the Ocean Beauty Salon… Unique Display Opportunities

Ocean Beauty Salon, in Redondo Beach, California, offers a unique way of displaying their retail products. "I think each product line I carry has its own personality. I have a unique display that reflects the essence of each. For example, one of the men's hair care and skin care lines has an industrial look and feel. The display is stainless steel with a sleek look. My upscale, *prestige* women's hair care line is in a curio cabinet lined in velvet for a regal look. The more casual skin care or body care lines are housed in a classic wood shelving unit." The entire look of the space is eclectic, with each piece of display furniture linked by common accent colors in the props or with the signage so the space looks united.

to be visible, inviting, and accessible. By keeping the largest percentage of the merchandise placed in a controlled format, the products that are featured in ways that do break from that format will get even more attention.

Another way you can attract attention to feature items and smaller items is to place them on eye-level shelves, while placing larger items on bottom shelves.

When creating a repeating pattern through the mass merchandising approach, *size* matters, as does *color;* but *common sense* trumps them both. The arrangement of the merchandise should be governed by the left brain's common sense and given the final touches that only the right brain can interpret esthetically.

## Hair, Skin, and Body Products

The primary directive most often guiding the placement of hair, skin, and body care products is common sense. It is best to assume the shopper is familiar with the notion of a product line or system, for example, shampoo, conditioner, mousse or cleanser, toner and moisturizer. To reinforce this point that products work together, it is important that the service provider educates the customer during the service. For example, an esthetician will talk about the products used and share information about maintaining the skin during a facial. The discussion should include the regimen of cleansing, toning, moisturizing, exfoliating, protecting, and so forth.

Assuming that prior customer education is given, there are three main ways of displaying products: by usage, by chronological order, or by skin or hair type.

### Displaying by Usage

Displaying by usage means that products are presented in a way that reveals the products' features, functions, and benefits through the groupings of the display. For example, hair care products are grouped by their usage, such as shampoo, conditioner, styling lotion, etc. You can group different product lines on the same shelf, keeping the usage the same, as in Figure 7-8.

### Displaying by Chronological Order

Another approach is to line the products up in the chronological order of usage in a home care program and keep all product lines together. For example, in skin care products, all of Brand X is together in a shelf and lined up by cleanser, toner, exfoliate, etc.

Figure 7-8
Product grouped by usage.

Some exceptions can be made to the chronological order approach, depending on the dimensions of the fixture. For example, cleansers and toners would appear first on the top left corner of the shelf and continue moving from left to right. However, as a category they are consistently top sellers, so their popularity might influence an intentional relocation to the bottom shelf where they will be easy to reach; this leaves primary visibility on the top shelf to be reassigned to a product that needs more time in the spotlight.

## Displaying by Hair or Skin Type

Another display variation is to group the product collections according to the hair or skin type they are formulated to treat. Keeping a collection together subtly encourages the customer to think in terms of using the entire product regimen, which can help foster multiple purchases. In a skin care example, specialty cleansers, toners, and skin treatments that would be recommended for certain skin types would be placed together, as opposed to being placed on separate shelves by product type. This technique works in a similar fashion for hair care and even nail care.

## Shelf Sculpting

Once the products have been sorted from a logical point of view, the right-brain display artist is now free to factor size, shape, and color into the formula. Placing the largest products in the center of the shelf, pyramid-style, can be more visually appealing than an uneven row. Keep in mind that even the tallest packages should allow for enough room at the top so that the shopper will not have to worry about knocking over the merchandise when making a selection.

Additional steps in **shelf sculpting** further the visual appeal and balance of a display. Turning all of the pumps so that they are facing in the same direction would make the products look more uniform in appearance. Further, when it comes to enhancing the impact of different color packaging, using what is called the **color block** method is recommended. This means that if different collections or brands have different colored packaging, the like-colored ones should be kept together as a group so that the block of color can have impact.

## Additional Display Considerations

A handful of other exceptions may require a different display strategy than what has been previously discussed. First, there is a general rule that the more expensive an item is, the fewer should be placed on display. A prominently featured display of a single high-ticket item will make it seem even more special. So, for items that are pricey or unique—less is more. Second, if shoplifting is of concern, high-ticket or easily "pocketed" items might warrant placement in a locked case. When you decide that this must be done, bear in mind that shoppers may hesitate to request access to that item. Therefore, the sales staff must be trained to offer their assistance in opening the locked case as soon as a customer appears interested.

Some other categories that may warrant their own designated section include:
- Men's products
- Products for babies and children
- Sun care products
- Products to straighten or smooth hair
- Products for lifestyle/hobbyists, such as runners, gardeners, golfers, swimmers
- Unique product collections, such as organics, essential oils, custom-blend products, local handmade goods, etc.

## Cosmetics

Most vendors make the display concept for cosmetics a bit easier by supplying a tester stand that is specifically constructed to display

**shelf sculpting.** Arranging items on a shelf so the outline is visually appealing by size, shape, and color, for example, from smallest to tallest, in a pyramid shape, or keeping the color packaging of a product line together.

**color block.** Keeping like-colored items together for visual impact in merchandising.

the product and sometimes, house the additional back stock. However, problems can arise when that unit is not in keeping with the store's décor or when the unit would necessitate the purchase of more product than is desired in order to fill it up. Today, many companies specialize in the creation of pre-made and custom-designed fixtures that are just right for the display of cosmetics.

The display of cosmetics will be more eye-catching if it is arranged with ample consideration given to the "flow" of the color spectrum, especially when displaying items that come in a full range of colors, such as eye shadows. Again, the vendor representative is likely to have a professionally designed schematic of the recommended sequence, and may even assist with the merchandising as part of their product support program. Employing this individual's expertise will take much of the guesswork out of the process. Beyond the issue of color though, the display of cosmetics will follow the same general guidelines that have been established for other merchandise, with regard to lighting, visual appeal, neatness, and signage.

The entire salon and spa industry is one of transformations and nowhere is this more fundamental than in the area of cosmetics. Unlike the glass-encased cosmetics displays of the past, that have been largely phased out of the department stores, the newer displays allow the customer access to product testers and actually encourage experimentation. You might expect to supply any or all of the following, and in some salons and spas, all of this might be expected:

- Some basic makeup removal supplies, such as milk cleanser, toner, cotton, and tissues
- Adequate light for accurate color assessment
- A bit of personal space for privacy (in case her personal "art" project falls short of expectations)
- An ample supply of disposable brushes, swabs, and pads (necessary for sanitary application)
- A tester station that is clean and sanitary
- A waste basket to dispose of applicators and tissue

Many cosmetic tester areas also have non-disposable brushes available for consumer use. This would be acceptable when the brushes themselves are being featured as a retail item, as it allows the shopper to see and feel how the brushes apply makeup to the skin. But "common use" applicators raise issues about sanitation and some states have laws in place that govern the use of non-disposable brushes. You must be certain that compliance with any of these

© Yuri Arcurs/www.Shutterstock.com

regulations is being followed and note the purpose of displaying such items in signage to make it clear to the customer. We will discuss testers further in the end of this section.

If these things are in place, the stage is set for shoppers to be the artists of their own beautiful creation. Of course, a skilled makeup artist will be able to take this primary configuration to the next level by providing the personalized guidance and expertise that most women crave.

Cosmetics as a category are associated with higher rates of shoplifting, so most of the actual stock is housed where the client will not have direct access to it. This means that while price stickers may be helpful for the cashier and for inventory purposes, most of the price information, for the customer's benefit, will need to appear on or adjacent to the display/tester unit. A label printer can create small, but easy-to-read, labels of various sizes to fit directly on the unit, stating the product's color name, or code, and price. A plexi-glass top that will cover the labels will catch the falling particles of powder-based products and keep the labels clean. The alternative is a price card that lists the retail price of each type of product such as eye shadow, mascara, lipstick, etc., that can be framed and placed to the side.

## When Shelf Talkers Speak

Some retail managers have moved away from the use of all signage to visually streamline their retail presentation. By placing

shelf talker. The official
term for signage that gives the
shopper a thumbnail sketch
of the product or collection.
It is placed near products
to communicate value to
customers.

a premium on simplicity, they have actually complicated the shopping process from the client's point of view, and potentially sacrificed the opportunity for the spontaneous sales that can be generated by a shopper's natural curiosity.

The more dominant segment of salon and spa retailers, however, all agree that **shelf talkers**, when used with style and restraint, can solve a host of problems by serving as a silent sales associate. A shelf talker is the official term for signage that gives the shopper a thumbnail sketch of the product or collection. It communicates product details such as price, features, and benefits. It can also remove the confusion of multiple languages that now appear on most cosmetic packaging.

Since shelf talkers became the ubiquitous form of retail communication, they have continued to evolve into a virtual art form. These usually diminutive signs, when artfully crafted and cleverly worded, can speak as if directly conversing with the shopper. Product vendors should be able to supply their standard version of shelf talkers, but if there is an aggressive focus on building brand identity, the copywriting task may best be kept in-house. By creating original shelf talkers, every aspect from the paper to the font to the tone of the language and perhaps even the use of a decorative frame can reinforce the thematic message of the establishment. (When the text is written, have the vendor representative do a quick read-through for accuracy, and keep the text on a disk or CD for changes and updates.)

Here are a few additional shelf talker guidelines:

- Shelf talkers are best used to summarize the details that apply to a group or collection of products (such as nail polish remover, cuticle treatments, nail polish, etc.) and then, in order to remain short and concise, highlight only one key benefit of an individual product.
- Placing the shelf talkers to the outside or end of the shelf makes the shelves look consistent and visually appealing.
- When using shelf talkers, the products should be placed in the order of mention on the sign. This will make finding the product much easier for the shopper.

## Picture Perfect

After all the thoughtful planning, custom design, and costly acquisition of merchandise, it can be disheartening to look around at what was once a glittering retail area, and now see dust bunnies, dog-eared signage, and the fingerprints of a month's worth of shoppers. Salon and spa retailing is unique in that it strives to provide products that reflect and sustain the treatments that are offered. If housekeeping measures are not up to par, clients may suspect that the same less-than-professional attitude toward cleanliness is being applied in the treatment rooms and service areas.

## Maintaining Testers

Placing a tester or a sample in front of the product removes several barriers. It allows the more tactile customer the satisfaction of touching, smelling, and handling the product. It makes the connection between sampling the product and buying the product clearer. Testers are often available from vendors at a rate below regular retail, due to their minimal packaging. Some vendors will even supply testers as part of the opening order.

The benefit of allowing the client to experience a product before purchasing is invaluable, and as many industry experts will point out, an important component of the feminine shopping experience. That experience, however, might backfire if the testers are not maintained after being set on the shelf. A gunked-up pump bottle or a lint-covered lipstick is as unappealing as it is unsanitary. The presence of testers requires a daily commitment to maintenance. Retail attendants need to set a schedule for their cleaning and then enforce it, perhaps even imposing some sort of good-natured fine for spotting a tester that is below the standard. If the upkeep of the retail area is always relegated to when "down time" occurs, then the upkeep is never viewed as a priority.

# PRESENTATION AND DISPLAY FOR APPAREL AND APPAREL-RELATED PRODUCTS

Apparel is increasingly becoming a central part of the salon and spa retail experience, especially if the salon and spa is located in a resort or hotel. Customers expect the same attention to detail in the area of apparel as they do in the rest of the boutique.

## Fixtures and Shelving

The art of displaying apparel items is just that, an art. When you lay out the floor and wall fixture plans, choose fixtures

HERE'S A TIP

Neat cubes of color-coordinated scarves and attractively styled mannequins displaying the latest in loungewear will make a far better impression than racks of tangled hangers and jumbled stacks of t-shirts tossed on a table.

appropriate for use with apparel. Many of the fixtures used for skin care products may be similar, but there are some fixtures that are used only for apparel. Using these fixtures will enable you to showcase the apparel in ways that will make customers eager to try on and purchase these wares.

### Two-Way or T-Stand

These freestanding fixtures in a "T" shape are known also as two-ways. The name comes from its design, which has a center post with two arms extending from it, hence the T shape. These are great for small or awkward spaces where larger units will not fit. They are also used for highlighting small new groupings of merchandise. It is best if these have locking wheels for easy floor arrangement. These are only for apparel.

### Four-Way

The four-way is another freestanding fixture, a little larger in size than the two-way because it has four sides with extensions. Both the two-way and four-way fixtures can accommodate straight arms, waterfall arms, and even small shelves. To make apparel fixtures more interesting, a mix of the options are available. Having a four-way with four straight arms is less interesting than two straight arms and two waterfall arms. Also, the arms on the fixture can be set at varying heights, mixing it up to create visual interest. Locking wheels are a necessity for these fixtures.

### Round Rack

This is only mentioned as a "don't" in the salon and spa retail environment. These are typically used in department stores to load a lot of merchandise on, quite typically markdowns. They have an inexpensive connotation about them and most spas try to avoid them.

### Cubes

These can be two-sided or one-sided. The two-sided cube fixture is designed for freestanding use with merchandise placed in the cubicles on each side. The single-sided cube fixture should be placed against the wall, cube side out, unless the flat side is being used as a backdrop or divider for a display. Of course, in this instance, the backside of the cube fixture must have a finished look. Cube fixtures are very simple and versatile. They can be used for many products, including skin care, gift items, slippers, headwear, and basic apparel items such as t-shirts, or even a large fluffy robe that has been folded and placed by itself in a cubicle.

## Wall Unit/Slat Wall

This can be a built-in fixture that is made of the same materials used in other areas of the salon and spa's retail, for example, the cash/wrap counter. Another type of fixture that can be integrated into the wall is called slat wall. This is a type of wall covering that has grooves every few inches to allow for the placement of shelves, arms, etc. Either of these can make a great wall display that is appealing and holds a lot of merchandise. These can incorporate shelves for folding garments, bars for hanging (which typically should be on the lower part of the wall), and face outs (which are best on top) to display apparel facing out. Again, a combination of all these options will create the most interesting visual merchandising. This type of fixturing can be used for most product classifications. Each of these fixtures has accessories that can change and enhance the basic fixture design.

## Tables

Single tables or nesting tables (usually two or three tables of varying heights that are grouped together) are perfect for creating attractive visual displays. These are usually placed in areas that draw attention to a promotion or salon and spa theme.

## Mannequin Forms

Every boutique that sells apparel needs several mannequins. These can be used freestanding on a floor pedestal type base, or just as a bust sitting on top of a display table (or possibly in a wall unit on a shelf). Mannequins typically come with what is called a finial, or neck block, to create a more finished look at the top of the mannequin. They help to enlighten customers about how a garment might look when worn. Studies have shown that more than 50 percent of shoppers say they get their ideas for clothing purchases from a display incorporating a mannequin.

There are several shapes of women's forms, typically dress, bust/blouse, or torso with legs for pants, as shown in Figure 7-9. The bust/blouse form is by far the most versatile. The other two forms are very difficult to dress to look natural and keep clothing from pulling. The bust form usually drops below the waist approximately three to four inches, creating a hip area. This bust form works perfectly for almost every type of apparel to be displayed other than swimsuits or lingerie panties.

© new vave/www.Shutterstock.com

Figure 7-9
A mannequin provides an attractive display.

## At the Augusta Salon…
## Take It from the Pros

The Augusta Salon in Denver, Colorado, gets its inspiration from top-notch retailers in the industry. Zach, the manager, makes it a priority to scout leading department stores to get ideas on how to display merchandise creatively. "Who knows better than the retailers at these chains regarding creative ways to blend props and color schemes in clothing and gift items? I ask my team to snap quick photos on their phones and bring them in so we can create eye-catching displays modeled after these retail superstars. I try to involve the team whenever possible and even award my top-selling stylists a space to merchandise. The whole team is excited each month when we do these changes."

### Hangers

Hangers may seem to be background items that will be hidden by the apparel they hold, but if you have spent a lot of time and money to create a beautiful and inviting salon and spa retail area, you should not scrimp with this accessory, because hangers do make an impression on customers. Plastic will cheapen the appearance of the apparel selection. Hangers should blend with the overall fixturing—for instance, a dark wood theme requires dark wood hangers, chrome accents in a modern environment would require chrome. Figure 7-10 shows an example of clothing displayed on wood hangers.

Figure 7-10
High-quality wood hangers give an upscale impression of clothing.

© GoodMood Photo/www.Shutterstock.com

Hangers come in many different shapes and styles. For women's merchandise, the retail area will need dress or top hangers and skirt hangers (with clips) to hang bottoms. Suit or coat hangers are never used for tops, sweaters, sportswear, pajamas, etc. These will be too wide and will stretch out points on the shoulders of the merchandise, making it undesirable for a customer to buy. Also, they make a woman's garment look very masculine. The only time a larger jacket hanger is used is to hold outerwear-type jackets or possibly robes. Salons and spas that carry men's apparel will need the wider hangers made specifically for men's size garments.

## Contoured/Display Hangers

These are special hangers that typically are a little thicker and sometimes have a drop with pant clips on them. These are used on the front of two-way or four-way fixtures to display an outfit. They are thicker to give the impression of having real shoulders inside filling out the garment a little more. The drop with clips allows you to clip a matching bottom extending out of the top, suggesting to customers how the entire outfit might look on the body. This is the next best thing to having a mannequin at the front of every fixture, which is not feasible.

## Cap Tree

Available at any fixture store, this standing fixture is similar to a coat tree but has flat discs on each arm tip, which makes it perfect for caps and hats.

## Rolling Rack

This rack is used more for the back room to hang and steam garments, then to roll the merchandise out to the floor when stocking fixtures. These racks can be easily broken down for storage in the back room.

## Wall and Free-Standing Mirrors

These are placed strategically in the store to allow shoppers to hold items up or even try them on to see how they look without going into a dressing room. You can have mirrors cut and mounted from a local glass/mirror store, or from the fixture store where the apparel fixtures were purchased. They will have mirrors that can bolt to the wall as well as freestanding styles that have an easel-type base.

## Preparing Apparel Inventory for Display

As merchandise arrives at the salon and spa, it should be prepared for the sales floor. Hang all apparel on the proper hangers, cut off any dangling threads, clean dark garments with a lint roller, and steam all garments. While a small hand-held steamer may work in a pinch for this task, a good, quality steamer is recommended. Look for a full-sized commercial steamer that has a weighted base on wheels with a water reservoir, a pole with a hook to hang a garment hanger on, and the steaming head at the end of a hose.

Consistency is necessary when hanging garments. The hanger hooks at the top should all face the same way. Tags should also be consistent. Vendors will usually put their hangtags on the left side of the body, sleeve, waist, etc. The salon and spa's price tags go in that same location or, if stickers are used, they are placed directly on the vendor's hangtag. Customers don't like to dig and hunt for pricing information. Size information can also be added to the price tag so that all the information the customer needs is in one location.

Garments that are folded on a shelf or in a cube require additional sizing stickers on the bottom right fold line so customers can easily find their size. In other words, if they are looking at a stack of folded merchandise, they should see a stack of size stickers. Without these stickers, customers will get frustrated digging through the stack or may decide not to dig at all. The stacks will become increasingly sloppy with the more digging they have to do, which in the end leads to more housekeeping.

## Making Room for Books, Gifts, and Accessories

Books or CDs, candles, and essential oils may be the perfect gift items in a retail salon and spa environment. The standard cubes and shelves may not seem quite right for displaying these types of items. When trying to add gifts to your retail offerings, it is important to remember that cramming these items in a small space will not show each item to its fullest. Often, it is the way you display the items that has the greatest impact on sales.

While it is tempting to shelve books with the spine out, it is essential to show books face out. Studies show that books displayed face out sell five to eight times better than when shown spine out. Salons and spas report that this display technique has increased their book sales four to 10 times. As a rule of thumb, only display gift items that you can readily sell. For example, have you ever entered a boutique and fell in love with the blouse of the mannequin, only to find that it was out of stock or it was the only one available? Pulling the last blouse off the mannequin is a deterrent to the buyer. Therefore, only display an item when you have additional stock on hand, unless you have the items in a clearance section.

Similar rules apply for gift items, such as candles, jewelry, or other accessories. These items can have a positive effect on the bottom line when salon and spa professionals commit to giving them the retail space to be visible and attractive to customers.

## Display Techniques

You can have fun with gifts and accessories with creative visual merchandising that is not confined to cubes, shelves, or hangers. You might use props that people would find in their homes or favorite hotels; for example, picture frames instead of sign holders, crystal bowls instead of ring holders, silver trays or sushi plates to stack soaps, or baskets full of rolled-up towels.

As in the section discussing storefront windows earlier, we discussed the idea that displays can tell a story or support a theme; for example, "Lavender Days of Spring." On a table, have lavender soaps on a tray or in a bowl, with a book about lavender, and perhaps other lavender-scented products such as sachets, room sprays, or candles in a small basket. On this table, have a vase with dried lavender and a sign announcing "Lavender Days of Spring" in a nice frame that ties to the theme (smart retailers will have the frame in stock in case a customer wants to buy it). Next to this table could be a T-stand fixture on either side with clothing such as resort/loungewear and robes that tie to the lavender theme. Now the retail space has made a statement about lavender!

Jewelry and accessories like bags, hats, and scarves that relate to clothing should be as close to that clothing as possible and shown or displayed with or on the clothing it is intended to go with. The actual inventory may not be housed with the clothing, but should be displayed adjacent to the apparel in appropriate fixtures for its type. Figure 7-11 shows a common display used for a necklace. The space should make it easy for customers to find what they're interested in, so if a pendant is displayed on a mannequin, the jewelry fixtures should be close enough that the customer doesn't have to trek to the other side of the retail space to find a similar pendant.

Figure 7-11
A jewelry showcased on a necklace
display.

© v.s.anandhakrishna/www.Shutterstock.com

Jewelry requires special fixturing and, depending on value, may need to be kept in locked glass cases. You know that any merchandise accessible in an open-sell environment to the customer will have a higher sell through than items kept behind counters or locked away that require the customer to ask for assistance. Common sense should guide where jewelry and other high-ticket items are displayed.

Many retailers have success with small baskets of inexpensive bracelets or small earring/necklace fixtures on the counter top at the register area. The key is not to clutter this space, as it also must accommodate guest check in/check out and other business transactions.

Vendor-supplied fixturing can be a great option, especially when it is designed for a certain type of product (e.g., sunglasses) that the salon and spa may have available from that vendor or others. This type of fixturing will improve visual display and sell through of the product. However, it may come with the vendor's logo or other "commercial" messages, so you must decide if that is appropriate for the retail setting and space. Selective use is a good idea, but too many vendor fixtures can distract customers with logos and different styles/colors/finishes that may not coordinate with your salon and spa's design and décor.

# MERCHANDISING TIPS: PUTTING IT ALL TOGETHER

After all of the fixtures, displays, mirrors, products, and signs have been placed, it's time for you to take an objective look at how it all fits together. It should be beautiful, pleasing to the eye, easy to maneuver through, and arranged in harmony with your salon and spa's philosophy and brand. In addition to lighting, which was discussed in-depth earlier in this section, two areas that can make a difference in the overall visual picture of the retail area are signage and props.

## Banners, Posters, Product Brochures, and Other Signage

When looking over the store's profile, signage should never be the primary feature of the landscape. Effective signs and posters will blend with the store's image and with other signage. Customers should be drawn to the merchandise. As they get close to it, the signage helps to explain or sell the products to which they were initially drawn.

Signs are silent salespeople that can be used to educate customers by offering information about the merchandise that might not be clear from looking at the product alone. For example, a sign or poster that has a photograph of a model with a new shade of blue nail polish gives the customer an idea of how it could look.

Signs can show brand identification by displaying the logo of the product line on it. They can also promote the store's image. Signage or sign holders throughout the store should match or coordinate well together.

Most salon and spa retailers apply a minimalist approach to product-centric banners and posters, and pass completely on their vendor representative's offer to drape the entire store in the vendor's company logo. Instead, they opt to emphasize the brand image. The one exception is during a special promotion or event. An eye-catching banner or poster announcing a fleeting opportunity or a new product launch can truly create excitement; otherwise, this type of signage is best kept to a minimum.

Product brochures, on the other hand, are a great way to supply your clients with a portable and somewhat more extensive form of the shelf talker. Since they generally feature the manufacturer's entire product line, they are only appropriate if the salon and spa has a significant portion of those featured goods; otherwise, they can generate a lot of interest in products that are not available to be purchased from the salon and spa.

Another effective type of signage is the magazine mention, or what is sometimes referred to as a "tear sheet." These are editorial endorsements of a specific product, or name-dropping of celebrities who use that product. They may appear in trade publications, or even better, consumer publications. These mentions can give any product a trendy and sophisticated aura that no other type of advertising can provide. They have been shown to be a consistently powerful in-house marketing tool. Again, vendors are usually more than happy to put them in spa professionals' hands on a monthly basis. For the most impact, place the actual product mentioned in front of the signage to make a clear connection in the shopper's mind.

## Accessorizing with Props

Last but not least, when assembling displays, you may want to use a few props. Props are items that are not sold in the store. Creativity and budget are the only limitations to the kinds of props that can be used in visual displays.

- Clay or ceramic tiles—possibly the same ones used to construct the salon and spa
- Stones—there are many sizes and colors to pick from

- Towels—these should be unused. They are the most effective when rolled up and stacked in a display. All white creates a clean, pure look. For a color story, get some towels that tie into the theme.
- An umbrella to use for a summer display about sun protection
- Picture frames
- Plants
- Fresh flowers
- Baskets—large to small
- Vases
- Thematic props—for instance, giant glass Christmas ornaments in a window display can promote holiday shopping.
- An interesting chair or bench
- Screens or sheer curtains for backdrops

## Keep It Fresh

Customers love to be entertained, so try to treat them to a fresh shopping experience whenever they visit. Creating featured displays that are always changing, and moving products to new areas, will give the feeling of something new and will draw customers to the shelves. Featuring new items or seasonal items in displays will keep the customer purchasing highlighted products, while changing the displays every four to six weeks allows the salon and spa to feature specific products and increase product sales.

Here are a few other tips from the merchandising pros:

- The average height of women is 5'5", making most top shelves difficult to reach. Eye-catching displays are the best way to effectively use this shelf.
- Featuring new items or seasonal items in spotlighted displays will draw attention to products that otherwise would blend into the larger shelving units.
- Rotating out-of-season items to the bottom shelves keeps shelves looking updated and fresh.

Creating retail displays with impact requires just as much art as it does science. The best in the business approach it with both sides of the brain and plenty of experimentation. When a display scores high marks with comments from consumers and increased sales, remember to photograph it and keep it on file for future use.

The floor displays will need to be rearranged as often as new products come in (possibly as often as weekly). Merchandise that is selling down (inventory is getting low) may need to be consolidated and moved to a less prime location. The new merchandise is placed in key focal points. That will keep customers noticing the newer merchandise. Fixtures may need to be added or taken out on occasion to accommodate more or less merchandise. A couple of times per year, you might want to plan a complete floor fixture reset—just to keep things interesting. Regular customers will be more likely to shop if they perceive the merchandise as new.

## Make Customers Want to Shop

Nothing can repel a customer more quickly than a messy retail area, not to mention the shock of having to pay full price for an item that looks as though it were at a rummage sale. Cleanliness and simplicity make a positive impression on customers. Keeping shelves clean, stocked, and straightened on a daily basis makes shelves approachable and will aid in the reduction of theft. Spacing products evenly gives the appearance of clean lines and a more modern look. Placing product signage to the outside or end of the shelf makes the shelves look consistent and visually appealing. Facing products, including pumps, in the same direction will simplify the look of the shelves. Face the pumps out for testers and face them sideways for non-testers.

Incorporating daily housekeeping tasks into the retail staff's duties will go a long way toward keeping the retail area in a condition that encourages customers to stay, shop, and buy. Each morning or evening, someone needs to walk through the store and check the store through the eyes of the customer. The list below is a basic reminder of the elements of cleanliness and order that will enable your store to make a great first impression:

- All displays are correctly arranged. Make sure a customer hasn't pulled a piece of merchandise out and left a hole in the display. If so, fill it in and tidy up the display.
- All mannequins and front display hangers are still dressed properly.
- Shelf talkers are with the correct product and straight on the shelves.
- Testers are cleaned up and no litter or product is spilled on the table.

- All products are still organized in the proper order. When doing this, check to see whether more inventory from the back stock needs to be brought out.
- All the fixtures, shelves, and mirrors are dusted and clean.
- Fresh flowers are looking attractive and wilted flowers are thrown out.
- Cash/wrap area is organized and clean, with no clutter.
- The store windows are clean with no handprints, nose prints, or smudges.
- Any burned-out bulbs are replaced.
- Dressing rooms are clean with no merchandise left behind.

# CHAPTER SUMMARY

- Before beginning the design of your salon and spa retail area, take a look at the retail spaces of the competitors and local retail boutiques in your area for ideas.
- Windows can be the most important location to make a first impression.
- Making the floor plan flow will guide customers through the retail space and encourage them to enjoy the experience.
- The cash wrap area is a great space for placing small items suitable for impulse purchases.
- Think of your retail space as real estate, with those areas having the best view and most foot traffic as prime.
- The percentage of space occupied by product classification should be in line with the percentage of contribution to your sales plan.
- Consumer surveys indicate that shoppers prefer to test skin care and cosmetic products before making a decision to purchase them.
- Mass merchandising is a great way to showcase products, show consumers that the salon and spa believes in the product, and cuts down on storage.
- The three ways to display beauty products are by usage, chronological order, or by skin or hair type.
- Testers must be hygienic and regularly maintained so the products look inviting to the guest.

# LEARNING ACTIVITIES

## Learning Activity 7-1: Creating Harmony

Salon and spa professionals are always looking and always watching. They continually shop the retail areas just as their customers would. Walk through your retail area, observing it with a customer's eyes. Find one area that is not as appealing as the rest of the space, or a place where the merchandise does not seem to be moving off the shelves. Analyze why this area is not in harmony with the rest of the retail space. Using the ideas in this chapter, redesign the area to make it more visually appealing. Track the sales of the merchandise in the redesigned area to determine if the redesign positively affected sales.

## Learning Activity 7-2: Thematically Speaking

Select one of the following themes and create a window, table, or wall display to support the theme. Select products in your spa that relate to the theme and enhance one another. Try to include products from several different classifications of merchandise to maximize the effect of the display. Themes to select from are:

"New Year, New You"
"Best Foot Forward"
"Girls' Night In"
"When Lights Are Low"
"In the Pink" (or choose another color)

# REVIEW QUESTIONS

1. Retail window displays are changed every four to six weeks:
   a. To prevent regular customers from getting bored with the same display.
   b. To prevent merchandise in the window from becoming faded by the sun.
   c. To give the retail staff something to do in their spare time.
   d. To highlight discounted and on-sale merchandise.

2. Which of the following statements about the mass merchandising style of retail display is FALSE?

    a. It encourages theft, because customers feel that no one will miss one item from a large display.

    b. It allows customers to navigate their shopping experience independently.

    c. It cuts down on storage costs.

    d. It is familiar and comfortable to most shoppers.

3. Sylvia, a new guest at the Urban Salon and Spa, is admiring a display of relaxation merchandise with an Eastern feeling. A single, beautifully bound book of Zen meditations is placed near a Zen sand garden, a grouping of candles, and a stack of relaxation CDs. The table display is near the inventory of sand gardens and candles, but further away from the books and CDs, which are stored spine out in a small bookcase under the window. Sylvia is interested in the book, but decides not to purchase it. What is the most likely reason for her decision?

    a. She already has a book of Zen meditations at home.

    b. She thinks that the book is only a prop in the display, because she doesn't see any additional books for sale.

    c. She is allergic to candles, and the display seems to indicate that they are sold as a package.

    d. She doesn't think that books should be sold at a spa.

4. Bree places three jars of conditioner and a single flower in a vase onto a shelf. What display technique is she using?

    a. Temporary installment

    b. Showcasing

    c. European

    d. Artistic

5. A high color-rendering index (CRI) on a light fixture means that:

    a. Colors will appear brighter than they really are.

    b. There will be too much glare for customers to be comfortable.

    c. Colors will appear as natural as possible.

    d. The light will create visual clutter.

6. Which of the following statements is TRUE about shelf talkers?

    a. They take the place of informed sales staff.

    b. They are unnecessary and serve to confuse shoppers.

    c. They provide extensive details about the products to which they refer.

    d. They are placed to the outside or the end of a shelf for visual appeal.

7. Tess owns a hair salon with a small facial and nail space. When she divides up her retail space, she should:

    a. Devote 60 percent of the retail space to skin care products, as this area needs to gain more exposure.

    b. Devote 75 percent of the space to hair care, as it represents the bulk of her sales plan.

    c. Divide the space equally between the three product areas.

    d. Devote 50 percent of the space to hair care and the rest to skin care and nail products.

8. Franz is designing the boutique of an Ayurvedic salon and spa that is due to open in six months. He designs the retail area to have a relaxed environment that is easy for customers to stroll through. He sets up comfortable stools with makeup testers and mirrors for customers to try on new products. He designs an antique-style counter at which customers can sample lotions in front of a large, gilded mirror. What style of design is Franz using?

    a. Grid

    b. Racetrack

    c. Free-form

    d. Bookstore

9. Which of the following are the standard guidelines for retail goods?

    a. They must be visible, inviting, and accessible.

    b. They should be displayed properly and affordably priced for the spa's customers.

    c. Perishable goods should always have the date of manufacture.

    d. All of the above.

10. Which of the following retail housekeeping tasks is not performed daily?

    a. Clean handprints and smudges from windows and mirrors.

    b. Change the outfits on the mannequins.

    c. Clean testers and face them in the same direction.

    d. Return merchandise from the dressing room to the sales floor.

# Marketing

## INTRODUCTION

Having a beautiful, well-stocked, smoothly functioning retail space takes an investment of blood, sweat, tears, and dollars. But what good is having all of this merchandise if no one knows about it? The next step is to make those bottles and jars fly off the shelves and go home with your guests and other customers. But how do you get the word out about what to buy, when to buy, or what's featured at your salon and spa?

A focused and concentrated marketing and promotion plan makes the difference between retail inventory collecting dust on the shelf and having happy, enthusiastic salon and spa guests who can extend their experience and maintain their results at home.

Through a variety of marketing techniques, you can direct and focus customers' attention on the services and retail opportunities that are available within your establishment. Because services and retail are so closely linked, this chapter shows salon and spa professionals how to create sales excitement within your salon and spa for both services and retail products. The ultimate goal, of course, is to increase your total revenue, but along the way, marketing also strengthens customer relationships and increases public awareness of the salon and spa and its philosophy.

## WHAT IS MARKETING?

Quite often, people will confuse marketing with advertising, as the two areas are related, yet quite different. **Marketing** is

Chapter **8**

© Milady, a part of Cengage Learning. Photography by Visual Recollection.

## LEARNING OBJECTIVES

After successfully completing this chapter, the reader will be able to:

- Identify the purpose of retail marketing for salons and spas.
- Conduct a SWOT analysis to evaluate the salon and spa, its retail area, and its competitors.
- Use a customer profile to determine marketing goals and direction.
- Develop a retail marketing calendar.
- Describe the strengths and weaknesses of various external and internal marketing strategies.
- Plan and execute a retail marketing plan.
- Identify opportunities for a variety of marketing promotions.
- Evaluate the effectiveness of marketing efforts.

235

SALON AND SPA SNAPSHOT 8.1

## At the Urban Salon and Spa…

Reuben put down the trade magazine he'd been reading. The article mentioned that more and more men were beginning to frequent day spas—but the Urban Salon and Spa certainly wasn't seeing much evidence of that, even though it had both a men's grooming center in the salon side and spa services and products geared toward male customers.

"What we need," he said to himself, "is a marketing campaign to bring more men in." Unfortunately, the marketing budget had been set at the beginning of the year, and a campaign to bring in new male customers hadn't been on his radar when he budgeted for November. "Still," he thought, "we ought to be able to generate some kind of interest, even if we don't have a lot of money to do it with."

Reuben called a staff meeting to brainstorm ideas for the new marketing campaign. Monte, Colby, Patty, and Bree were eager to share their thoughts. Reuben explained the general concept. "I'm thinking about a 'Guy's Day Out,' maybe the day after Thanksgiving, when everyone is out Christmas shopping. Or maybe we should make the theme, 'Shave and a Haircut—True Bliss.' After all, a professional hot-lather shave is about the closest thing to heaven a guy can experience, right?"

Colby chuckled. "So you say, every time you have one. But if a man's never experienced that, how is he going to know how terrific it is and be motivated to come in? And we'd need something they could take away, too—like a free travel grooming kit or 20 percent off any men's skin care product."

"You know what would be really terrific?" mused Patty. "If you could get that morning-show DJ to talk about us on the radio. Everybody listens to him. Man, if you could get him in here for a hot shave and a terrific haircut, and he talked about it—we'd get tons of new customers, I bet."

"We could do a full-page, color ad in the *Metropolitan Male* magazine," suggested Colby. "That would certainly hit our target audience."

"It's also very expensive, and we don't have a lot in the ad budget right now," said Reuben.

"Okay, so how about a quarter-page ad in the Sunday sports section of the newspaper?" Colby replied. Reuben grinned. Now that he could afford.

He jotted down that idea. He had barely finished writing when Monte jumped into the conversation. "And what about all those men who buy gift certificates for their wives and girlfriends? Don't we have their names the database to remind them when the next

(continues)

## At the Urban Salon and Spa...

(continued)

big holiday is coming up? We could use that same list to invite them to do something for themselves for a change!"

Bree bounced in her chair. "Let's send a special e-newsletter to our entire database about the promotion," she said. "We can follow up with an e-mail blast a couple of weeks later to reinforce the message."

"That sounds great!," said Bree. "Women who have husbands and boyfriends and brothers and sons … maybe we can offer the women an incentive for bringing a guy in during our promotion. Maybe a gift card for $20 off their next service or retail purchase when they bring in the man in their life."

"I can do a post on our Facebook page, and put some eye-catching pictures on there too," Monte added. Reuben continued writing as fast as he could. "That's great! I guess I'd better place an order for more men's products," he said. "It looks like we have a campaign to deliver!"

---

defined as the activity of creating, communicating, delivering, and exchanging offerings that have value for guests. It is a blend or mix of activities done to reach new and existing customers. It is your strategy or roadmap for attracting and maintaining your customer base. Marketing activities should all be targeted to reach your target market and align with your brand. Activities such as advertising, networking, promotions, e-mail campaigns, and making outbound calls to customers are all part of marketing. The right combination of these activities becomes a part of your marketing plan to sell your products and services.

**Advertising** is a component of your marketing plan. It is the ad you place in the paper, on the Internet, or in a coupon to get the word out about your business. It is a part of your overall marketing strategy.

In the next section, we will discuss the importance of marketing, how to create a marketing plan, and we will lightly touch upon branding as it relates to your marketing plan. Finally, we discuss how to execute the plan so you have a well-managed roadmap for attracting customers.

**marketing.** The activity of creating, communicating, delivering, and exchanging offerings that have value for guests.

**advertising.** Calling attention to one's product or service through announcements in media including newspapers, magazines, flyers on the Internet, or radio.

© Login/www.Shutterstock.com

## How Does Marketing Benefit Your Business?

There are some common questions that come to mind when the word "marketing" is mentioned. For example:

- "Why should salon and spa professionals do marketing? Won't 'word-of-mouth' be enough?"
- "Can't the products speak for themselves?"
- "Won't it cheapen the salon and spa's image to offer specials or promotions?"

There are five reasons marketing promotions are a perfect fit for the salon and spa environment. Namely, promotions can do these five key things:

1. Create retail and service excitement.
2. Give the shopper a reason to buy *now*.
3. Stimulate the staff.
4. Strengthen customer relationships.
5. Increase brand awareness.

### Create Retail and Service Excitement

Successful salons and spas utilize promotions, events, product launches, or monthly features to keep shoppers excited and browsing in the retail center. With so much competition in the marketplace, shoppers are always looking for value and what's new. When planning promotions, remember that products have a higher margin than services. You can be creative and offer promotional packages that combine services with product discounts to stimulate business in both areas. For example, "Purchase our new 'Cucumber Mint' facial and receive a cleanser and toner at 30 percent off." You can have a promotion for multiple services that include product, and discount both. For example, "Receive 25 percent on your haircut and color services if you pre-book. Receive a complimentary conditioner as our gift."

## Give the Shopper a Reason to Buy Now!

An effective marketing plan helps to direct shoppers' attention to what they need to use at home. Promotions draw their eye to the products and let them know that there is something on the shelves that can benefit them. Once the guest leaves your salon and spa, the sale becomes much more difficult. You need to overcome the unspoken objection of "I'll buy that later." Guests need to look at products while the experience of their service is still foremost in their mind. They will be more inclined to buy while they are still feeling the tingle of a facial, the relaxation of a massage, or while running their fingers through the silky smooth texture of their newly styled hair. At that moment, they determine whether they want to extend those same benefits through your salon and spa's retail products.

## Stimulate the Staff

The salon and spa staff will develop blinders to what is on the retail shelves. Frequently changing promotional themes keeps the staff excited and prevents boredom. If you stock multiple lines, the staff can get overwhelmed deciding what brands or individual products to feature. When you implement a four-to-six-week promotional plan, the staff is able to focus on the featured service and a limited number of retail items.

## Strengthen Customer Relationships

If your salon and spa can fill customers' needs and expectations, profits should follow. But before customers will hand over their money, they must feel a bond with your salon and spa and its retail offerings. Your customers want to feel that the salon and spa staff cares about them. They want to feel special. Marketing can create and bolster those feelings that will encourage customers to return often to "their" salon and spa to receive the special attention they desire and deserve.

All too often, marketing promotions are directed toward bringing in new customers.

"Offer good for new customers only" seems to be the mantra of many retailers. But why would a business ignore the customers it already has? Studies have shown that it costs 10 times as much to acquire a new customer as it does to retain an existing one or reactivate an old one. You may find that your limited marketing dollars would be better spent encouraging current customers to buy more often, rather than trying to attract new customers who may or may not answer the call of the marketing promotion.

Special offers, personalized messages, follow-up phone calls and e-mails, invitations to private classes and events, rewards for referrals, and frequent guest or VIP programs all make customers feel as if they are among the salon and spa's elite. Extending the personalized attention that guests receive in the treatment room to your retail promotions is sure to increase customer satisfaction, as well as revenue.

Customers who feel special may also be more open to referring others to enjoy the special attention they have enjoyed at the salon and spa. Referrals are the least expensive and most effective form of marketing, but you must ask for them. Offering a "referral reward" of a $25 gift card to thank customers who refer new guests is one way to encourage customers to spread the word.

## Increase Brand Awareness

Increasing brand awareness means letting people know about the salon and spa's community involvement, its beliefs, and its specialties.

Examples of awareness marketing include:

- Sponsorship of a booth at a community wellness fair
- Complimentary chair massages for participants in an American Cancer Society Relay for Life
- An educational, public service interview in a local newspaper article with the salon and spa manager, for example, on causes of stress and how to relieve it
- Participation in a radio talk show about the salon and spa's community service project, for example, providing services for women at the domestic violence shelter

What do any of these things have to do with increasing retail sales? Directly, perhaps nothing. These activities do place your salon and spa in the minds of potential customers. So when a potential customer is wondering where to go for a much-needed haircut, pedicure, or massage, he or she may remember seeing the Urban Salon and Spa giving chair massages at the Relay for Life. When it is time to book an appointment, your salon and spa will get the call. Print ads work in the same way. When a potential customer is considering gift certificates as a reward for a work team, the article in the local paper on stress relief will come to mind.

## Your Brand

The **brand** is what a company stands for and what brings people into your salon and spa. It is a perception or image of your business, which sets you apart from the competition. Brand equity is the value the brand brings in terms of customer loyalty. Think of a company brand as an element attached to the vision, and mission, and philosophy of your salon and spa. All of the marketing and advertising strategies and activities should be aligned with the brand so you can communicate and reinforce what your salon and spa stands for.

### An Example of a Solid Brand

Branding can best be explained by providing a well-known example. Starbucks Coffee is a company with a well-developed, highly recognizable brand. When one thinks of Starbucks, the first thing that usually comes to mind is the image of those tables and couches with people enjoying good coffee. Starbucks is a convenient place to go to chat with a friend or meet with a business associate. In fact, the Starbucks mission is about bringing people together so they feel at home. It is a second home to many students and has become the "virtual office" for many people. Starbucks caters to business people and students with laptops, papers, and books. There are plenty of tables with electrical outlets conveniently located throughout and free Wi-Fi. Couches are also available for the solo person reading a book.

The team members (called partners) wear signature green aprons and greet each customer with enthusiasm. They work together and make the drinks and prepare the food. You never feel pressure to choose a higher-priced drink from the menu, even though you may just order a regular coffee. People go to Starbucks for the coffee, but what stands out in their mind is the comfortable, welcoming environment. Starbucks is a great example of a company focused on selling their brand, with their partners fully engaged and representing what they stand for.

When you think about your marketing plan and how you will go about spreading the word about your business, assure every element aligns as closely as possible with your brand; this way, you reinforce what your salon and spa stands for. In the following sections, we will discuss marketing your salon and spa business as a whole, with the understanding that your retail operation is a part of the plan.

**brand.** The attributes of a company and the image that is communicated through marketing and advertising. It is a perception or image of the business that sets it apart from the competition.

**DID YOU KNOW?**

Marketing isn't always directed toward the salon and spa's products and services. It can also promote image and philosophy, making the public aware of the salon and spa and what it stands for.

# PREPARING A MARKETING PLAN

Planning your marketing plan or strategy is one of the keys to the success of your business. Your **marketing plan** is a detailed strategy in a document form that states how you will promote your business, build a customer base, and how you will make a profit. The marketing plan will be a section of your overall business plan. It is important to have such a plan in place to drive your entire operation, not just the retail efforts. Your business plan will contain essential elements that tell you and potential investors or lending institutions what your business will do and how you will do it. Although this text is not designed to show you in detail how to create a business plan, it is important to discuss this briefly. Below we go over the main parts of a business plan so you know how your marketing plan relates to that.

## A Business Plan

**business plan.** A written document that conveys important aspects about a business for planning and tracking growth over a given period.

A **business plan** conveys important aspects about your business so you can plan and track your growth over a 5-year period. The aspects generally covered in a business plan are noted below, and the details covered in the marketing plan are expanded upon in the next section.

- Executive Summary: Objectives, who you are, what you do, mission statement, projected sales, keys to success
- Company Summary: Ownership, detailed business description, location
- Products and Services: What do you offer?
- Market Analysis Summary: Who are your customers?
- Marketing Strategy and Implementation Summary: What is the message? When will it be implemented? (time frame)? What department? Why is the promotion needed? How does the customer take action?
- Management Summary: Who is the leader? How is the staff organized, how will you staff the business?
- Financial Plan: Projected income, breakdown between products/services, break-even amount
- Appendices: Attachments, figures, charts

You can find step-by-step tutorials on business plan creation on the Internet. In the following section, we will discuss the finer points of the marketing plan as mentioned above.

## Marketing Plan

When creating a marketing plan, savvy salon and spa retailers use a twist on the reporter's old formula of "5 Ws and an H" to make the cash register ring. The marketing plan answers the following questions:

- Who is the target market for the promotion? Is it current customers, sales leads, resort/hotel guests, VIP clients, neighbors to the salon and spa, or association lists such as the chamber of commerce?

- What is the message? Clearly define what customers need to know. Does the salon and spa want men to come and buy gift certificates? Is the salon and spa trying to cross-promote its nail customers to the hair designers or massage customers to the esthetic department? Is the salon and spa offering a special on summer sun care products? Is the salon and spa announcing its participation in a community wellness day?

- When is the focus time frame? How long will the special take place? Is it a limited time offer—only good for 30 days? Plan the marketing cycles around the business cycles of customer traffic. If the salon and spa traffic is on a four-to-six-week cycle, featured promotions will more than likely be on the same time frame. In addition, schedule the frequency of marketing messages to keep the salon and spa name in front of customers often, but without becoming overbearing.

- What department is involved with the marketing message? Does it only affect hair designers, makeup artists, or massage therapists? Does it cross over to skin, body, and nails? Is the salon and spa as a whole the focus of the message?

- Why do customers need the promotion, service, product, or information? In order to get shoppers to spend their money, marketing messages and promotions must appeal to their needs, wants, and desires.

- How does the customer take action? An effective retail promotion tells the shopper *exactly* what to do: "Pick up the phone and call the Urban Salon and Spa." Or: "Come into the salon and spa between specific days and hours." "Log on to the website and register by midnight Thursday to win a total make-over."

## Identifying the Salon and Spa's Customers and Competition

To establish the foundation of your marketing plan, you will need to do research to learn more about your salon and spa, your customers, and your competition. By learning about your salon and spa and the competition, you can better position your products and services in the minds of customers and prospects. It is important to identify what makes your salon and spa better or different from your competitors. Use that difference to create a niche, or what is also referred to as a **value proposition**. Those points of difference might include your salon and spa's philosophy, the hours, exclusive treatments and products, the location, or your staff. By learning about your customers, you will be better able to tailor marketing promotions to connect with what is important to your customers and their needs.

**value proposition.**
The attributes that make your business unique and make it stand out from the competition.

### SWOT Analysis

One common way of discerning information about your salon and spa, and your competitors, is through a SWOT analysis. SWOT stands for Strengths, Weaknesses, Opportunities, and Threats. The ultimate goal of this analysis is to determine how well your business is serving current markets. By taking the time to do a SWOT analysis, you will uncover many ideas for your marketing plans. An example of a SWOT analysis is shown in Figure 8-1.

To do a SWOT analysis, a company does the following:

- Examine the internal and external environment in which it operates.
- Determine the strengths and weaknesses of its operation.
- Consider what opportunities exist for growth.
- Determine what threats exist from competitors or changing trends.

### Customer Profile

Creating a profile of your customer base will help you determine marketing strategies (see Figure 8-2). Are your customers young, single professionals with high-pressure jobs and lots of disposable income? Or are they women with families and limited time for indulgences? Knowing who is likely to frequent your salon and spa will make a big difference in both the kinds of marketing messages and the way they are delivered.

Figure 8-1
Sample SWOT Analysis

| | Seasons Salon and Spa | Competitor A | Competitor B | Competitor C | Competitor D |
|---|---|---|---|---|---|
| **About the Salon and Spa** | | | | | |
| **Year started** | 2009 | | | | |
| **Type** | Resort salon and spa/Medical | | | | |
| **Sq. Footage** | 9,000 | | | | |
| **Number of annual clients and visits/ demographics** | 6,500/13,000 visits 85% female, 35–55 yrs old married | | | | |
| **Guest frequency** | First time - 40% Frequent - 19% Infrequent - 41% | | | | |
| **Brand** | Upscale elegant with focus on relaxation | | | | |
| **Staffing** | 15 ft, 8 pt | | | | |
| **Mission statement** | Seasons Salon and Spa is a progressive facility offering the most medically advanced, noninvasive treatment. Our salon team is world class and our impeccable customer service is our trademark. | | | | |
| **Website** | www.seasonssalonandspa.com | | | | |
| **Charities** | United Way, Race for the Cure | | | | |
| **Advertising** | Internet, SpaFinder, Networking, Chamber of Commerce | | | | |
| **Events** | Charitable events supporting, Monthly product focus events | | | | |
| **Strengths** | Science-based practice, Great location World Class service, Expert Service team | | | | |
| **Weaknesses** | High support staff turnover, Low % of frequent guests | | | | |
| **Opportunities** | Capture local customers, Implemented a new referral program. | | | | |
| **Threats** | New Dermal Spa and Men's Grooming salon opening in area. | | | | |
| **Market advantages** | Reputation and service/product guarantees | | | | |
| **Key target market** | 35–55 yr old females with average income of $75,000 | | | | |
| **Other key attributes** | Service staff has remained since opening | | | | |

(continues)

Figure 8-1 (cont.)
Sample SWOT Analysis

| | Seasons Salon and Spa | Competitor A | Competitor B | Competitor C | Competitor D |
|---|---|---|---|---|---|
| **Retail Operations** | | | | | |
| **Types of primary products** | 3 hair care lines<br>2 nail care lines<br>2 skin care lines | | | | |
| **Lines carried** | Superior Formulations<br>MD RX<br>Nutria Advanced | | | | |
| **Themes philosophy** | Natural, organic | | | | |
| **Retail events** | New product launches Monthly promo | | | | |
| **Charities** | United Way, Race for the Cure | | | | |
| **Strengths** | Vendor relationships Training | | | | |
| **Weaknesses** | No formal retail staff, we miss sales | | | | |
| **Opportunities** | Retail sales for every customer has room to grow. Adding a make-up line | | | | |
| **Threats** | No one available to manage daily retail goals | | | | |
| **Market advantages** | Exclusive line of products | | | | |
| **Other key attributes** | Staff very familiar with products | | | | |

© Milady, a part of Cengage Learning

## Goal Setting

When you know what you want your marketing plan to accomplish, you can then develop programs and promotions to reach those goals. A good place to look for your goals is your retail plan (discussed in Chapter 2). Most marketing efforts are created to make that plan succeed. For instance, if the retail plan states that the salon and spa will sell $2,000 in bath and body products in June, then marketing efforts would focus on a bath and body promotion rather than a makeup promotion.

Examples of possible marketing goals include:

- Increase the number of new customers by 10 percent during the next six months.
- Increase retail purchases by existing customers by 15 percent over the previous year.
- Increase the percentage of retail sales per ticket.
- Introduce a new line of body care products for customers with sensitive skin.
- Increase the sales of packages and gift certificates; increase the redemption rate for gift certificates.

Figure 8-2
Spa Client Profile

---

**Seasons Salon and Spa**
**Retail Data**

**General Demographics**
- Number of clients
- Number of visits
- Age group
- Gender
- Race
- Education
- Estimated income
- Marital status
- Children
- Employment
- Average time as a client

**About the Retail**
- Average number of retail purchases by Product Classification
- Average number of retail purchases per client/visit
- Average number of retail purchases per square foot
- Types of guests: first time, infrequent, frequent
- Key group clients: weddings, parties, corporate
- Reason to purchase: maintenance, recreate the spa experience, replenishment, impulsive, gift, promotion
- Where else can guests purchase your products?

**Other**
- How do guests like to be informed: e-mail, direct mail, printed materials texts, Facebook, Twitter?
- Frequently requested items
- Frequently out of stock items
- Challenges

# Budgeting

Budgeting for marketing begins even before your salon and spa is open for business. The location of the salon and spa, and how much that location costs, are the first marketing decisions business owners must make. Paying for market research or demographic information is another up-front marketing cost of a new salon and spa that is often overlooked. This is a significant cost, however, and can range from a few hundred dollars in a small market to several thousand in a larger metropolitan area. Along with marketing, signage is an important part of the marketing budget which must be considered before the salon and spa even opens.

In today's competitive marketplace, flooded with rapid change, a new salon and spa will have only a few months to proclaim to the market that it is "new." Therefore, pre-opening and launch marketing dollars are critical for your salon and spa to have the opportunity to create that great first impression, which will result in the best form of marketing—positive word-of-mouth proclaiming the wonders of your business.

## Budgeting Amount

After your salon and spa opens, a marketing budget can be developed. This budget can be created using a general rule of thumb: marketing dollars as a percent of gross revenue.

If your salon and spa is part of a resort/hotel, the budget will be about 5 percent of revenue for marketing. In this setting, part of the salon and spa's marketing is absorbed by the overall marketing efforts of the resort/hotel to draw guests to its location. Too often, resort operators assume that the hotel's guests are a captive audience for the salon and spa, inferring that the salon and spa itself does not have to do as much external marketing for customers. The fact is that a successful resort/hotel salon and spa will need to achieve a 50 percent contribution from the local market. The mission is not simply to sell that 5 p.m. massage service on Saturday afternoon, but to market to the local customers who may be willing to come to the salon spa for a relaxing massage or nail treatment at noon on Tuesday and who may go home with $20 or $30 of retail merchandise.

In the day spa industry, marketing costs as a percentage of gross revenue may be as high as 10 to 12 percent, depending on the competition and the type of services rendered.

With an established salon and spa, marketing costs can be thought of as an incremental accumulation of costs. You will start with the basic marketing items, such as a website and flyers, and add to those items additional marketing costs until the salon and spa has reached capacity for that given time. As each layer of marketing is added, the cost is budgeted for that particular layer.

In the spa industry, the *Uniform System of Financial Reporting for Spas* references the "top-down" budgeting method. In the top-down method, management sets a gross revenue goal. Once the gross revenue goal is set, the manager will add layer after layer of marketing resources until the gross revenue goal can be achieved. This application can be easily used for salons as well.

## Website Development

One of the single largest expenses for marketing can be the development of a website. The development of a website satisfying most of the business's marketing needs can vary greatly in cost, depending upon whether or not you choose to create it in-house or through the use of a professional developer. It is best to do some research on the Internet and look up the websites of similar salons and spas in your area. The website developer or "powered by" attribution is often located at the bottom of the page. This is usually the contact information for the company responsible for creating the website. You can then contact that company for a consultation.

© Gizele/www.Shutterstock.com

Another alternative is to create the website in-house from a template offered through a leading hosting company. You can search on the Internet for resources or simply ask people in your network. Regardless of the avenue you choose, it is highly recommended that you obtain a website for your business, as your clients want to have easy access to your service menu. Once you have your website created, you will want to factor in the monthly fee for hosting the site on the Internet. This may be a separate fee sent to the salon and spa directly or it can be negotiated with the website professional. We will further discuss website development later on in this chapter.

## DID YOU KNOW?

The website is the salon and spa's online brochure and can meet many of the marketing needs, from newsletters, product promotions, and educational articles to online retailing and online scheduling.

## Other Costs

Other marketing costs vary based on the number of printed pieces, size of audience, and amount of work needed to produce the marketing message. The key to selection of external marketing options depends on the particular medium's ability to reach the target market. In marketing terms, this is measured in "reach" and "frequency." "Reach" measures how many of your salon and spa's target customers will receive the message. "Frequency" measures how often the message will be received by your target customers. For example, if a billboard is seen by 20,000 drivers daily and 4,000 of the drivers fit your salon and spa's target market demographics, you can easily calculate the cost of reaching the target market by dividing the cost of the billboard by 4,000. On the other hand, an advertisement in the bridal section of a large metropolitan daily newspaper might cost more than a billboard, but a greater number of the people who see that ad will fit your target demographics, making it a better use of marketing dollars.

Television, usually considered the most expensive marketing medium, can be the least expensive, if used judiciously. The ability to select cable markets that have a specific audience as well as the ability to select particular television programs that your target markets watch can drive down the cost of reaching your target customers. The up-front cost of producing good quality commercials for television must be considered in the overall cost.

Figure 8-3 shows a sample marketing budget for February.

When preparing your salon and spa's retail marketing and promotional budget, there are several important questions you will want to consider, including:

- How many promotions are planned through the year?
- What is the depth and breadth of each promotion? For example, one promotion may feature an e-mail message, information in the salon and spa's newsletter, on-hold message recordings, and staff recommendations—all items that take very few dollars to achieve. However, a promotion that involves planning multiple postcard

Figure 8-3
Sample marketing budget

| Monthly Marketing Budget February | | |
|---|---|---|
| 1 | Website maintenance | $50.00 |
| 2 | E-mail marketing system | $120.00 |
| 3 | Monthly rotating on-hold messaging service | $85.00 |
| 4 | Postcard promotion (mailing costs, postcards) | $2300.00 |
| 5 | In salon new signage for promos | $250.00 |
| 6 | Balloons outside for promo | $175.00 |
| | **Total budgeted marketing costs** | **$2,980.00** |

campaigns, brochure mailings, special signage, and a media blitz will require you to budget additional funds to cover these expenses.

- Will you need to hire outside experts for any promotions, such as graphic designers, printers, and public relations experts?
- What financial assistance will your vendors provide for these efforts?
- Will you tie a blog into your website so you can write articles and get comments from your readers? Blogs are a great way to share expertise and keep customers coming back to your website.
- Will the retail calendar include any major media blitzes? Will media promotions include media tours or just promotional/information communicated to the media?

## Creating a Retail Marketing Calendar

When outlining a retail marketing calendar, you will have more opportunities than you can humanly manage within a calendar year. A variety of promotional categories define ways that marketing can boost service and retail sales.

- Seasonal Promotions: These are tied to calendar events, such as the changing seasons and holidays.
- Season-less Promotions: These promotions are not tied to any recognized annual holiday.
- Cross-Promotions: These promotions target key services and products across boundaries. To boost service and retail sales in the nail department, for example, you can offer your body massage clients a special offer to try the new nail services. In a destination salon and spa, you can cross-market by tying the salon and spa in to other amenities in the resort, such as tennis, golf, swimming, health club, and child care (so the parents know they can leave the kids to visit the salon and spa).
- New Service or Product Launch: When you invest in a new service or product, or make a financial commitment to a product line/brand, you need to have a master roll-out plan to launch the new line.
- Vendor Promotions: Check with your vendors to learn what promotions they are planning throughout the year. If those promotions fit with the philosophy and marketing goals of your salon and spa, you can include them in your marketing calendar as well.

### HERE'S A TIP

Before planning your marketing calendar, take a look at magazines that your clients read and study the advertisements. Is there a new beauty product or new technology that is getting a lot of press? Is there a new hot color in accessories, hair, or makeup that you need to be aware of? If so, how can you take advantage of the press? For example, if a popular magazine has ads for a new hair care product that you carry, you can feature the product in your promotion and say, "Featuring SunSation sunscreen for hair, as seen in *Glo* magazine." Be creative. Anything you can do to leverage the media buzz will lend support for your promotion.

- Corporate Business: Salons and spas can work with local businesses to develop a reward program for employees, or develop relationships with local businesses for cooperative marketing ventures. Resort/hotel salons and spas can tie into any host groups and meetings that are on the resort/hotel calendar. Savvy managers work with the hotel's meeting planners to make the salon and spa personnel available for spouse programs or attendee rewards. Regardless of your situation, you can develop relationships with the local convention and visitors' bureau and chamber of commerce to mine corporate opportunities through those organizations.
- Consumer Trade Shows: Local trade shows, health fairs, and bridal events can provide a venue for highlighting your salon and spa's services and retail products.
- Wish Lists and Gift Registry: A gift wish list or gift registry online and inside the salon and spa can help increase your gift certificate and retail sales.
- Product Feature of the Month: At the very least for a promotional effort, you can select one to three products to feature every month. For a very small salon and spa, this may be enough of a product focus to boost sales by 20 to 30 percent.
- Specialty Clinics or Seminars: Consumers are looking for expert health, beauty, and wellness advice. Your salon and spa can host an educational seminar in-house or off-site and match key products and services to each seminar topic.
- Demonstration Days: You can host an in-house demo day. Hair salons have traditionally hosted Super Saturday events where product reps are in the salon to demonstrate the latest product introductions and application lessons. You can also bring in an out-of-town expert to help drive retail sales. When a product representative closes the sale, it tends to carry an attitude of prestige to your customer.
- Runway Events: Your salon and spa can participate in local fashion shows as a way to promote the hair and makeup services. If you stock clothing, participation can expand to include providing models and clothing for the fashion show. You might also host a trunk show for your VIP clients to give them a sneak peek at the newest fashions.

- Resort/Hotel Guests: If you are located in a resort or hotel, work with the resort/hotel to turn guests into salon and spa customers. Ideas include: offering VIP gift cards; inviting key hotel guests to the salon and spa to pick up a complimentary logo t-shirt, sun visor, or sunscreen; offering a 10 percent savings card on product purchases during their visit; slipping an inspirational book or message card from the salon and spa onto the pillow during the turn-down service; ensuring that there are plenty of your music CDs in the guest rooms if CD players are provided.

# DELIVERING YOUR MESSAGE

After defining your marketing plan, you will determine the marketing vehicles that will deliver the message to your target audience. To be effective, multiple methods will need to be used in combination to create the desired effect. These will include both external and internal marketing pieces.

In order for a promotion to succeed, customers need to see the marketing message, preferably more than once. Successful salon and spa professionals plan a full-spectrum marketing program to get the customer's attention.

There is no such thing as doing too much when it comes to showing and telling about a promotion. One message one time at the front desk will not be enough.

Common ways to drive the point home include messages that are:

**FYI**

The average consumer is hit with more than 27,000 visual messages a day. It's necessary to cut through the clutter to have your retail message stick in the shopper's mind.

- Presented on signs at the front desk, front door, in the retail area, in the locker room, in the lockers, in the treatment rooms, in the hotel rooms, at the hair station, at the nail station, and/or in the pedicure area
- Posted on the salon and spa's website
- Sent in an e-mail message
- Sent in a postcard
- Included in the salon and spa newsletter
- Featured in the salon and spa's on-hold message

Brochures and other media such as direct mail, magazine ads, newspaper ads, television ads, radio ads, and billboard ads—and other marketing venues—have different strengths and weaknesses that you will want to consider when developing your marketing plans.

It is a nice idea to ask your clients how they want to receive information about your salon and spa. You can collect this information on your client profile form. Many clients dislike e-mail and prefer a quick text. Others love a direct mail brochure. Whatever your approach, a blend of three or more vehicles, sent at different intervals, is best for reinforcing your message and catering to the various communication preferences in an integrated marketing campaign.

## External Marketing Pieces

External marketing pieces are those that go out from your salon and spa to reach customers in their own environment. Some options, like television advertising, can be expensive; others, like e-mail, are virtually free.

### Print Media: Brochures and Flyers

Brochures and flyers are print pieces that provide detailed information about a product or service, or even a general overview of your salon and spa. They are useful for educating customers about new products, because they can go into more detail than a postcard, which has a limited space for content.

A common size for a flyer is 8.5 × 11. A typical brochure is a tri-fold, which is sized to fit a standard No. 10 envelope for mailing, but which opens out to six panels for copy and graphics. These are the most common sizes, however you can be creative and look at other formats that have a more artistic approach. The brochure should be attractive, easy to read (no small type), and include contact information so customers can follow up for more details. Providing the salon and spa's address, phone numbers, e-mail address, and website address in the brochure makes it easy for customers to get their questions answered, which will encourage them to come in and buy. While a brochure can be sent as a direct mail piece, it can also be used as a pick-up piece at the front desk, or even on a brochure rack in the treatment areas or retail space.

### Postcards

Postcards are inexpensive to create and to mail, but they are limited in the amount of space they have to deliver your salon and spa's message. Postcards are best used as part of an integrated marketing campaign. Postcards can urge customers to "save the date" for an upcoming event, follow up on an e-mail message or e-newsletter story, or announce a new product or service. Many times, vendors will have postcards available for co-op advertising, which lessens your costs for this form of marketing.

While postcards are more expensive to create than an e-mail message, they have the advantage of being a physical entity, something customers can hold onto, put on their refrigerators, or stick into their purses or folders. This physical presence and portability makes postcards ideal for offering a call to action that will entice customers into your salon and spa: "Bring in this postcard to receive a free gift!"

## Newsletters

A newsletter provides marketing information in a casual and less-structured format that is often perceived favorably by customers because it does not seem like advertising. Newsletters can be produced in a print format or in an electronic format that can be sent by e-mail and/or posted on the salon and spa's website.

Newsletters can be produced as frequently as needed to present the salon and spa's message; monthly or bimonthly are probably the best for keeping the salon and spa's name in front of the customer's eyes without seeming obtrusive. Content can include information about upcoming promotions and events, new products or treatments, profiles of employees, articles about wellness and beauty-related topics, and fun activities for readers. Every issue should include contact information for the salon and spa, as well as its days and hours of service.

## Electronic Media

E-mail. Sending e-mail messages is one of the least expensive ways to reach customers, but you must treat this medium with care. Federal regulations about spam, or unsolicited e-mail messages, require businesses to be open with customers about collecting their e-mail addresses and ensuring that customers are willing to receive e-mail messages from them. This is known as "opting in." You cannot simply take guests' e-mail addresses from their business cards and add them to a database. You must ask for the address and explain to guests how their e-mail address will be used by the salon and spa. Also, any e-mail messages sent to customers must include information about "opting out," or asking to be removed from the mailing list so as not to receive further e-mail communications from the salon and spa.

© Yuri Arcurs/www.Shutterstock.com

E-mail is a quick medium. People don't want to scroll through a long, copy-heavy message. Even e-newsletters focus on short copy with website links for more detailed information. E-mail is best for reminders about upcoming events, news about retail specials, or ads for new products. The e-mail message provides the "sizzle" or excitement about the salon and spa's message, while a link to the website sends customers to the "steak," which is the details about the particular marketing promotion.

There are several online marketing tools that you can use to manage your database of customers and to send out professional promotions using templates. Constant Contact and Vertical Response are just two of the many commonly used services. These do-it-yourself services have an ability to track if your e-mail has been opened, who has opted out, and even if your e-mail was forwarded to someone else in the recipient's network.

**Website.** A website can be a one-stop shop for customers to find out everything they need to know about your salon and spa and its offerings. Today, most people expect that a business will have a website. But there is more to having a Web presence than simply tossing a few pages of content and pretty images up onto a page. You may want to invest the money to have a professional Web designer work with you to create a site that achieves the salon and spa's marketing goals and is in line with your image and brand.

A website can be as simple or as complex as you want it to be. The style of the website is a reflection of the theme and philosophy of the salon and spa. Choices of imagery, music, and print style (font) all say something to the Internet user about your brand and what you stand for. As mentioned previously, before beginning the process of establishing a Web presence, you can visit the websites of other salons and spas and high-end retailers to get ideas of what works and what doesn't. Some key points to consider include how customers will find the website, how they will navigate the site in a way that's both effective and pleasing to them, what they want to learn from the website, and whether or not you want to use the site for online retailing.

- How customers will find the website: Make sure that your website address is included on every piece of promotional material that goes out from the spa. Include your website address on your business cards, your letterhead, and the signature line of your e-mail messages. Also include key words on your site (known as metatags) that enable search engines to find your website when a potential customer enters information into a search engine. A Web designer can provide guidance on helping the website to get the exposure it needs to succeed.

- Offer options to viewers: If the website has a long introduction with a photo montage, give the viewer the option to "skip intro" and go directly to the home page. If the website features background music, there should be a "music on/off" option. While music may help to set a tone for the salon and spa's website, it may also alienate customers who dislike website music interfering with the music they choose to play on their computers. Because people have computers with varying capabilities, websites might want to give viewers the option of "HTML only" or "Flash." That way, potential customers who have a slower connection won't become frustrated at the time it takes for their computer to load fancy graphics and animated images.

- Think about what customers want to know: What information should be included on the website? At a very minimum, hours of operation, location/map, menu of services, salon and spa news and events, and contact information are musts. Many salons and spas include their mission statement or philosophy on their home page. Beyond that, the sky is the limit. A photo gallery, gift certificate information, monthly specials, web-only specials, online store, online reservations, news releases and recent media exposure, and information about the salon and spa's charitable endeavors can all help customers to learn more about the salon and spa, its products, and services. The website can also include a place where visitors can sign up to receive the e-newsletter or e-mail messages from the salon and spa.

- Make decisions about extra features: Animated graphics, streaming video, and pop-ups may seem like essentials for the modern website, but you may want to think twice about the effect these can have on the Internet-savvy customers. Certainly, a pop-up announcing the upcoming Spring Fling special seems like a great idea, but many people consider pop-ups to be intrusive and annoying. If you have an upbeat, trendy salon and spa, this may fit in with the hip, upbeat visitors you want to attract. If you are a traditional spa, these features will send the complete opposite signal of a relaxing experience. Streaming video may serve the purpose of demonstrating the salon and spa's latest treatment, but it might also freeze someone's computer—not exactly the way to stimulate positive feelings in a prospective client.

- Consider all facets of online retailing: Purchasing salon and spa products online may seem a logical extension of your mail order program, but you must be honest about whether you are able to handle online sales. Consider how you will process online credit card orders. Will you take other online payment options, such as PayPal? Will you have enough staff to process, pack, and ship online orders in a timely fashion? Today's online shoppers have come to expect quick turnaround from online retailers—with shipments going out within 36 hours of placing their order. If you don't have the staff availability to turn around customer orders speedily, you may want to hold off on offering that service.

## Online Marketing Through Social Media

**social media.** A virtual communication tool that connects people online with applications such as Facebook and Twitter.

**Social media** is an internet-based communication tool that connects people virtually. Social media is an internal marketing vehicle that can be viral, quickly spreading the word about your business as existing customers share your business with their network.

When creating an online marketing approach, you will want to consider the different pathways that can drive business your way. The two major channels you will want to consider when designing your online presence through social media are Twitter and Facebook. These social media channels have allowed people to network without even leaving the comfort of their own home.

For example, Twitter is an information channel where the account owner can enlist "followers" that become an audience for their "tweets." These tweets are small bits of information that are 140 characters long or less, announcing quick updates on events or news about your business. You can then re-direct recipients of your tweets to your website or Facebook page for more information. Twitter is a free service and is best used as a secondary online marketing channel, to support other channels.

Facebook is a great interactive portal where people can join your business page and become "fans" or "members." You can update your "wall" to include photos, news, and events. Facebook allows you to interact with your members, and members to interact with one another through posting messages or photos—either on your wall or on their own wall, about you. These postings allow people to convey longer messages than Twitter. Facebook also has an ads page, where you can create ads that are targeted to a specific demographic. These ads run alongside the pages of Facebook members meeting your target criteria. Once clicked, the person is taken to your website to make an appointment or purchase a product, join an interest list, etc. Facebook, like Twitter, is a free service, but the ads feature is a fee-based program.

Yelp is another social media application that can be very relevant to your business. Yelp functions as a customer review message board and allows consumers to post a review of your business and supply a detailed description of their experience. This can work in your favor, since positive reviews can function as a means for gaining new clients. When you have enough reviews on Yelp, you can track reviews and gain insights about your customers. You can post messages to your reviewers and even post deals. Your business may already have a review on Yelp without you even knowing about it. People can review your business and voice their opinions, both good and bad. When potential customers do an Internet search for "hair salons in Boulder, Colorado", if you have a Yelp review, your review page may come up before your website does.

Social media activities get the word out about your business to a broad audience and can reinforce your monthly product promotions with a common theme. All social media elements can be aligned so they support one another. For example, you can align your monthly newspaper promotion for hair conditioning treatments with a Twitter announcement about the promotion, directing customers to your website for further information. You could also have the promotion duplicated on your Facebook page.

Once you get your social media accounts established, you will want to have a plan to manage each account and keep it fresh with up-to-date information. Because social media information is accessible 24 hours a day and is "on demand" it is extremely important to keep your content fresh and change it frequently. As a guide, you may want to look at the Facebook and Twitter content of your competitors or companies in your industry and assess how often new content is delivered. Nothing is worse than a tweet once per month or a Facebook posting that is weeks old.

## Billboards

Billboards can be part of an integrated marketing campaign, but because of their limitations, they are seldom the only marketing piece to deliver the salon and spa's retail message. Studies have shown that someone driving past a billboard can read only seven words before passing beyond sight of the billboard. Certainly, commuters passing a billboard on a daily basis might be able to read a longer message over the course of several days

### At the Creative Touch Day Spa...
### Social Media to Launch a Retail Campaign

**SALON AND SPA
SNAPSHOT 8.2**

Creative Touch Day Spa in Madison, Wisconsin, shows the power of integrating social media into their marketing campaigns. Carla, the manager at Creative Touch, realized that every business she knew of had an online presence—at minimum, a Facebook page. She had a personal page on Facebook, but knew that to be professional, she needed a page for her business.

"I needed a business page where people could focus on beauty and wellness. So I created a Facebook fan page and populated it with articles, advice, and specials so people would be encouraged to visit. References were always made from Facebook to the website to gain further information and vice versa." Carla encouraged her staff to promote the page. Two weeks after creating the page and launching a product and service special, the page already had 100 fans and the spa had 25 services pre-booked!

or weeks—but only if they are highly motivated to do so.

Billboards do a good job of communicating with a striking or vibrant image, the salon and spa's name and logo, and a brief message. For Mother's Day or Valentine's Day, a salon and spa billboard might show an image of a woman luxuriating in a massage, or enjoying a pedicure, with the phrase, "Skip the flowers this year." The salon and spa's name and a phone number or Web address completes the message.

© Tsian/www.Shutterstock.com

## Broadcast Media

Radio and television advertising can reach a substantial audience, but it can also be the most expensive type of marketing unless you carefully target the exact audience you want to reach. You may be able to keep your costs down by negotiating trade-outs: an exchange of goods and services for advertising space. Working with a media buyer can also help you negotiate the best deals with various media entities.

Another way to get exposure is to invite media personalities to participate in salon and spa events or programs. Every time the station announces, "Donna DeeJay will be appearing at the Urban Salon and Spa's Super Bowl Sunday Kick-Off for Women, January 29, from 3 p.m. to 6 p.m.," the salon and spa gets another free on-air mention. Of course, Donna DeeJay gets free services for herself, but you will attract many more customers to your special event than if you didn't have that exposure to all of the radio station's listeners.

## Print Advertising

Advertising in magazines and newspapers can be a good way to reach new customers, but you need to make careful decisions about where you will advertise, how often, and what you will promote. Magazines and newspapers commonly publish editorial calendars that let advertisers know when they will be covering certain topics. Also, newspapers tend to run certain topics in their "lifestyle" pages on the same day each week, for instance, health and wellness on Tuesdays, community profiles on Wednesdays, or entertainment news on Fridays. You can tailor your advertising schedules to match the publication's editorial content. Targeted publications, such as those for brides, lawyers, the theater, etc., will be more effective than general interest publications.

For salons and spas with limited marketing budgets, print advertising should promote a specific event or message. Just like broadcast media, publications may offer trade-out arrangements with advertisers (ad space in return for products or services) or offer partnerships that benefit both the publication and the salon and spa. Image ads do nothing but get the salon and spa's name out in front of the public, and there are many less expensive ways to do that. Instead, a print ad should include:

- Features and benefits of the product or service
- A call to action—"Come to the Urban Salon and Spa on Wednesday for your free travel kit."
- Awards or accolades that set the salon and spa apart—"Voted Best Salon and Spa in the Midwest," "As Featured in Elle Magazine."
- Your value proposition or niche that makes your salon and spa unique

## Press Releases

Press releases, also known as news releases, are a way for salons and spas to get free exposure in the media. You can create a local media list of newspaper, radio, and television reporters to whom you can send frequent news releases about a variety of salon and spa-related events. These can include new product launches, special events, awards, new staff members, new treatments, participation in community or charitable activities, or commentary on issues and trends. Press releases can include photographs and invitations for media people to visit the salon and spa for more information.

Unlike paid advertising, there is no guarantee that a newspaper or broadcast station will use a press release, but when it does, the exposure is free and is often more positively perceived by potential customers, because it is news and not advertising. Sometimes, newspapers will run a press release as it was written; more often, reporters will use the release as the starting point for a story they write themselves. They may also file the press releases for future reference, remembering the salon and spa the next time they need an expert source for a salon and spa-related article. You can also post your press releases on your website for customers to read there.

For members of ISPA, you can take advantage of media coverage from ISPA's media query service. This member benefit, in which spas respond to media requests for information for articles and stories they are research-

ing, is another way of getting good press and getting your name into consumer and industry trade magazines, newspapers, television, radio, and online media without having to pay for advertising.

# INTERNAL MARKETING PIECES

As the name suggests, internal marketing pieces are used within the salon and spa to repeat and reinforce marketing messages in small and subtle ways. These internal pieces show customers that the salon and spa is excited about its marketing promotion and wants to be sure that customers have every opportunity to get the message.

## On-Hold Message

The first contact a customer may have with your salon and spa is when he or she calls in and hears a promotional message. While every effort is made to minimize on-hold time, it will be common during busy times to place a caller into the queue for assistance. Instead of listening to dead air, the salon and spa can provide commercials that will be played during this time. On-hold messages can range from 10-second blurbs to a 60-second commercial. It is best to coordinate the salon and spa's audio message with corresponding print media advertising.

## Message on the Front Desk

When the customer is checking in or checking out at the front desk, they should see your promotional message front and center. This will be the first and last place clients have the opportunity to spend their money. You can capture their attention by setting up a mini-display of products along with a stable, self-supporting sign holder. Typically, this sign will be 8.5" × 11", but not smaller than 5" × 7".

## Message in the Retail Area

You can call attention to your featured retail products on the actual shelf where those products are displayed. This can be done with shelf clips that hold a promotional card, or with easel-backed cards placed next to the apparel, gifts, accessories, or products being featured. It is important to make it easy for customers to know which products are being promoted during their visit.

## Handout Cards at the Front Desk

When guests check in at the front desk, the receptionist can hand them a promotional card or flyer. They can read this while waiting for their service to begin and it will plant the seed for items they might want to buy from the beginning of their visit, instead of waiting until the very end of the visit to think about buying retail.

## Message Behind the Front Desk

When guests are standing at the front desk, what do they see? Do they see your logo? Do they see promotional messages? The area behind the desk is an ideal place to tell the salon and spa's retail story.

## Staff Recommendations

In order for any promotional campaign to be successful, you must enlist the support of the entire staff. It is necessary to allow time and budget to train the staff to sell the salon and spa's current campaign. The staff will need to be confident and competent in their sales messages to make the cash register ring. All staff members have the power to educate and influence salon and spa guests and their home care experiences—but only if they know what to say.

# PEOPLE MAKE MARKETING HAPPEN

Marketing doesn't happen by itself. People must work together to design, carry out, and follow through on all salon and spa marketing initiatives. You will need to work closely with employees, vendors, and outside people to implement your marketing plans.

## Internal Marketing Staff

If you are a large operation with a marketing department or a salon and spa in a resort/hotel, involve staff members in the marketing from the beginning of the development of your marketing plan. This is important for many reasons, including the following:

1. You want to assure the corporate marketing department is in support of your ideas and that your efforts will not conflict with the resort/hotel marketing calendar.
2. Guidelines are established from the top of the organization concerning verbiage used for copy, logos, placement, etc.
3. The marketing department may have resources you can leverage, such as a budget, or connections for public relations and advertising.

## Salon and Spa Staff

Enlist the help of the team to come up with a retail marketing plan. You may have key staff members, such as supervisors from esthetics, massage, hair, and nails, and the retail manager all contribute ideas to the plan. By participating in its development, the staff is more likely to support its implementation and assist with helping the salon and spa to meet its marketing goals. Creating staff support from the start puts wind into the sails of the marketing strategy.

Once you are ready to launch a promotion, make sure every team member knows how it works. Who needs to know? Everyone: the inbound call center, front desk, concierge (in a resort/hotel spa), service providers, and everyone who has face-to-face contact with the customer needs to know about the event.

When you launch a new product or service, ensure that every team member involved with the event has been trained to execute the new service and sell the new product. Methods for getting the message out internally include providing sales scripts tailored to each department and hosting a promo plan kick-off meeting to launch each new season or special.

## Vendors

Part of a salon and spa's long-term success is building solid, integrated relationships with product vendors. You want to be proactive and meet with each company to enlist its participation in the salon and spa's promotional calendar. A promotional event doesn't necessarily have to match the vendor's "stock" monthly deal sheet, although it can make planning a little more convenient.

Your salon and spa is responsible for creating a master calendar and then enlisting the support of product companies. (Revisit the vendor relations section in Chapter 3 for more ideas on how to solidify a true partnership with selected vendors.)

Many vendors offer their clients cooperative promotional material, or "co-op." Some include free product or monies back on advertising. Many will pay a percentage of a radio, television, or print media advertisement. You can ask vendors to provide detailed spec sheets on how you can qualify for their co-op dollars. Some may offer in-store incentives and support for VIP salon and spa accounts. Vendor contributions can help decrease the salon and spa's costs and also save you from having to reinvent the wheel. In other words, if the vendor already has a promotional brochure, postcard, or press release, there is no reason for you to invest the time and money to create the same thing.

## Other People

You may know a lot about operating a salon and spa and its retail operation, but you do not necessarily know how to write and design marketing pieces. Rather than create postcards, brochures, press releases, or a website that look shoddy or amateurish, you may want to consider working with professionals who specialize in those disciplines.

As noted above, vendors may be able to provide postcards, press releases, brochures, tent cards, and other marketing collateral. For original pieces, you can seek out writers, graphic designers, and Web designers who work for agencies or on a freelance basis. Print, radio, and television outlets will have professionals who work with advertisers to create ads that meet the needs of both the advertiser and the medium. The salon and spa may work with a public relations agency to coordinate its media exposure.

For media coverage that is not paid advertising, you will want to cultivate positive relationships with media people, including reporters, editors, and on-air personalities. You can send news releases on a regular basis to your media list and suggest story ideas where appropriate. You can position your salon and spa as an expert source in the salon and spa field and serve as an articulate, informed source for news features. Remember to thank writers and editors for their coverage of your events and also highlight media placements in the salon and spa newsletter and website, providing recognition for the medium in addition to the coverage in that medium.

# PUTTING THE PLAN INTO ACTION

Once you have a master calendar full of events to drive sales, you must remember to connect the dots for the ultimate sales success. A marketing and promotion worksheet will keep you organized and enable you to have all of your information in one place. Information such as:

- The launch date
- Featured products
- Inventory requirements
- Display areas
- Roles and responsibilities of staff
- Total sales and ROI

Using a promotion worksheet makes it easy for you to keep track of the various components of the plan, such as theme, target audience, launch date, goal, and budget. After noting what key products and services will be featured during the promotion, you can list out any additional inventory requirements that need to be acquired for the promotion.

Buying can be motivated by emotional needs, and emotions are often triggered through the 5 senses of sight, sound, touch, taste, and smell. For instance, if the salon and spa is launching an orange whipped facial and body cream, it can tie in orange teas to drink, orange smoothies, and a big bowl of fresh, juicy oranges. If the salon is promoting a holiday hair care gift set, with a peppermint scent, you could have peppermint candies, candy canes, and a display of pre-wrapped packages. Multiple sensory connections can help pique the shopper's interest in what the salon and spa is offering and will evoke an emotional motivation to buy.

As a final step before the marketing promotion begins, you walk the promotion through the salon and spa and facilities and add any additional props that will help tell the story. Visual merchandising anchors will show your guest what is being featured.

# MARKETING PROMOTIONS

While most salon and spa professionals may think of marketing in terms of specific promotions and events, it can also include year-round sales of products through mail order, as well as marketing and sales of gift certificates.

## Mail Order

Mail order business and direct mail programs are a good way to drive repeat business for the salon and spa retail operation. Some salons and spas have been able to increase their retail sales by 20 percent to 40 percent with an effective mail order process. After all, the easiest customer to sell is the one who has already purchased product from the retail operation.

A database of customer e-mail addresses and mailing addresses, along with guest preferences and purchasing history, can form the basis of a successful direct mail program. The salon and spa can notify a guest when her favorite moisturizer is on sale, when there is a manicure special, or when new loungewear by her favorite designer is available for purchase.

## Gift Certificates and Gift Cards

Gift certificates and gift cards are always good for any special event as they can bring a new customer into the salon and spa and entice multiple purchases.

Printed gift certificates should be:

- Pre-numbered consecutively
- Contain an authorized signature
- Show an expiration date if one is assigned
- Include the recipient's name
- Indicate the dollar value or the services the gift certificate is good for

You can increase the chance that the gift certificate will be redeemed by sending recipients a reminder notice encouraging them to visit the salon and spa, and enclosing the menu of services.

You need to realize that people who come into your salon and spa because they have a gift certificate are prospects and not yet customers. The goal for the salon and spa is to turn that prospect into a repeat customer and not just a one-time visitor. A small retail gift for redeeming a gift certificate for service, and an invitation to join as a frequent guest (or an offer of a member loyalty program), may encourage a peripheral customer to become a regular.

For all occasions, gift certificates can be a suggestion for undecided customers. However, you must check with your state's guidelines on gift certificate redemption rules. While 20 percent of all gift certificates are never redeemed and some feel it is free money, some states have implemented very strict rules and regulations regarding what businesses have to do with unclaimed money. It is prudent to check with the state attorney general's office and the salon and spa's legal counsel.

# A YEAR OF PROMOTIONS

Salon and spa professionals should never feel at a loss for a marketing promotion. There is enough happening throughout the year to create hundreds of opportunities to bring customers into the salon and spa and encourage them to buy by showcasing products and offering "mini-services."

## Big Bang Holidays

There are three holidays on every salon and spa's master plan, and for every retailer, for that matter. They are Valentine's Day, Mother's Day, and the winter Holidays, and these represent the best gift-giving opportunities and the best gift certificate sales opportunities. They are only the beginning, though. Truly successful salons and spas look beyond these three for marketing hooks for their merchandise.

### Valentine's Day

A holiday for lovers, and who wouldn't love a gift of relaxation, wellness, or beauty? With male salon and spa visits on the increase, you can tie in his and hers service with retail. If you have a spa, you might offer a massage for two with a gift of massage oil, body lotion, and bath soak as a package, or his and hers facials with a skin care kit for two. This is the time to think of wine and roses, a chocolate mud bath, and a chocolate soufflé whipped body moisturizer. For salons, you can offer a manicure and pedicure combination or a his and hers combination package. This can be a real crunch time. Most Valentine's Day gift certificates will be purchased within 72 hours of the holiday. You will have to ensure adequate staffing for all those men running in and logging on at the eleventh hour.

### Mother's Day

Men buy for their wives and women buy for their mothers, stepmothers, mothers-in-law, grandmothers, daughters, stepdaughters, daughters-in-law, and maybe even for themselves. Target your marketing message to both the male and female shopper. You might package a big, comfy robe with a half-day spa package. Or package a makeup box with a haircut, facial, and makeup lesson. You might offer a pedicure and manicure and offer a great foot scrub, leg mask, polish, and slippers. Another opportunity is to offer a mother-daughter day of beauty and pampering. How about a multi-generational package to get all the women in for a service and have a retail package that goes along with it?

### Winter Holidays

Most salons and spas gear up for four months to promote winter holiday gift sales. While offering wide selections of half-day, full-day, or monthly series of services, successful salon and spa professionals also remember to tie in some retail product with each gift idea. They stock up on impulse items for the holidays. Corrective skin care will take a back seat for gift giving. A salon and spa's inventory mix will expand for the holidays.

## Seasonal Promotional Events

These marketing options are calendar driven. There are times throughout the year when salons and spas can make an extra effort to promote their offerings to consumers.

### First Quarter Options (January–March)

New Year, New You. Consumers are blasted with "New Year, new you" messages in every media. If a salon and spa offers any type of diet, exercise, or nutritional counseling, or beauty makeovers, now is the time to highlight these services. For retail sales, salons and spas can tie in cosmetics, firming body creams, vitamins, and nutraceuticals to the event.

SALON AND SPA SNAPSHOT 8.4

### At the Chapparosa Salon and Day Spa… Girls Night Out

Chapparosa Salon and Day Spa of Kansas City, Kansas, utilizes in-house events as a means of featuring new products and spotlighting services. Mina, the owner, recently held her monthly "Girls Night Out" party and encouraged her clients to bring a friend. "I want to build my business from the existing clients, and there is no better way than through referrals. By asking my guests to bring a friend, the client receives a percentage off her next service and the guest receives an introductory special for her service. Each month we feature a new product or service at these events and we are building a reputation as the place to go for fun and beauty."

**Post-Winter Blues.** If your salon and spa is located in an area of the country that suffers from seasonal affective disorders, or SAD, you can feature chromatherapy services and products. You might offer specialized massage programs to fight the mid-winter blues or offer a mid-winter makeup touchup or self-tanning promotion.

**Pre-Spring.** Now is the time to promote laser hair removal, sclerotherapy, and cellulite treatments, as well as hair brightening services, such as highlights. Many consumers don't book these services until late spring and summer is in full swing, so a carefully planned marketing push can bring these customers in sooner.

## Second Quarter Options (April–June)

**Spring Fling.** Salons and spas can tap into spring fever by showcasing new hairstyles and styling aids, and new fresh faces for spring with new makeup looks. They can sell post-winter skin repair with exfoliates and hydrating serums.

**Spring Cleaning.** Your salon and spa can use this theme by featuring all cleansing items on sale: "Save 10 percent off all facial cleansers, shower gels, and shampoos."

**Secretary's Day.** Become a hero when your salon and spa suggest that bosses send their right-hand person in for a service. Include an administrative professional's basket of retail product.

**Graduates.** Treat those hard-working college students to a day in the salon and spa to beat the stress during mid-terms and finals.

If your salon and spa is located in or near a college town, it can offer a parents' package (great for parents' weekends and alumni events, too). The special promotion can offer an indulgent package to the parents because they survived their kid going to college.

Father's Day. This holiday can be an exciting new sales opportunity. Many men would love to receive a massage, facial, and pedicure, even a hair color enhancing technique, such as grey blending. Spas can tie in a great collection of shaving products for the guys. They might offer shaving cream, razors, brushes, or even self-tanners or bronzers.

Proms. This is a time for salons and spas to drive makeup, hair, and nail services. Prom-going girls (and guys) are dropping into the salon and spa for their Prom Packages. It's a perfect opportunity to tie in a makeup touch-up kit that includes powder, blush, lip gloss, and lip liner.

## Third Quarter Options (July–September)

Bridal Biz. Bridal-related events are big business today. It used to be that the salon and spa bridal business was promoted only during the month of June—not anymore. You can target a year-round bridal business with the biggest opportunity for bridal bucks from April to October. Think bridal showers, bridal parties (bride, bridesmaid, mother of the bride, future in-laws, and all those groomsmen), wedding days, and honeymoon services.

Cool Looks for Hot Days. Smart retailers look for ways to beat the summer slump. A salon and spa in Manhattan, for example, may suffer from a mass exodus to the Island. In L.A., there may be a slump when it's a wrap for sitcom season. For the rest of the country, regular salon and spa guests may skip appointments or drag them out. Only in resort salons and spas are the employees working overtime to facilitate vacationing guests during peak periods. This is one season where salons and spas will weather the consumer storm of feast or famine.

Back to School. Back-to-school time does not typically drive the masses into the salon and spa. It can, however, spike sales when directed to specific target markets.

- Teachers: Offer local teachers a back-to-school special. Kick off the school year with a new look and new products.
- Kids: The smell of new crayons and the thrill of the back-to-school wardrobe brings back many happy

memories. A salon and spa specializing in troubled skin treatments can offer a back-to-school skin special. Add a service for a fresh, new haircut, and you have an ideal "back-to-school" package.

- Mom: She deserves a medal for getting the kids back on the school bus. Host a "Whew ... Back to School for Mom" special.

## Fourth Quarter Options (October–December)

**Happy Halloween.** Does the salon and spa have a great makeup department? Can it feature makeup tips or classes where Mom can learn how to create ghosts and goblins or turn the salon and spa into Hollywood Central for the day? Clients can get dressed up at the salon and spa while the team creates the hair and makeup looks.

**Fabulous Fall Looks.** Ever notice how fat those magazines are, the ones that stuff mailboxes this time of year? Consumers are preprogrammed to look for new clothes, hair, jewelry, and makeup. Your salon and spa can host its own Fall Looks Review, which shows guests how to recreate the look at home with your professional products.

**Preferred Customer Thank-You.** Treat VIP clients to a preferred customer sale. Instead of just sending them a Thanksgiving Day card, you can reward them for being loyal customers by offering a limited-time sales event.

**Holiday Dazzle.** You will need to make a branding decision as to how early to launch the winter holiday promotions. Following traditional mass retailers, winter holidays usually get displayed while Halloween is still being sold. Nordstrom does not launch winter holidays until Thanksgiving night when its bevy of elves goes in to transform all of its stores. Most salons and spas split the difference and launch winter holidays around November 15.

## Season-*less* Promotional Ideas

There are many ways you can promote your services and retail products that are not tied specifically to the calendar.

### Annual Series Sales

Think of a service package tied to specific products and create a signature sale. Let this be your trademark that is anticipated yearly. For example, everyone knows about half-yearly sales at Nordstrom's. Georgette Klinger has made every August the time all of their series packages go on sale. This event is one of their staples.

## Anniversary Special

Celebrate the salon and spa's annual business anniversary. Since most small businesses fail within the first five years, every year you are open is worth a celebration. Host an annual event to thank loyal customers for their support. Offer limited-time-only anniversary specials. If you have been open for 11 years, offer an 11 percent discount on all retail products the week of the event. Offer VIP clients a special gift with purchase.

## On-Site Services

You can provide services for special events and market the salon and spa to participants and spectators at the event.

## Kiss and Makeup

Every spring and fall the major fashion magazines feature all the hottest new colors and styles. Tie in a promotion twice a year with a makeup event.

## Reward/Loyalty Programs

One master retailer is Chico's, a clothing and accessory store for women. Chico's offers a Passbook to Savings so those who shop at Chico's reap the rewards. Customers sign up, shop, and when their purchases hit $500, they get an additional 5 percent off every purchase thereafter. Members get birthday bonuses, free shipping on online orders, discounts on gift certificates, exclusive sales, easy check writing privileges, and invitations to special parties and events.

## Frequent Buyer Programs

With this promotion, you can reward shoppers for selecting your salon and spa. Establish reward levels for frequent shoppers and/or big spenders. For example, spend $500 and receive a free makeup kit. Spend $750 and get a free body scrub and body lotion. Buy 6 haircuts and the 7th one is free, and the customer qualifies for a free shampoo and conditioner. You can even design a program where customers receive points for purchases that can be redeemed for rewards. From time to time, you can offer double or triple points for the purchase of selected items.

## Makeover Contest

Full-service salons and spas can host a makeover contest. They can partner with a local radio or television station or magazine. They capture the before and after results. This type of contest lets them tie in any apparel, hair, skin, and makeup products. The salon and spa can then show potential customers how to take care of themselves beautifully from top to toe. If you are a salon only, you can partner with a local spa (and vice versa) to put on the event. This joint venture could be the beginning of a referral relationship that can boost both business entities. Just be sure that the business you partner with does not offer the same products or services as you.

### Extreme (or Not-so-Extreme) Makeover

With television shows like "Extreme Makeover," consumers are pre-programmed to look for make-over services. You can let customers know what services you offer that can be positioned as a total make-over package. In a spa, you may offer lifestyle coaching, diet and nutrition, exercise, wardrobe analysis, non-surgical face lifts, and laser hair removal. For salons, you can offer hair redesign, hair extensions, makeup lessons, manicures and pedicures, and even spray tanning. You can always tie a home care product into the package. If you are offering an "extreme ticket" (meaning that it costs big bucks), build the retail promotion around the package. You will drive retail sales simply by including a maintenance kit in the package price.

### Face in a Bag

If your salon and spa focuses on skin care, or has makeup services, you can have clients bring their home care products in for the staff's review. You can offer new clients an incentive to get rid of the products that may not be giving them the best results. For example, offer the new client an instant 10 percent savings on any new products they purchase on their initial visit. Makeup clients typically have dozens of products that they purchased that do not work. Ask them to bundle up the items and have a makeup lesson or consultation. The makeup artist or technician can get them to toss what doesn't work and help them select products that do.

# EVALUATING THE SALON AND SPA'S MARKETING EFFORTS

Once your promotion is over, you will want to take time to recap the event. What lessons have you or your staff learned? What would you do the same or differently for the next event? And the most important questions of all: What was the bottom line? and What were the overall sales? There is a place on the bottom of the event planning form for recording this information.

You can analyze the success of each promotion and keep the form on record. The promotional evaluation form would indicate a description of the promotion, costs, and retail sales results. To determine the contribution of a specific promotion, you subtract the cost of the promotion from the retail sales generated, less the price of the inventory for the promotion (at cost). The form can include an area for comments, as it is difficult to remember a year or two later what the results of the promotion were and whether it should be repeated or modified.

## CHAPTER SUMMARY

- Marketing activities should be targeted to reach your intended audience and align with your brand.
- The most successful salons and spas market continually to their current customers and potential customers.
- Marketing isn't always directed towards the salon and spa's products and services. It can also be a way of gaining brand awareness.
- Creating a marketing plan is a tool to strategically promote your business so you get the most impact from your investment.
- A website will attract customers and potential customers to your business and serve as a living brochure.
- Knowing your competition is an important piece in creating a solid marketing plan.
- Your value proposition, or niche, is what makes your business unique. Keep it in mind when you create your brand and your promotions.
- Integrating your website with social media channels such as Facebook and Twitter will gain interest and create excitement for your products and services.
- Holiday and season-less promotions in your salon and spa will enable you to offer mini services that will generate future bookings.
- Each quarter brings a new opportunity to create promotions that keep your calendar fresh.

# LEARNING ACTIVITIES

## Learning Activity 8-1: SWOT Team!

Using the form in Exhibit 2, conduct a SWOT analysis of your salon and spa and three of its main competitors. Using the information you gather, find at least three points of difference that your salon and spa has to offer customers. Develop those points into a statement of your unique selling proposition.

## Learning Activity 8-2: Angling for a Promotion

Select one seasonal and one season-less promotional idea from this chapter and develop a marketing plan for your salon and spa on those themes. Use the promotion worksheet in Exhibit 10 to ensure that you are following all of the steps necessary to have a successful promotion. Track sales of the product or products featured in your promotions before, during, and after the events. Were the promotions successful? If not, what would you do differently next time?

# REVIEW QUESTIONS

1. Which of the following is a weakness of news releases as a marketing vehicle?
    a. Because they are not paid for, they are not taken as seriously as ads.
    b. They are time-consuming and expensive to create.
    c. There is no guarantee that the media will use the information provided.
    d. Little happens at a salon and spa that is truly newsworthy and journalists get annoyed by frivolous news releases.

2. A "unique selling proposition" is:
    a. That which sets your salon and spa apart from its competitors.
    b. A special promotion that happens only once a year.
    c. A promotion offering special pricing on one-of-a-kind merchandise.
    d. An offer that can't be refused.

3. Angela Avery wants to buy her sister a manicure/pedicure package and some related retail products for her birthday. Angela is not a regular visitor, but she selects the Urban Salon and Spa for her gift purchase because she remembered its participation in the downtown area's "Walk for Wellness" last month. What type of marketing influenced Angela's decision?

    a. Seasonal promotion
    b. Staff recommendation
    c. Customer loyalty
    d. Salon and spa awareness

4. Jazmine decides to include a "New Year, New You" promotion in her retail marketing calendar. She is taking which of the following into consideration?

    a. Vendors' promotions
    b. Holidays and seasons
    c. The salon and spa's retail plan
    d. New product launch

5. Reuben has put together a new "Birthday Club" for his guests. When guests register for the club, they receive a birthday card that includes an invitation to visit the salon and spa and receive a percentage equal to their age off any single retail purchase during the week of their birthday. This type of promotion is designed to:

    a. Create retail/service excitement
    b. Strengthen customer relationships
    c. Build awareness of the spa's philosophy
    d. Give the shopper a reason to buy now

6. Guests at the Seasons Salon and Spa can sign up to receive news and special offers by e-mail by completing a form at the front desk or by going online and submitting their e-mail addresses in the sign-up box on the website. This activity is called:

    a. Opting in
    b. Opting out
    c. Spamming
    d. Phishing

7. Bree, the retail manager at the Urban Salon and Spa, approaches Reuben with an idea for marketing the new collection of Zen sand gardens—host a sand sculpture contest for corporate teams and have the host of a popular TV talk show emcee the event. Winners would get a spa prize package featuring the new sand gardens. This is an example of a(n):
   a. Big Bang promotion
   b. Seasonal promotion
   c. Internal marketing promotion
   d. Season-less promotion

8. Jazmine wants to evaluate whether the salon and spa's June marketing event promoting its line of body care products for people with dry skin was profitable. To do that, she looks at which one of the following:
   a. Were product sales of the line higher this June than last June?
   b. After subtracting the costs associated with doing the promotion, were product sales of the line higher this June than last June?
   c. Did they sell out of products in that line?
   d. Did they gain any new customers?

9. What does the "O" stand for in SWOT analysis?
   a. Outsiders
   b. Outside influencers
   c. Overtures (internal and external)
   d. Opportunities

10. Which of the following external marketing pieces are inexpensive to create and mail but are limited in the message they can deliver?
    a. Brochures
    b. Postcards
    c. Newsletters
    d. Website

# Salon and Spa Retail Opening

## INTRODUCTION

Opening a new salon and spa is an exciting endeavor, which is often a milestone in the career path of many beauty and wellness professionals. The skill set required to be successful in opening a new salon and spa is quite different than the skill set required to be a successful technician or designer.

To discuss the complete list of business skills, planning steps, and other requirements involved in starting a salon and spa from the ground up lies outside the scope of this book. For further information about beginning your new venture, visit milady.cengage.com and refer to *Successful Salon and Spa Management,* Sixth Edition, by Edward Tezak, published by Milady, a part of Cengage Learning. This chapter is designed to lead salon and spa business owners and managers in the development of the retail entity within a new or already operational salon and spa.

Chapter **9**

## A SYSTEMATIC APPROACH TO PLANNING

When you become involved in the development of a new retail boutique in your salon and spa, you can benefit from a systematic approach to planning your retail operations.

One systematic approach is to use a six-month countdown plan to the opening. The following is an example of the activities contained in such a plan, starting with tasks to accomplish months in advance and ending with tasks you will expect to do just weeks and days before you open.

### LEARNING OBJECTIVES

After successfully completing this chapter, the reader will be able to:

- Integrate the components of the previous chapters into a six-month plan for opening a new salon and spa retail operation.

- Gather information about competitors through the use of a market survey.

- Understand the components necessary in designing a logo.

- Select point-of-sale computer software to maximize efficiency and profitability.

- Explore components necessary for the retail product offerings.

## At the Seasons Salon and Spa…

SALON AND SPA SNAPSHOT 9.1

© Andresr/www.Shutterstock.com

Jazmine sank gratefully into the restaurant booth across from her friend and mentor, Dahlia. It was the first time the two salon and spa professionals had found the opportunity to meet since Jazmine had been promoted and charged with opening the retail boutique in Printemps, a new "sister" salon and spa to the Seasons Salon and Spa.

"I can't believe how many meetings it takes to bring a new salon and spa to life, and I'm just leading the boutique construction," Jazmine told Dahlia. "Architects, designers, contractors, vendors … if I didn't have my 6-month plan to keep track of all the decisions I need to make, I'd be completely disoriented. This seems like the first time I've sat down in a week."

"Still, it's rewarding to watch those blueprints start to turn into walls and rooms and whirlpools right before your eyes, isn't it?" said Dahlia, who was an old pro at salon and spa openings. "By now, Printemps must be starting to look like a real salon and spa."

Jazmine nodded as she glanced over the lunch menu. "I can't wait for you to see it when we're ready to open—I'm sure the next three months will fly by. You know, I can hardly make a decision about what to eat. It seems that all I've been doing lately is making decisions—about products to align with our treatments and services, meeting with vendors and testing samples, and so forth, and now reviewing employee applications. What I need more than lunch is six more hours in a day!"

"I remember those days," Dahlia sympathized. "I know you probably just want to get away from business for an hour or two, but I'm dying to know just a few more things about your new place. What's your retail space like? Is it larger than the space at Seasons? What kinds of products will you be carrying? Have you found any unique items to offer?"

Jazmine's face fell. "Unique retail items? Don't get me started! I practically got into a fistfight with the architect over built-ins, and I'm still not convinced I have enough room to do the boutique justice. And products … to be perfectly honest, I've just been testing products and focusing on the initial core product choices." Dahlia heard a hint of desperation in her friend's voice. "I'm not even sure I know how much I'm supposed to order … after all, I've got nothing to base my figures on. I'm starting to think I don't have what it takes to open a new retail boutique."

## Opening Countdown

6 months:

- Conduct a market survey.
- Finalize the retail design and layout.
- Create the logo.
- Develop a merchandise plan and budget.
- Select the point-of-sale computer system.
- Explore core retail treatment products.

4 months:

- Establish sales and inventory procedures.
- Establish a commission strategy.
- Finalize the opening inventory value and begin merchandise purchases.
- Develop the retail marketing plan.
- Develop processes for retail direct mail and mail order.
- Select a packaging and gift wrap program.
- Source remaining retail merchandise.

3 months:

- Recruit a retail supervisor and/or retail specialists.

2 months:

- Finalize the retail commission structure.
- Purchase operating supplies.
- Finalize the gift certificate program.
- Establish reorder/restock procedures.
- Determine pricing strategies.

4 weeks:

- Hire staff and set training schedules.
- Bring the point-of-sale system online.
- Start receiving and ticketing merchandise.

2–3 weeks:

- Arrange fixtures, supplies, and packaging.
- Prepare merchandise for display.
- Enter merchandise data into the computer system.
- Continue product/retail and point-of-sale training.
- Audit purchase order ledger to ensure all goods have shipped; request tracking numbers.

1 week:

- Finalize retail space setup/begin setting merchandise on shelves.
- Purchase visual props to enhance product presentation.
- Complete merchandise training for all products.

**DID YOU KNOW?**

The most successful business owners and managers have a solid foundation of business skills such as accounting, project management, problem solving, and decision making.

**DID YOU KNOW?**

Using a systematic approach to planning will help you to maximize your retail sales, maximize your profits, and track your milestones, leading to the launch of a retail operation.

- Conduct staff training on register procedures.
- Assign associates to specific merchandise responsibilities.
- Open the retail area for business.

# SIX MONTHS FROM OPENING

Depending on the size of your spa retail operation, preparations for opening may begin anywhere from six months to a year before the projected opening date. At this stage of planning, consider big-picture issues, including market competition, customer demographics, facility design and layout, logo creation, merchandising budgets, and point-of-sale computer selection. The decisions made at this point will affect nearly every other decision concerning the opening of the salon and spa retail operation.

## Conduct a Market Survey

Whether planning a resort/hotel salon and spa, day spa, or salon, one of the first things that must be done is to check out the competition. This competitive analysis or market survey will typically focus on the service delivery, the service menu, the product lines, number of treatment rooms, nail stations, styling stations, and the level of similar activity at the competitive business. The competitive analysis would not be complete if it did not include a thorough understanding of the retail component. You will want to thoroughly understand the market before you make any purchases, whether of merchandise or retail fixtures.

For example, if the salon and spa down the block offers some of the same products as your retail area, you will want the price points to be aligned. Also, your salon and spa can offer those and also offer more unique products within the same classification. There is more on what to look for in marketing surveys in the section below.

For a resort/hotel salon and spa, the competition will encompass more than salons and spas located in the immediate vicinity. Market surveys would include the resorts from which the new salon and spa hopes to draw its future guests. Day spa retail operations may want to consider including in their market survey local beauty retailers and discounters in addition to neighboring salons and day spas.

---

**HERE'S A TIP**

If you are opening a large retail space with its own entrance, you may draw customers that would never become guests of the salon and spa. On the other hand, the retail area becomes its own entity, and potential clients may walk out of the salon and spa door without noticing your retail. Increase the awareness of the services offered by adding a tag phrase to the logo such as "Salon and Boutique" so customers of the retail space are reminded of the service side of the business. Have retail staff mention the service menu to retail guests so they are encouraged to learn more.

---

**DID YOU KNOW?**

Surveying the competition and understanding the particular characteristics and points of distinction of other salon and spa facilities in the market will help you create the proper product mix and price points.

Understanding the salon and spa market is a strategic task that is done as a part of determining the overall business concept. The complete study will include broader areas pertaining to the overall business, but for the focus of this section, we will look at the areas relevant to the retail operation. When conducting the market survey, you will want to look at an average of four to six salon and spa retail operations, focusing on facilities that are within 5 to 10 miles of the new business, that are similar in customer profile, and that are on the cutting edge of salon and spa retail operations. Information gathered during the survey pertaining to retail includes:

- What is the size of the retail area or areas?
- Is the retail in open areas within the salons and spas or inseparate shops?
- Do they have dedicated retail staff?
- What merchandise is sold? This information is recorded by retail classifications and subclassifications—for example, bath and body products, hair products, makeup lines, nail lines, skin care lines, private label, apparel, gifts, accessories. (The market survey forms—see Figure 9-1—should have a space to write the names of the lines, the number of products in each line, and a column to indicate approximate pricing.)
- Do competitors offer any special retail promotions?
- Do they offer any exclusive or signature merchandise lines?
- What are their gift certificate/gift card processes?
- Do they offer gift packaging programs—and if so, do they charge?
- What are the competition's strengths and weaknesses?
- What are their retail philosophies?
- Is there a product satisfaction guarantee given?
- Is there a customer loyalty program?

## Sample Market Survey Form

After gathering the market survey information, analyze the data to determine how the new salon and spa retail operation will fit into the existing retail environment. As the information is reviewed, consider the following questions:

- What opportunities are not being met by the current salon and spa retail market?
- What are the areas of differentiation among the competition?
- What attributes of each competitor have the most effect?

Figure 9-1
Sample Competitive Spa Retail Survey

| Criteria | Location A | Location B | Location C | Location D |
|---|---|---|---|---|
| Proximity from your location | | | | |
| Impact from local business | | | | |
| Customer profile/demographics | | | | |
| Household income | | | | |
| Store design/lighting | | | | |
| Square footage | | | | |
| Product assortment (List all retail classifications) | | | | |
| Vendors | | | | |
| Logo product | | | | |
| Private label | | | | |
| Pricing strategy or perceived value | | | | |
| Products | | | | |
| Gift packaging/bag program | | | | |
| Overall traffic | | | | |
| Customer service | | | | |
| Customer comments | | | | |
| Overall design | | | | |
| Strengths | | | | |
| Weaknesses | | | | |
| Hours of operation | | | | |
| Spa menu | | | | |

- How can the new retail operation create its own market niche?
- How will the new retail operation express the philosophy of the salon and spa through the products it offers?
- What kinds of store designs—fixtures, lighting, flooring—were most effective?
- How is the retail merchandise displayed? What ideas can you utilize on visual displays?
- If a logo is used, is it used on private label products, apparel, etc.? Purchase an item in a retail space that you find appealing. Record details of this example to utilize in your own design process.

## Customer Demographics

Part of the planning process is to understand your potential customers so you can closely match your retail merchandise offerings. You can achieve this by establishing a demographic profile of potential salon and spa customers. Consider the following questions when creating a profile:

- Who are the target guests? What are their ages? Household income? What percent male and female?
- Will the guests be young professionals or more mature guests?
- Is there a large residential area or concentration of office buildings near the salon and spa that may result in regular treatment guests?
- Will there be a membership component?
- How close by are traditional retail outlets and/or discounters for health and beauty products?
- Will the salon and spa do significant wedding business or special women's outings?
- What percent of guests are price sensitive vs. luxury brand consumers?

In a Resort/Hotel:

- Is the property of a prestige level that guests will want logo wear? What do other outlets in the resort/hotel sell? Is their logo the same or different from the salon and spa?
- What percent of business will be local and what percent tourist?
- What percent of business will come from group business and what percent from independent travelers?
- How many fitness guests will the salon and spa have each day? Is the salon and spa located in an area that will have foot traffic near the retail space that may contribute additional customers?

## Marketing Considerations

Use the information gleaned during the research phase of pre-opening to direct the salon and spa's marketing plan. Marketing questions to ponder include:

- Who is the salon and spa's retail target market? Consumers in the surrounding area?

- Is the pricing strategy in line with target customer demographic?
- Are there other salons and spas are in the vicinity? If so, what are their marketing strategies?

In a Resort/Hotel:
- Will your guests be property guests? Wedding groups? What clientele does the resort/hotel cater to?
- Is there an opportunity to develop retail packages or baskets for VIP meeting groups?
- Will the salon and spa retail area have window displays for merchandise or the opportunity to display merchandise in other areas of the salon and spa or resort?
- Is it possible that the hotel room amenity program could feature salon and spa products to promote usage and retail sales?
- Is there any merit to doing in-room retail promotions such as a display of bath salts and oils for guests' in-room bathing?

## SALON AND SPA SNAPSHOT 9.2

### At the Monarch Hill Salon and Spa... Planting Seeds of Awareness

The Monarch Hill Salon and Spa, in Fort Lauderdale, Florida, leverages the hotel to draw guests. Signature spa products are offered in the rooms, and the salon and spa menu is placed on the nightstand and on the vanity. All of the restrooms on the property use the signature products and display samples of the menu. Although this is not unusual for a salon and spa, the marketing is taken still further. Guests are offered an opportunity to receive complimentary bath salts, lotions, and shaving products by visiting the salon and spa retail area and showing their room key. Jeff, the manager, implemented this sampling program over a slow season and saw an increase in retail and service bookings. "This simple act of giving complimentary samples brought people here that would have never crossed the threshold. Once they arrived, we offered them a cold beverage and brought them into the retail space to select their sample products. Afterwards, we gave them a quick tour of the spa."

## Community Partnerships

For the creative salon and spa manager, there are many potential business partnerships within the larger community. For example:

- For day spas and salons, are there any local inns or hotels that do not have a spa or salon component that could be a strategic marketing partner?
- Is there an opportunity to work with local realtors to pass out gift certificates and retail products as a promotion to new home buyers?
- Is there an opportunity to do fashion shows at nearby restaurants?

After evaluating the competition, the customer base, and the marketing options, you will be ready to create the appropriate merchandise mix and retail environment.

## Finalize the Salon and Spa Retail Design and Layout

A well-planned retail layout, design, and fixtures can spell success for a salon and spa retail operation. As retail revenue has such a significant impact on overall business profitability, you will want to initiate a discussion on retail layout and fixtures with the development team very early in the planning or construction process. Most architects and interior designers are not experts in the specific skills of retail design and layout. It is important to evaluate their experience, and, if it is limited, perhaps hire a retail consultant to assist with the layout and fixture selection.

There are two main types of retail fixtures: built-in and freestanding. Built-in units are part of the retail area's structure and are discussed early in the process. The architect is generally responsible for drawing the detail design of the built-in units, which will be given to a millwork contractor to construct. Check the design against the overall merchandise classifications to make sure that the various product classifications have appropriate space and fixtures allocated for their display.

© Mayer George Vladimirovich/www.Shutterstock.com

## HERE'S A TIP

Fixturing needs to be flexible enough to accommodate or change shelving to hanging or vice versa. Since the nature of retail is evolutionary, fixtures will need to accommodate new and possibly different products in the future.

You will need to think about how your merchandise will be displayed. Good questions to ask include:

- Are the shelves designated to display your products adjustable?
- Are there enough shelves to maximize the display?
- Will there be storage built into the bottom of the shelving units or will the display extend to the floor?
- If you are carrying apparel, will it be displayed folded or hanging?
- If hanging, do the built-in units have adequate hanging bars?

You can easily get ideas for displaying merchandise by going to a high-end specialty store and observing how they present the different categories. The market research you conducted previously will also give you an idea of ways to display products.

Freestanding fixtures need to be flexible enough to house several different types of merchandise, and should be easily moved about the shop to maximize retail exposure. The object is to create fixture and traffic patterns that showcase the products with the highest dollar per square foot in revenue. To achieve this, fixture style and positioning should guide the guests to walk through as much of the retail area as possible. Chapter 7 also provides a wealth of information that can assist in planning a new retail layout.

Laying out the retail space involves more than just fixtures for merchandise, though. Other considerations include placement of the retail counter, the electrical needs for the counter, data lines for the point of sale, and sufficient counter space for gift wrapping and storage of packaging supplies if that service will be offered.

Good lighting is essential in retailing and contributes to the ambiance and character of the retail environment. There are countless choices of light sources available, from recessed lights built into each shelf to spotlights on a ceiling track positioned to highlight the merchandise. Discuss the plans with the architect early in the process and also review the accent lighting placement for the merchandise display as well as the task lighting over the retail counter.

Since you will not put your entire inventory on display, assure you account for back room storage or for understock storage drawers or cabinets. When designing an efficient back room, the objective is to create an area for merchandise storage, a desk or work station for the retail manager (if that position is planned), and work space for merchandise check-in, tagging, steaming apparel, and packaging supplies. Also, if you plan to sell any apparel, the design should include a dressing room that is at least three feet by four feet.

## Create the Salon and Spa Logo

Next to the salon and spa itself, the logo can be one of the most valuable assets to your business and brand identity, as it is unique and exclusively yours.

Not only is the logo a tremendous revenue source, it offers advertising opportunities as well. Many consumers enjoy collecting logo wear as a badge of the many destination spas or resorts they have visited. Logo apparel can serve as a subliminal marketing tool when the guest, who is now back home, puts on her favorite sweatshirt and reminisces about the wonderful time she had at your salon and spa, and makes plans to return soon. A guest wearing a t-shirt with your logo may cause others to comment, "I see you're wearing a t-shirt from the Seasons Salon and Spa. I have considered going there myself; how was your visit?" leading to endorsement advertising for the Seasons Salon and Spa. If your business is based upon a local clientele, t-shirts and hats are a powerful advertising tool to establish your name around the community.

To get the most creative, quality design possible, you may wish to enlist the services of a graphic designer or company with experience in creating logos. The designer/company will need to know all of the potential logo applications that the salon and spa plans to use, because intricate artistic details may not translate well to embroidered pieces or screen-printing. It is important to consider the possibility of private label products and souvenir items such as hats and shirts. A professional embroidery tape digitizing service or screen printer will be able to determine if the logo artwork will adapt to embroidery or silk screening.

## Logo Application Using Embroidery

When considering embroidery work for salon and spa apparel, familiarize yourself with the methods, costs, and logo requirements prior to choosing a company to do your work. You can find potential vendors at trade shows or through your network of professionals. As when choosing product vendors, open up your schedule to

© Essl/www.Shutterstock.com

**FYI**

Think of your logo as the signature or symbol representing your business. Consistency and superior quality will establish the logo in the consumer's mind.

conduct some research and invite potential vendors to submit their proposals and show examples of their work. You will also want to provide examples of logo apparel that you like. Reflect on your market survey data and get ideas from quality clothing examples. When considering the quality of the embroidery, you may choose to specify the thread color and type. Because this can be a confusing and complicated process, consult with the logo artist or the embroiderer for their recommendations, as they are the experts. There are three major thread manufacturers, who produce charts that show samples of thread with a corresponding color number.

When selecting thread type, content is extremely important. There are five types of thread:

1. Cotton: The least popular, may bleed, shrink, and fade.
2. Rayon: Currently the most popular, is the most expensive of the five. Offering the largest color selection, rayon is colorfast and has the most luster, which enhances the logo quality.
3. Polyester: Proven successful for industrial use. For example, uniforms that withstand industrial cleaning need polyester thread because of its durability and colorfast quality.
4. Acrylic: Because of new thread technology, now offers an expanded color selection and is gaining strength in the industry. Although acrylic is the most durable and colorfast, rayon still remains the most popular.
5. Metallic: Becoming very popular and is price competitive with rayon. Silver and gold are standard, but colors are available by special order.

## Logo Application Using Silk Screen Printing

Screen printing or silk screening is a process that stencils a design or logo onto a product bottle or on fabric using special screen printing inks. Many products, such as bottles, t-shirts, sweatshirts, and tote bags, are silk-screen printed. If you are involved in developing private label products, put considerable attention into the silk-screening design of the bottle label, as the amount of detail and colors in the logo affect the process. In general, the logo will be very small on a bath product, reducing the amount of detail that can be screened on the bottle's logo. Furthermore, each silk screening pass to apply an additional color will add cost to the final product. Silk screening is a popular process for labeling your private label products or wearable logo items such as shirts and hats.

Silk screening is a very straightforward process. A screen printer stretches fine meshed fabric (silk, polyester, nylon) over a wood or metal frame and adheres a stencil to that fabric. Ink is then squeegeed across the stencil, leaving the impression. Some inks must be heat cured by sending the printed product through a drying tunnel. When using silk screening on fabrics, assure the print is pre-tested to determine whether ink will adhere to the product and remain colorfast.

When considering a silk-screening project, as with any vendor, do your research and interview several potential vendors. Bring in examples of products that give an idea of the design and quality you would like. Most screen printers use automatic equipment that allows printing of multicolor designs or logos with excellent registration. When supplying a screen printer with logo artwork, it is important to understand their requirements so you receive the best results possible.

## Develop a Merchandise Plan and Budget

When opening a new salon and spa and retail operation, the challenge is that there is no history to draw upon to determine the capital you should provide for purchasing retail inventory. A lack of history does not mean that you randomly pick a number and buy haphazardly until the budget is spent. In the operational business plan for the initial development of the salon and spa, there will be an assumption of retail revenue or, at minimum, a treatment revenue assumption. This point was briefly discussed in Chapter 8, when the components of a general business plan were mentioned.

This next example will recall information previously covered in Chapters 4 and 5 concerning inventory turnover target and cost of sales. Assume that the Printemps Salon and Spa is under development and the business plan calls for $300,000 in annual retail revenue.

- The next step is to determine the inventory turnover target. Assuming a four times turnover would result in an opening inventory at retail value of $75,000 ($75,000 × 4 = $300,000). If the spa then assumes a 50 percent overall cost of sales, the salon and spa professional should plan on spending approximately $35,000 to $40,000 for the retail inventory ($75,000 ÷ 50 = $37,500).

- The next step is to plan purchases by retail classification. There are no industry standard statistics to determine retail sales by classification or mix of sales for salons and spas. Sampling was done with the writing of the *Uniform System of Financial Reporting for Spas,* which suggests a potential distribution of revenue for a resort/hotel salon and spa (shown in the Financial Tools section of that book).
- Depending on the service makeup of your salon and spa, you will want to distribute your inventory investment accordingly. For example, a spa with an emphasis on skin care and body treatments may wish to allocate 50 percent of the inventory dollars on treatment products, 30 percent on apparel, and 20 percent on gifts and accessories. A salon will distribute the retail purchasing budget differently, with perhaps 50 percent on hair products, 30 percent on nail products, and 20 percent on makeup.

Using an example for the Urban Salon and Spa, where there may be many more styling stations than treatment rooms, the distribution of revenue may look more like this: Hair products, 47 percent; makeup, 10 percent; skin care, 20 percent; bath and body, 14 percent; and gift and accessories, 9 percent.

## Select the Point-of-Sale Computer System

Technology has increased the sophistication of point-of-sale systems to include perpetual inventory and open to buy schedules. Therefore, the sooner a system is selected for the retail operation, the better. You can begin using the system in the planning stages, smoothing the transition from planning to actual business. Early purchasing of a point-of-sale system will also give employees adequate time to train and understand the system. Many people will use the selected system every day. The system will need to adapt to the individual needs of the particular facility. If the retail operation is part of a larger operation such as a hotel or resort, you may look for a system that interfaces with other revenue areas such as a restaurant or accounting department.

You can investigate many different systems, doing thorough research as the system can represent an extremely large capital investment. You will want to request at least three references from the manufacturer of any hardware/software, following up with a call or a visit to each reference.

**FYI**

To find the most effective point-of-sale system, you should include all affected personnel in the decision-making process. They are often able to contribute details about what they will need the system to do.

An abundance of point-of-sale software is available to address the operational needs of the salon and spa business. Consider several factors when weighing the options of each type of software. First and foremost is an understanding of the salon and spa's requirements. Performing calculations, tracking ability, and reporting capabilities required by the operation can help determine the level of automation required of the system. In addition, evaluate the ease of use, speed, reliability, and whether there is a strong customer support service. Once you are comfortable with these factors, you can narrow the options further to include items that are perhaps not as vital, but can greatly enhance the system.

The requirements of each operation can differ significantly, but important to all salons and spas is the ability to track information about guests' preferences, previous purchases, and important guest notes. This is one of the benefits of implementing point-of-sale software, as capturing these details is nearly impossible without a certain level of automation. Ideally, software should simplify the process of identifying guests, selecting the items they wish to purchase, and processing the transaction with their chosen payment type. For convenience, the chosen system should have the capability to input new guest information as required for first-time visitors. The ability to query existing guest information and pull it into a transaction is also essential for accurate tracking and accumulation of sales. The capability to scan products at point of sale can reduce user error as well as prove to be a real-time saver. In addition to recognizing a UPC label, some systems can generate their own labels, providing an integrated approach from inventory management to retail sales.

The right system builds upon the close relationship between inventory maintenance and product sales—product sales should have the effect of reducing inventory while returns should offer the option of replacing to inventory. To assist the salon and spa in keeping a model/par stock (the amount of inventory to keep on hand), reporting should reflect a reorder point and quantity. This information eases planning for purchasing additional inventory. The ability to place and track purchase orders is an added benefit to any point-of-sale system and is an important aspect of maintaining accurate inventory counts.

The ease in which the system can perform special calculations is important. For example, the salon and spa may offer certain incentives to promote product sales, which could include a commission paid to staff members. These commissions should be captured. Additionally, the system should have the ability to capture the sale of promotional products, which are either given at no charge (such as a gift with purchase), or buy one and get second item at 50 percent off. The ease with which a software application can handle these functions can have an effect on the length of time involved in processing these transactions. For this reason, a system that can be configured based on the salon and spa's requirements so it can then respond as it should during the sale, avoiding the need for the staff members to perform additional steps. Where discounts are applicable, a combination of pre-configuration and manual intervention may be necessary. For example, automatic discounts applicable to specific types of guests or certain individuals should be programmed within the system to trigger automatically where appropriate, whereas discounts offered at the salon and spa's discretion will have to be determined on a case-by-case basis. In both cases, reporting should have the ability to reflect the discount amount and reason. Reporting should also have the capability to provide assistance in balancing at the end of a staff member's shift or end of day as well as to produce a variety of methods in which to analyze sales, payroll, and transaction information.

Additional security can be offered in a software system that provides the ability to distribute sensitive functions such as discounting and returns on a privileged basis, as determined by management. Audit tracking ability can provide a means of investigating any suspicious transactions as well as researching transactions on behalf of clients. For accurate balancing and for clients' records, the capability to generate detailed invoicing is paramount and is essential where gift certificate sales and redemptions are offered. The ability of the system to produce customized gift certificate formats can alleviate the need to purchase them through a separate vendor.

In keeping with the security efforts suggested by major credit card companies, the ability to handle payment information with discretion is becoming more of a priority. Therefore, more salons and spas are adopting credit card masking—the ability to display only the last four digits of the card number. The ability of the system to process these payments, as well as allowing guests to combine payment methods in any transaction is also highly important. At a resort/hotel salon and spa, if the software is not part of a larger property-wide system, its ability to interface with a variety of property management systems (PMSs) should be an important consideration as it can facilitate guestroom charges. Similarly, the capability to interface with a member billing system can provide a means to process charges to a variety of member accounts if the property includes a membership base.

While retail is an important source of revenue for salons and spas, the services themselves are still the basis of an individual's introduction to the business. For this reason, a point-of-sale system geared for the salon and spa industry should have the ability to quickly pull up reservation information for settlement at the point of sale where products can then be added to the transaction. Important to service sales will be the ability to track commissions payable, applicable service charges, and any discretionary gratuity administered by the guest. Also important will be the ability to acknowledge product recommendations estheticians or stylists make during services where a commission or incentive program exists. For ease of use, an ideal system should offer seamless integration between database appointment booking, guest check-in, and point of sale, as these areas are key to the salon and spa's contact with the guest.

In summary, some important factors for consideration are:
- Ease of use
- Speed
- Audit tracking
- Ability to perform returns
- Database capability
- Scan capability to avoid user error and the need to select from the menu
- Capability to produce UPC labels
- Ability to print invoices
- Ability to process various payment types and methods (split payment, transfer charges)
- Ability to quickly track guest information, preferences, and purchase history
- Ability to categorize item types being processed
- Reports to provide sales data by type, terminal, etc.
- Ability to track seller for calculating commission
- Security features (credit card masking, tracking, etc.)
- Entry of all items to be processed at POS, including flexibility in how items are grouped, price changes, stock levels, reorder levels
- Touch-screen compatibility

- Gift certificate sales, full and partial redemptions, tracking and reporting
- Reports to capture discounting
- For some resorts, the ability to interface to member billing systems and PMS systems to streamline billing functionality
- If using a member billing system, the visibility of the member number at POS is helpful, or guest type (as an indicator to the front desk)
- Note triggers to relay information pertinent to processing and completing guest transactions
- Opportunities for upselling
- Privileged/restricted functions for management only (e.g., price modifications)
- Ability to capture promotional products with or without a charge
- Offer a variety of discounting options (automatic, manual, percent, flat, specific items, guest type, etc.) that can be tracked
- Tips and service charges can be automatically calculated and distributed

Some other things to consider when reviewing point-of-sale systems for a new retail operation include features that make cumbersome processes easier; for example, you might look for automatic reordering triggers to help with inventory management. Look for software that provides the ability to create purchase orders and on-order logs, communicates directly with vendors electronically, and provides a self-directed system for inventory counts. Computerization, no matter how intimidating, should be seen as a management tool. Salon and spa professionals think of it as an automated consultant—it knows what to look for, finds the information, and gives it to them to act on. Look for a reputable vendor who knows and understands the salon and spa business. Look for a software program that is simple to use, but powerful in the information it provides. Great management software is a tool needed to operate the business efficiently today and grow the business for tomorrow.

## Explore Core Retail Treatment Products

As discussed in Chapter 3, selecting the right products for your services and retail operation are critical steps in making your salon and spa a success. Retail products must not only align with your philosophy and brand, but they must also help maintain the results the client experiences in the salon and spa. In addition to the questions covered in Chapter 3 regarding vendor selection, there are several things to consider about vendors and products before selecting your retail lines:

© argo74/www.Shutterstock.com

- What are the minimums for opening retail orders and reorders, and the lead times to get products in? What is the vendor's timeline for initial orders? For reorders?
- What evidence can the product representative provide that demonstrates retail sales by other salon and spa facilities (without divulging confidential information)? Vendors can provide statistics on best sellers and slow movers.
- How wide should the product order be to sell at-home regimens?
- What is the product's sales history, by item, to assist in determining opening par levels?
- What retail support marketing can the company provide, such as training, samples/testers, promotional help and marketing, collateral or co-op programs?
- What is the product's shelf life?
- Does the vendor provide indemnity insurance?
- What are the guidelines for samples and testers?
- What are some pricing strategies beyond the suggested retail price? Describe for your vendor the potential demographics of the salon and spa's guests and determine how well the products can target your guests' needs.
- What are the payment terms?
- Does the vendor have a return policy?
- What promotions does the line conduct during the year?
- In addition to training for the service providers, does the vendor provide training for retail sales associates or reception personnel?
- Does the vendor have a retail training guide for the products?

- What kind of collateral will the vendor provide to be given to salon and spa guests?
- Does the vendor have retail shelf talkers to assist guests in learning about the benefits of a specific product?
- Where else is the product sold in the area, and what are the vendor's national key accounts?
- Does the product labeling drive consumers to the vendor's website for reorders? If so, this will undermine your retail profits.
- Will your salon be listed on the vendor website as a retailer of their products?
- Will guests return to the salon and spa as suggested on the vendor's website?
- Will the vendor ship within the salon and spa's shipment and cancel date windows?
- Will the vendor reship backorder items at no cost?
- Are environmental considerations that are important to the salon and spa, such as packaging, met by the vendor?

# FOUR MONTHS FROM OPENING

Much work has already been done in preparation for the salon and spa retail opening, but there is still much left to do. Each step brings you closer to a trouble-free grand opening.

## Establish Sales and Inventory Procedures

Depending on the size of the salon and spa operation, the step of establishing sales and inventory procedures is done about four months before opening. Larger salons and spas with extensive product lines and inventory may require a longer lead time. One important step you will need to take is to establish charge accounts with each of your vendor partners. A quick way of doing this without continually searching for the information is to work with the accountant, if you have one, to create a credit form that contains all of the pertinent credit information about the salon and spa. This saves the time of completing individual credit applications from the many vendor partners with which the salon and spa will be working.

## Inventory Management

Accounting for your retail product is a big part of assuring your business is profitable. As discussed in Chapter 4, you will need to decide the frequency of retail inventories, and how you will handle transfers from retail inventory to professional products. This is such an important topic that it will be summarized here once again.

Unless it is appropriately recorded on a transfer log, the cost of the product may not get charged to professional products and may end up inflating the retail cost of goods sold. In Chapter 4, there is a much more detailed discussion of transfers.

Transfers may happen in some resort/hotel salons and spas where the resort gift shop also sells salon and spa merchandise, in which case the movement of merchandise from your retail space to another shop must be recorded. There is also a potential issue with resort VIP gifts, where the sales or catering manager will simply walk into the salon and spa retail area and pull some merchandise to give to a VIP guest. Well before the entire salon and spa opens, it is important to establish guidelines for what the sales or marketing departments (if such entities exist) will be charged for the merchandise, and whether it will be at retail or at cost. It is suggested that some standardized gift ideas are created for VIP gifts, either with costs or gratis. In addition, an authorization form must be in place very early, since spa gifts may be given out for promotions months before the facility opens. It may be wise to order a separate stock for VIPs and marketing use, so that the salon and spa retail operation does not face the service predicament of being out of stock for the paying guests.

It is customary to extend employee discounts to salon and spa employees for retail merchandise. Standard discounts are 25 to 30 percent for resort/hotel salon and spa employees, 30 to 50 percent for day spas or salon employees, and 40 to 50 percent for managers and executives. If employees are allowed to make purchases at cost, you need to decide whether the item will be subtracted from inventory value or if the purchases will be shown as an employee discount, and factored into the overall cost of goods sold for the retail department.

Other questions to consider at this stage include: What will be the retail department's policy with respect to returns? Will the salon and spa charge postage/courier charges for retail products mailed to the guest's home? Review the market survey to determine the standard shipping charges from competitors. If you are part of a resort/hotel, look at how this is handled at other retail outlets on the property.

## Establish a Commission Strategy

Four months before opening is the right time to construct the preliminary commission plan. Before you begin to recruit retail leadership, retail consultants, or even the service providers, develop the basic retail commission plan. Who should be included in any retail commissions—the supervisor, just the service staff, front desk staff, and/or retail consultants? Will the policy be a flat percentage commission or will retail goals be established for each staff member, with the commission calculated on a tiered scale based on achievement? Will the commission structure be tiered according to the profit margin of the item sold? It is important when management starts interviewing potential employees that they are able to communicate any retail commissions that will be part of the employee's compensation. Commission suggestions are discussed in more detail in Chapter 2.

## Finalize Opening Inventory Value and Begin Merchandise Purchases

Although the pre-opening retail planning example used previously would suggest that the salon and spa should have an inventory value of $40,000, the fact is that the dollars to purchase the inventory must be included in the overall pre-opening budget. It is important, therefore, to finalize the amount that can be spent for opening retail inventory and to make any classification allocation adjustments before the retail merchandise purchasing process begins. The initial purchases for retail inventory are not an expense of the salon and spa on the statement of income, but are recorded as an asset on the balance sheet.

Each month, starting with the beginning inventory, add to that any merchandise at cost received during the period, and subtract the ending inventory to determine the cost of goods sold. Remember, inventories are still a "cash" transaction and the salon and spa must have the capital resources to purchase retail merchandise. Thus it is essential that a final purchasing plan be developed to avoid a situation where the salon and spa has committed to $40,000 worth of retail purchases, only to discover that it no longer has $40,000 to allocate to retail inventory, but only $30,000. This would mean that the salon and spa could not make any additional commitments unless adjustments were made to purchasing plan.

Purchase orders (POs) must be used for all of the retail purchases to maintain appropriate records. For products that are used both as a treatment (professional product) and a retail product, you will use separate POs for each purchase. Vendors will often provide a purchase confirmation that can be checked against physical purchases for errors and retained along with the original purchase order. Record all retail purchases on an "on order log," which is organized by delivery date. Individual files can be set up for each retail vendor as purchases are made. To develop harmonious vendor relationships that meet the salon and spa's needs, establish an earliest delivery date and a date after which the salon and spa reserves the right to cancel the order. You will not want boxes of new retail merchandise stacking up for a month or two before the doors open for business. It is appropriate to ask for the merchandise to be delivered three to four weeks before the anticipated opening. It can then be stored in a secure area separate from other operating supplies.

## Develop a Retail Marketing Plan

Time is needed to plan a specific salon and spa retail promotional direction. Some promotional and sales opportunities are easy, such as fall and winter holidays, Valentine's Day, and Mother's Day, but those three annual events will not result in a plan to maximize retail revenue.

In Chapter 8 there are numerous suggestions for retail marketing plans and promotions. In general, some examples might include:

- Gift with purchase programs
- Special pricing for groups of products
- Buy one and receive a percentage off a second companion item

There are also countless seasonal promotions that can be implemented in addition to the typical holiday promotions. Examples might include:

- Summer promotions for sun products, waxing and pedicure treatments, promotions for swimsuits and sandals, special facials for sun-damaged skin, or even anti-cellulite treatments
- Father's Day special with men's treatments and products
- Graduation specials, as students have now graduated to care for their skin as adults
- Wedding promotions for the bride and groom—give them a special relaxation product basket to treat themselves after the big day or matching robes for bride and groom

- A makeup promotion for graduations or just before the holidays
- New product launches
- Seasonal apparel
- A winter promotion for dry skin in the cold of winter

There are hundreds of additional ideas limited only by the professional's imagination. The salon and spa's vendor partners can help identify cooperative promotional events or advertising opportunities and develop a promotional calendar for retail for the year, which can be reviewed on a quarterly basis. Discussion of these opportunities should be a regular part of the salon and spa professionals' dialogue with vendors. Even small/independent operators may be surprised at what is available to them if they consistently ask their vendors these types of questions.

## Develop Processes for Retail Direct Mail and Mail Order

The easiest customer to sell is the one who has already purchased product from the retail operation. All that has to be done is to establish a system to collect e-mail addresses, mailing addresses, or telephone numbers and to maintain a guest history card or program. For example, a guest buys a night cream that should last approximately 30 days. That guest would probably consider it a high level of service to receive a card or e-mail asking how they liked the product, and suggesting that additional product be shipped to them. Better yet, the follow-up promotion can tell the guest that the salon and spa is having a special offer on that product offering a 20 percent discount if they buy two or three of the products. Tell the guest that the salon and spa does not charge for shipping (if applicable) and invite them to call anytime they need a special product.

Some salons and spas have been able to increase their retail revenue by 20 to 40 percent with an effective mail order process. The names and addresses that are collected at the retail space can form the beginning of a database for direct mail programs announcing new products or treatments or highlighting special promotions throughout the year.

## Select a Packaging and Gift Wrap Program

Packaging is a vital merchandising tool. It is an excellent opportunity to create logo awareness and promotional exposure for the salon and spa. This, along with development of a saleable logo and its use on merchandise, are two very important steps in salon and spa branding. The packaging can also be used as a display tool inside the retail area. With packaging, the color, texture, and design are important. The interior design of the salon and spa should guide you in the packaging selections. A typical packaging program would include:

- Merchandise bags
- Gift boxes
- Tissue
- Gift baskets and fill
- Ribbon
- Wrapping paper
- Double stick tape
- Paper rack or bar cutter
- Price tags/hangtags
- Shipping labels
- Sales check/receipts forms

There are several choices for packaging suppliers. If you intend to include your logo on the gift boxes or merchandise bags, it is important to source the packaging materials four to six months before the opening.

## Source Remaining Retail Merchandise

At this point in the salon and spa's critical path countdown, the major product classifications have probably been selected, including key skin care, hair, and nail treatment products, plus the peripheral support lines for body treatments and bath and body products, if applicable. Additionally, for spas, final decisions have likely been made with respect to the spa robes and towels and sandals. The logo has been finalized, embroidery tapes have been produced, and basic apparel lines have been selected. Now it is time to source the other potential retail products such as accessories and home goods, for example.

Vendor suggestions for these additional retail products may be found in professional directories or on websites. There may also be a gift show or gift merchandise mart nearby where you can shop for potential merchandise. The competitive retail survey can provide vendor leads, as will an Internet search.

If you have a spa, one of the challenges with spa retail is coming up with a unique retail "feel," since most spas will feature bath and body products, skin care lines, candles, robes, and so on. Just as most people look for distinctive shops and retail stores when they travel, hoping to find more than just the same old stores in every town, the same holds true for the spa guest. They are looking for points of difference as they shop.

It is important to stay true to the salon and spa theme and to select products that remain consistent with the core purpose and philosophy.

Establishing your brand and remaining consistent is important to your salon and spa. It is also wise to capitalize on the unique characteristics or location that makes your salon and spa special.

For example, if your salon and spa is in the southwestern desert or on a northern lake, source products that will enable the guest to take home merchandise that will bring them back to the essence of their visit with you. If products do not adequately convey that essence, explore artisans in the area who may craft beautiful ceramic bowls that could be used to display towels in the master bath of the guest's home or Native American weavings or beadwork that will connect guests with history when they look at it back home. In some cases these artisans will be willing to work with you on a consignment basis, which means that the salon and does not have to commit inventory capital to carry the merchandise in its retail space.

Distinctive merchandise displayed in retail showcases or in the window of your retail area will act as a magnet to draw guests into the space. Whether or not they purchase that distinctive product, guests are likely to find other merchandise in the boutique that they will choose to purchase. Some salons and spas go overboard on finding unique products and miss opportunities to maximize sales and profits on their key items. A general rule of thumb is that "unique and different" should represent 20 percent or less, and core items should be the remaining 80 percent. In other words, items that you can reorder and that are consistent with the business should be at least 80 percent of sales and inventory. Whether core products or unique items, all retail purchases are made with the goal of matching the philosophy of the retail operation with the salon and spa's overall philosophy.

Small salon and spa operators, or salons and spas with limited retail space, may say that they do not have the opportunity to carry additional merchandise beyond the basic skin care, bath and body, hair, and nail merchandise. They should take into consideration that the salon and spa would be leaving retail sales dollars on the table as guests would be willing to buy these additional merchandise items if they were available. The key questions to ask are whether the salon and spa has the capital to invest in additional retail inventory and how well that merchandise can be displayed or whether additional design and fixturing is required.

# TWO MONTHS FROM OPENING

With only two months to go, you must now attend to details that will make the retail opening run smoothly for managers, employees, and guests.

## Recruit a Retail Supervisor or Retail Consultants

Retail in a salon and spa is handled in several ways. If the salon and spa is large with a dedicated retail area, it will probably have a retail manager or supervisor and dedicated retail consultants. In some cases, the retail is displayed in the reception area of the salon and spa, but retail floor staff works the area, asking guests whether they can be of assistance. In other salons and spas, the retail is simply another function of the reception desk staff. The salon and spa relies solely on the therapists or technicians to influence retail sales or for guests to find something of interest by themselves.

Often, the salon and spa director or the owner/operator of a salon and spa assumes responsibility for the retail department, yet may have very little expertise in managing a retail operation. One of the purposes of this text is to better equip the individual responsible for retail with the basic tools to manage a retail operation. Clearly, salons and spas that have dedicated personnel and provide training specific to retail selling techniques have demonstrated higher levels of sales and profits that justify their investments.

When looking for retail leadership, you can post positions on the job board associated with your salon and spa professional organization. In addition, you can advertise in the local newspapers or trade publications. If there is a college or university in the area that offers a merchandising program, make contact there for graduating students looking for employment.

## HERE'S A TIP

The ideal candidate for salon and spa retail would be someone who has been a supervisor for the cosmetics area of a traditional department store, or a health and beauty store operation, and who also has some merchandising education. Or it may be someone who has worked as a retail buyer for a specialty or traditional retailer.

It is unlikely that prospective hires will have all the knowledge needed to manage all aspects of the salon and spa retail department and they will need support from management. Some spas will contract with a retail buyer or consultant to handle the buying, inventory management, and merchandising on a part-time basis, including ongoing periodic reviews of the retail performance, and counsel and reports to salon and spa leadership.

## Finalize the Retail Commission Structure

At this point, you have identified the retail supervisor. Together, review the preliminary work done on establishing the retail commission structure and finalize the plan before recruiting the remaining staff.

## Purchase Operating Supplies

There's nothing more frustrating than reaching for a needed supply and not finding it. To avoid that problem, make certain to purchase office supplies well before opening day. You may want to consider integrating your logo or branding efforts into the printed supplies you use. Especially for resort/hotel salons and spas at the four- or five-star levels and higher-end day spas, consistency of style/type/colors and materials is important; use of an expert's eye (such as a graphic artist's opinion) would be helpful, even for supplies. The following list offers suggestions to help guide the process of gathering these items:

**Merchandise:**
____ Bulletin board/push pins
____ Cash register tape
____ Client books
____ Delivery scale and setup kit
____ Pins/pin cushions
____ Retractable knife
____ Sale and promo signage
____ Scissors
____ Seam ripper
____ Shipping boxes, tape, labels
____ Steamer
____ Tagger machine
____ Tagger gun and tags

**Office Supplies:**
____ Broom
____ Calculator/adding machine and tape

——  Calendars
——  CDs
——  Desk trays
——  Desk drawer organizers
——  Duster, window cleaner, towels
——  Dustpan
——  Envelopes
——  Extension cords
——  Fax machine
——  File cabinet; file folders and labels
——  Hole punch
——  Letter openers
——  Liquid paper
——  Markers/highlighters
——  Name tags
——  Notebooks and dividers
——  Paper
——  Paper clips and holder
——  Pencils/sharpener
——  Pens
——  Phone message pads
——  Post-it notes
——  Rolodex
——  Rubber bands
——  Ruler
——  Screwdriver
——  Stapler/staples
——  Tape/dispensers: transparent, double-sided, packing
——  Trash cans
——  Vacuum
——  Yellow pads/notebooks

## Finalize the Gift Certificate Program

Some steps to take before finalizing and offering a gift certificate program include:

- Research local and state laws regarding the purchase of gift certificates/cards.
- Determine whether gift certificates should be for designated treatment packages or dollar amounts.
- Establish records/procedures for the sale of gift certificates and related transactions.

## Establish Reorder/Restock Procedures

Retail inventory must be monitored closely to determine rate of sale for core products. Once established, you can determine stock levels and set reorder points to allow time to receive shipments from the vendor before the product sells out.

## Determine Pricing Strategies

When establishing retail prices, consider perceived value and what the market will bear based on distribution. You can review the market surveys you conducted several months earlier to get an idea of what your competitors' price points are, and also take into consideration the demographics of your target customers.

When setting initial markup (discussed in detail in Chapter 5), most salon and spa retailers settle on a 100 percent markup and operate at 50 to 55 percent margin. Therefore, an item that is $4 at cost with a 100 percent markup will retail for $8. If it retails for $10, the mark up is 150 percent and the margin is 60 percent. Many new or small retailers are enamored by the notion of paying $9 for a product and selling it for $30, but in reality their primary concern should be selling more volume. Pricing that is based on impressive markups may not help you achieve the goal of maximizing sales volume. As the old retail saying goes, "It is better to make fast nickels than slow dimes."

# FOUR WEEKS FROM OPENING

With only a month until opening day, everything starts to come together. Merchandise arrives, staff members begin training, and you ensure that all loose ends are tied up.

## Hire Staff and Set Training Schedules

The retail manager/supervisor, or other person designated to support management with responsibility for retail, now reviews applications and hires the retail consultants if any are planned for the retail department.

The key is training the staff. There is no question that you will want to arrange for a professional trainer or vendor trainers to come in and work with the service providers. It is important to include the guest receptionists and/or the staff responsible for retail sales in the retail area in this training, as product knowledge is the key to increased retail revenues. You may also want to consider training specific to retail sales techniques.

Create a Policy and Procedures Manual with a section on retail that will be the guide to organizing the training subjects. The product vendor partners can be a great help in providing merchandise-specific materials. The key for retail product training is to focus on the product attributes and benefits for the retail staff.

Other subjects to be developed for retail consultants are:
- Establishing customer rapport
- Selling skills
- Retail sales goals
- Stocking, folding, and retail aesthetics
- Daily operations
- Gift certificate sales transactions
- Returns
- Special orders
- Promotions
- Mail order
- Merchandising
- Employee discounts
- Product transfers from retail to professional products
- VIP gifts
- Daily sales reporting
- Opening and closing procedures

## Bring the Point-of-Sale System Online

Begin using the point-of-sale system and training other retail staff in how to use the software. Training should include learning all of the processes that will be used during a typical day, as well as procedures that may be unique, such as commissions, discounts, member billing, etc. It's better to find the bugs in the system and work them out before opening day.

## Start Receiving and Ticketing Merchandise

For a new salon and spa retail operation, keeping the merchandise receiving logs updated helps you to know just what retail merchandise has been received. Every effort is made to isolate received merchandise in one place separate from all other operating supplies. Some salons and spas will try to dedicate one of the treatment rooms to retail storage unless the backroom storage is of sufficient size and can be secured. This helps to

SALON AND SPA
SNAPSHOT 9.3

At Beauty 20/20...
Training Day Fun

Beauty 20/20, a salon and spa in Austin, TX, offers a wide array of retail items in a separate store next to the salon and spa. The retail space was designed to be a stand-alone entity, with a breezeway separating the service side of the business. Because Beauty 20/20 is planning an extensive grand opening, the dry run of the retail operation took the form of a "Friends and Family" night. Peter and Stephanie, the owners, knew what it was like to open a store, and wanted to provide a safe environment for the team. "In a safe environment, employees could practice ringing up real sales on the register, input client information, and practice the entire sales protocol. The festive shopping party resulted in a great opportunity to try out sales techniques, practice register operations, and to just shake off the jitters associated with opening day." Stephanie felt the team was more polished and less stressed on opening day because of the time to have the trial run.

avoid merchandise shrinkage and helps to keep the merchandise organized. As product is received, each box is marked with the contents then stored in the designated secure area or staging location until it is placed on the retail shelves.

# THE FINAL COUNTDOWN CHECKLIST

The last few weeks before opening may seem like crunch time, but if you have followed a solid six-month (or longer) pre-opening plan, you will feel well prepared for opening the doors to your guests. Only a few more details remain before celebrating a successful launch.

## Two to Three Weeks from Opening

- Arrange fixtures, supplies, and packaging.
- Prepare merchandise for display.
- Enter merchandise data into the computer system.
- Continue product/retail and point-of-sale training for staff.
- Audit purchase order ledger to ensure all goods have been shipped; request tracking numbers.

## One Week from Opening

- Finalize retail space setup, begin setting merchandise on shelves.
- Purchase visual props to enhance product presentation.
- Practice register procedures.
- Complete merchandise training for all products.
- Assign associates to specific merchandise responsibilities.

# CHAPTER SUMMARY

- A systematic approach to planning your retail operation will allow you to track your milestones leading to the launch.
- You will want to thoroughly understand the market before you make any purchases. A competitive market survey will focus on elements including the service delivery, service menu, and product offerings.
- You can get ideas for displaying merchandise by going to specialty stores and making observations.
- The salon and spa logo can be one of the most valuable assets to your business.
- You will want to distribute your inventory dollars in proportion to the service makeup of your salon and spa.
- Important factors to look for in choosing a POS system include ease of use, speed, database, invoice printing, touch screen capability, gift certificate processing, security features, and guest history.
- A well thought out marketing plan will increase exposure to the retail space.
- Mail order and direct mail are great ways to drive repeat business.
- It is important to establish the commission plan prior to hiring the staff, as it will be part of their compensation.
- Ideal retail managers are those with prior experience, either as a supervisor in a traditional department store (with merchandising experience), beauty store operation experience, or experience as a retail buyer.

# LEARNING ACTIVITIES

## Learning Activity 9-1: Be the Research Expert

Imagine that you are opening a new salon and spa and have been tasked with conducting a market survey of the competitors. Using the market survey form from this chapter, select two retail operations that are competitors to your salon and spa retail operation and complete the market survey form for both of them. Write a report that answers the following questions:

- What opportunities are not being met by the current salon and spa retail market?
- What are the areas of difference among the competition?
- What attributes of each competitor have the most effect?
- How can the new salon and spa retail operation create its own market niche?

## Learning Activity 9-2: Tell Me About Your Computers

After reviewing the information on selecting a point-of-sale system in this chapter, develop a request for proposal for a new POS system for your salon and spa's retail operation. Include items that you require in your system, as well as items that are not essential, but would be beneficial to improve your facility's inventory management.

# REVIEW QUESTIONS

1. Which of the following tasks are typically performed six months before opening?
    a. Establish a commission strategy
    b. Recruit a retail supervisor
    c. Purchase operating supplies
    d. Create a logo

2. An ideal point-of-sale system for a day spa or salon will include all of the following features, EXCEPT:
- a. Ability to interface with a property management system
- b. Ability to track information about guest preferences and past purchases
- c. Ability to place and track purchase orders
- d. Ability to mask credit card information

3. What type of retail fixture is often given to a millwork contractor to build?
- a. Built-in
- b. Freestanding
- c. Shelving
- d. Dress forms

4. Which of the following statements about a salon and spa's logo is FALSE?
- a. Consistency and superior quality establishes the logo in the mind of the guest.
- b. Many guests enjoy collecting salon and spa logo wear.
- c. Intricate, artistic details in a logo always transfer well to embroidered pieces.
- d. Logo apparel can be a subliminal marketing tool.

5. The Printemps Salon and Spa has budgeted $50,000 for opening retail inventory purchases. It has allocated 25 percent of that for gifts and accessories. Within that classification, it has allocated 75 percent for how-to books and relaxation CDs. How much money has been earmarked for books and CDs?
- a. $37,500
- b. $12,500
- c. $15,000
- d. $9,375

6. Jazmine attends an art fair that features the works of local artisans, looking for merchandise for the retail boutique of the new Printemps Salon and Spa. She is particularly interested in the work of an artist who incorporates delicate pressed wildflowers into a variety of products, including note cards, earrings, and sun catchers. Jazmine thinks that this artist's line meshes perfectly with the salon and spa's "springtime" theme. Each of the following statements supports her decision to purchase these products for the retail operation, EXCEPT:

   a. It is wise to capitalize on the unique characteristics that make this salon and spa special.
   b. "Unique and different" items should represent 20 percent or less of the salon and spa's merchandise.
   c. Salon and spa retail operations should carry merchandise that represents the basic experience, such as bath and body products, skin care lines, candles, and robes.
   d. Guests are willing to buy additional merchandise items beyond the basic skin care, bath and body, hair, and nail merchandise if they are available.

7. Which of the following candidates would be the best hire for retail manager of a large salon and spa boutique?

   a. Paige, an esthetician with three years of experience in retail.
   b. Marguerite, an assistant manager for the cosmetics department at a Marshall Field's department store.
   c. Leo, a food and beverage manager at a restaurant.
   d. Alana, a receptionist at a day spa with a small retail space in the reception area.

8. Jazmine collects information such as mailing addresses and e-mail addresses from all of the guests who visit the new Printemps Salon and Spa within its first month of business. She then sends a postcard inviting them to return to the spa within the next 30 days to receive 20 percent off their next purchase at the boutique. This is an example of:

   a. Seasonal promotion
   b. Vendor co-op
   c. Direct mail program
   d. Telemarketing

9. Establishing guidelines for how the retail operation will handle transfers of retail product for professional use, for sales to the resort's sales or marketing department, or for VIP gifts, typically happens:
   a. Two months before opening
   b. Six months before opening
   c. One month before opening
   d. Four months before opening

10. Robin is directing the opening of a new salon in a mid-size metropolitan area. It will open downtown and cater to business people. It focuses on quick service for the busy professional. Robin is conducting a market survey to find out what the competition is offering in retail. Which of the following operations would be most relevant to include in his survey?
   a. A hair salon that is 200 miles away.
   b. A store selling discounted beauty supplies on the same block as the salon.
   c. The day spa in a neighboring county that shares an owner with her new salon.
   d. Robin's former day spa in the suburbs, which he left to open this salon.

# Appendix 1
## RESOURCES FOR FURTHER STUDY

This book provides an overview of retail management for salons and spas. Many other resources are available that can provide further information and guidance to spa professionals who want to expand their knowledge of this important area of salon and spa management.

## Beauty Industry Resources

Milady, a part of Cengage Learning, Clifton Park, NY
    (800) 998-7498
    delmar.milady@cengage.com
    milady.cengage.com
Online continuing education for professionals
    Milady U: miladyonline.cengage.com
National Coalition of Estheticians Associations NCTA
    (201) 670-4100
    nceaorg@aol.com
    ncea.tv
Green Book. (2012). American Salon & American Spa. Questex Media
    Group LLC.

## SPA Industry Resources

International Spa Association, Lexington, KY
    (888) 651-4772
    ispa@ispastaff.com
    experienceispa.com
Certified Spa Supervisor and Retail Management courses, and Risk
    Management for Spa e-Learning course
Day Spa Association
    (877) 851-8998
    dsa@DaySpaAssociation.com
    dayspaassociation.com
Order these resources directly from the ISPA website at
    experienceispa.com
    ISPA 2011 consumer trends report. (2011). Lexington, KY: International
      SPA Association.
    ISPA 2011 spa industry study. (2011). Lexington, KY: International SPA
      Association.

Uniform system of financial reporting for spas. (2004). Lexington, KY: ISPA Foundation.

Diagonal Reports "USA Day Spa Market 2010," (2011). GSS Delegates ©Diagonal Reports 2011.

## General Online Resources

American Salon
  americansalonmag.com
American Spa
  spatrade.com/americanspa
Behind the Chair
  behindthechair.com
California Cosmetology Association
  the-cca.com

As you transition into your new career in the beauty and wellness industry, let us continue the journey with you. Be sure to check out miladyednet.com to prepare for your State Board Exam and gain access to additional resources to hit the ground running as a licensed professional, ensuring long-term success no matter where your career may take you.

Milady, a part of Cengage Learning
  milady.cengage.com
Modern Salon
  modernsalon.com
NailPro
  nailpro.com
Pro Beauty
  probeauty.org

## Distributor Resources

Salon Centric
  (800) 282-2843
  saloncentric.com

## Cosmoprof

Customer Service US: (888) 206-1192
Customer Service Canada: (888) 241-3330
cosmoprofbeauty.com

# FURTHER READING

AGM merchandising manual. (1999). Fountain Hills, AZ: Association of Golf Merchandisers.

Ander, W. N., & Stern, N. Z. (2004). Winning at Retail. Hoboken, NJ: John Wiley & Sons.

D'Angelo, J. M. (2010). Spa Business Startegies: A Plan for Success. 2nd edition. Clifton Park, NY: Milady, a part of Cengage Learning.

Dion, J. E. (2001). Retail Selling Ain't Brain Surgery, It's Twice As Hard. Chicago: Dionco, Inc.

Dion, J. E., & Topping, T. (2000). Start and Run a Profitable Retail Business. Bellingham, WA: Self-Counsel Press.

Falk, E. A. (2003). 1001 Ideas to Create Retail Excitement. Prentice Hall Press; Revised edition

Johnson, L., & Learned, A. (2004). Don't Think Pink. New York: AMACOM.

Milady (2011). Financial Analysis and Coaching Tools. Clifton Park, NY: Milady, a part of Cengage Learning.

Milady (2012). Retail Analysis and Coaching Tools. Clifton Park, NY: Milady, a part of Cengage Learning.

Phillips, C. (1995). In the Bag: Selling in the Salon. Clifton Park, NY: SalonOvation/Milady.

Phillips, C. Complete Carol Phillips Selling Library. (Audio/Video/DVD). Gainesville, VA: Encompass One.

Schroeder, C. L. (2004). Specialty Shop Retailing: How to Run Your Own Store. Hoboken, NJ: John Wiley & Sons.

Tezak, E. J. (2012). Successful Salon and Spa Management, 6th edition. Clifton Park, NY: Milady, a part of Cengage Learning.

Underhill, P. (1999). Why We Buy: The Science of Shopping. New York: Simon & Schuster.

Underhill, P. (2004). Call of the Mall. New York: Simon & Schuster.

Whalin, G. (2001). Retail Success. San Marcos, CA: Willoughby Press.

# Appendix 2
## REVIEW QUESTIONS ANSWER KEY

### Chapter 1

1. c
2. d
3. a
4. d
5. a
6. b
7. d
8. d
9. b
10. d

### Chapter 2

1. a
2. b
3. c
4. d
5. b
6. a
7. a
8. a
9. b
10. b

### Chapter 3

1. c
2. d
3. d
4. a
5. d
6. c
7. a
8. c
9. a
10. b

### Chapter 4

1. c
2. a
3. b
4. d
5. b
6. d
7. b
8. a
9. c
10. c

### Chapter 5

1. c
2. a
3. d
4. b
5. d
6. c
7. c
8. a
9. b
10. d

### Chapter 6

1. c
2. a
3. c
4. b
5. a
6. d
7. d
8. a
9. c
10. d

### Chapter 7

1. a
2. a
3. b
4. b
5. c
6. d
7. b
8. c
9. d
10. b

### Chapter 8

1. c
2. a
3. d
4. b
5. b
6. a
7. d
8. b
9. d
10. b

### Chapter 9

1. d
2. a
3. a
4. c
5. d
6. c
7. b
8. c
9. d
10. b

# Glossary

**Advertising.** Calling attention to one's product or service through announcements in media including newspapers, magazines, flyers on the Internet, or radio.

**Average Retail Inventory.** The sum of the beginning of the month inventory (retail value) for each month of the year.

**Average Retail Markdown.** A calculation used to evaluate the impact of coupons and discounts taken on the total retail revenue.

$$\text{Retail Markdown Taken} \div \text{Total Retail Revenue}$$
$$= \text{Average Retail Markdown}$$

**Booking Ratio.** A customer traffic ratio used for sales planning to determine retail sales opportunities.

**Brand.** The attributes of a company and the image that is communicated through marketing and advertising. It is a perception or image of the business that sets it apart from the competition.

**Brand Ambassador.** A member of the staff who serves as the subject matter expert and educator of a particular product line.

**Brand Identity.** The philosophy of a business that is communicated and experienced through the staff, service models, and décor.

**Business Plan.** A written document that conveys important aspects about a business for planning and tracking growth over a given period.

**Color Block.** Keeping like-colored items together for visual impact in merchandising.

**Compensating Errors.** Two or more errors that are set against each other so the accounts will balance.

**Compensation.** What an individual receives for working in the salon or spa. These include base pay, commission, benefits, training, and non-monetary rewards.

**Core Values.** The key principles that support the mission statement and guide decision making.

**Cost Complement.** Once the mark-up goal percentage is considered, the cost complement is 100 minus the mark-up goal.

**Cost of Goods Sold.** The direct cost, including freight, of merchandise purchased for resale. This number is typically expressed as a dollar amount but is converted to a percentage to become the cost of sales.

$$(\text{Initial Inventory} + \text{Purchases}) - \text{End Inventory} = \text{Cost of Goods Sold}$$

**Cost of Sales.** The profitability of retail sales expressed as a percentage.

$$\text{The Cost of Goods} \div \text{Total Retail Revenue} = \text{Cost of Sales}$$

**Education.** A learning process that builds up over time as knowledge is acquired, skills are developed, thought processes are changed, and lessons are learned through experience.

**Gross Margin.** The profit derived from sales after the cost of goods sold and before payroll and other expense items are deducted. It is calculated by subtracting the Cost of Sales percentage from 100.

**Impulse Item.** Any unplanned purchase a guest makes upon check out. These are usually small, inexpensive items chosen near the checkout counter.

**Key Item.** An item that is a consistent part of the store's inventory and which is reordered regularly.

**Maintained Markup.** The consistent amount above cost at which goods are sold.

$$\text{Gross Margin} \div \text{Net Sales} = \text{Maintained Markup}$$

**Margin.** The profit derived from sales after the cost of goods and other deductions are subtracted.

**Markdowns.** Any reduction in retail price after merchandise has been received into stock.

**Marketing.** The activity of creating, communicating, delivering, and exchanging offerings that have value for guests.

**Marketing Plan.** Part of the business plan that gives a detailed strategy about how to promote the business, build a customer base, and make a profit.

**Mission Statement.** An explicit statement that sets forth the purpose of the business that is publicly communicated and part of the brand and core values.

**Net Retail Revenue.** Subtracting the total retail adjustments (employee discounts, merchandise returns, and allowances such as overcharges or undercharges) from the total retail revenue.

**Open to Buy.** A budgeting calculation stating the amount of stock in retail dollars that the buyer is open to receiving into stock during a certain period.

$$\text{(Beginning of Month Inventory} - \text{Monthly Sales)} - \text{Markdowns} + \text{Purchases} = \text{End of Month Forecast}$$

$$\text{Planned End} + \text{of Month Inventory} - \text{End of Month Forecast} = \text{Open to Buy}$$

**Over-Assorted.** Carrying too many styles from a wide assortment of vendors.

**Par Stock/Model Stock.** The ideal number of items to carry based upon average sales and planned inventory turns. This may change due to seasonality. Par Stock is hotel/resort terminology; Model stock is retail terminology.

**Perishable.** Goods that lose their appeal over time.

**Philosophy.** A statement of the main beliefs conveying what a business stands for.

**Retail.** The sale of physical goods or merchandise directly to consumers.

**Retail Classifications.** A grouping that identifies merchandise with a similar end use.

**Retail Inventory Method.** Utilizing the retail value of goods (not cost) when calculating sales statistics.

**Retail per Service Ticket.** A calculation used to evaluate the average amount of merchandise sold per customers receiving services, allowing the retail per service provider to be tracked.

Total Revenue from Retail Service Tickets ÷ Number of Service Tickets = Retail per Service Ticket

**Retail per Ticket.** A calculation used to compare average retail sales to the number of tickets.

Total Retail Revenue ÷ Total Number of Tickets = Retail per Ticket

**Retail Plan.** A plan outlining the product lines carried, retail mix, budget, purchasing process, vendors, and pricing.

**Retail Sales Contribution by Classification.** A calculation used to evaluate the impact of a particular product classification on the total retail sales.

Classification Sales ÷ Total Retail Sales = Classification Sales Percentage

**Retail Sales per Square Foot.** A calculation to monitor retail revenue contribution within the salon and spa retail space.

Total Retail Revenue ÷ Total Square Footage of Retail Space = Retail Revenue per Square Foot

**Retail Sales Percentage.** A calculation used to evaluate the impact of retail sales on the total salon and spa revenue.

Net Retail Revenue ÷ Total Salon/Spa Revenue = Retail Sales Percentage

**Revenue Adjustments.** Adjustments to revenue, which may include employee discounts, merchandise returns, overages, and undercharges.

**Stock-to-Sales Ratio.** A calculation allowing you to keep the proper level of inventory on hand.

Monthly Sales ÷ Beginning of Month Inventory (at retail)
= Sales to Stock Ratio

**Sell Through.** A product performance percentage rate to tell you how well a product is selling.

Weekly Sales ÷ Beginning Inventory for the Week = Sell Through

**Sell Through Percentage.** A percentage comparing the amount of inventory received from a vendor in units against the units actually sold.

Units Sold ÷ Units Received = Sell Through Percentage

**Shelf Sculpting.** Arranging items on a shelf so the outline is visually appealing by size, shape, and color, for example, from smallest to tallest, in a pyramid shape, or keeping the color packaging of a product line together.

**Shelf Talker.** The official term for signage that gives the shopper a thumbnail sketch of the product or collection. It is placed near products to communicate value to customers.

**Shrinkage.** The difference between the actual inventory count on hand and what the records state.

Physical Inventory – Book Inventory = Shrinkage

**Social Media.** A virtual communication tool that connects people online with applications such as Facebook and Twitter.

**Spiffs.** Vendor rewards provided to staff to recognize sales achievements.

**Subclassifications.** Defining retail classifications further to show variables such as price, type, or brand.

**Target Market.** A specific group of people with something in common to whom you are selling, or wish to sell, your products and services.

**Total Retail Revenue.** The sum total of retail revenue from each product classification. Sales tax is not included in this figure.

**Training.** A process that aims to improve knowledge, skills, attitudes, and/or behaviors in a person to accomplish a specific job task or goal.

**Turnover.** The number of times an average inventory is sold within a specific time period, normally for one year.

Annual Retail Sales ÷ Average Inventory at Beginning of Month
for Each Month of the Previous Year = Turnover

**Value Proposition.** The attributes that make your business unique and make it stand out from the competition.

# Index

## A

accessories, display of, 222–224
advertising, 237–238
anniversary special, 274
annual series sales, 273
apparel
  preparing for display, 222
  presentation and display for, 217–224
  private label, 74
apparel fixtures/shelving
  cap tree, 221
  contoured/display hangers, 221
  cubes, 218–219
  four-way stand, 218
  hangers, 220–221
  mannequin forms, 219
  mirrors, 221
  rolling rack, 221
  round rack, 218
  tables, 219
  two-way or T-stand, 218
  wall unit/slat wall, 219
assortment strategy, 22–23
automation of inventory techniques, 88
Aveda lifestyle salon, 65
average retail inventory, 89
average retail markdown rate, 129

## B

back room storage, 290
banners, 225–226
beauty products. *See* skin, body, and beauty products
best sellers, 92
blog, 251
body products. *See* hair, skin, and body products; skin, body, and beauty products
booking ratio, 33–34

books, display for, 222–223
boutique items, 4–5
boutique layout, 204
brand
  awareness, 240–241
  defined, 241
  Starbucks as example of, 241
brand ambassador, 166–167
  training by, 181
branded salon and spa experience, 65
brand identity
  hangtags for, 69
  retail promotes, 5, 7
bridal-related events, 272
broadcast media, marketing through, 260
brochures
  product brochures, 225–226, 254, 266
budget
  *See* Retail Budget and Budgeting
  develop, 293–294
  retail plan and, 51
budgeting
  dues and subscriptions, budgeting for, 150
  marketing budget, 247–251
  *See also* retail budgeting
  top-down, 248–249
built-in fixtures, 289–290
business vision and mission, 20–21
buying trips, budgeting for, 150

## C

calendar
  retail marketing, 251–253
  spa seasonality, 36
  vendor, 34
cash register counter, 197
cash wrap counter, 197
challenge areas, 163–167
  brand ambassadors and, 166–167
  for front desk and other staff, 167–170
  massage therapists, 172–174
  overcoming common, 166

challenge areas (*continued*)
   for retail consultants in spas, 175–178
   for salon and spa managers, 165–167
   selling, 172
   for service providers, 170–172
chargebacks, 112
Chico's reward/loyalty program, 274
cleanliness, importance of, 216–217, 228–229
clearance items, 108
clients
   act of advising, 161
   customer surveys, 28
   know your, 28–33
   as retail partner, 11–12
   target market, 30
   *See also* customers
clinics, specialty, 252
coaching sessions, 10
coding errors, as budgeting variances, 155
color block, 213
color-rendering index (CRI), 201
color scheme, product line selection and,
       63–65
commission
   staff incentives, 44–45
   retail budgeting, 149
   structures, 41–44, 308
compensating errors, 132
compensation, 39–45
   defined, 39
   planning, 40–41
   retail management agreement, 40–41
competition, 244–246
consultation time, inadequate, 163
consumer trade shows, 252
contoured/display hangers, 221
contract service, budgeting for, 150
core values, 22–27
corporate business, 252
cosmetics
   displays for, 213–215
   medical spas offering, 52

cosmetic tester stands, 213–215, 217
cost complement, 138
cost of goods sold, 125, 132–133
   gross margin and, 141
   initial markups and, 137–138
   invoice discounts on freight and, 139
   maintained markup, 141–142
   markdowns and, 138
   merchandise movement and, 139
   physical inventory and, 139–140
cost of sales, 125, 128
   *See also* cost of goods sold, 125, 132–133
cost of sales percentage
   factors leading to high, 134–135
   factors leading to low, 135–136
   gross margin and, 141
   initial markups and, 137–138
   invoice discounts on freight and, 139
   maintained markup and, 141–142
   markdowns and, 138
   merchandise movement and, 139
   physical inventory and, 139–140
   retail budgeting and, 148
counter, cash wrap, 197
credit, with vendors, 66
credit card companies, security efforts and, 296
CRI. *See* color-rendering index
cross-promotions, 251
cube fixture, 218–219
cultural trends, 23–24
customer demographics. *See* demographics
customer profile, 244
customer relationships, marketing and,
       230–240
customers
   database of email and mailing addresses,
       268
   identifying, 244–246
   loyalty programs, 73
   retail protocol and, 185–186
   understanding experience of, 184–185
   *See also* clients

customer service, value-added, 186–187
customer surveys, 28–30

## D

data sorts, 30
delivery service, 187
demographics
    general, 29–30
    for market survey, 287
    trends in client, 28
demonstration days, 252
departmental income or loss, 154
direct contact vendor support, 71
direct mail programs, 268, 304
directors, sales facilitation by, 165
discounts
    cost of sales percentage and, 134
    *See also* markdowns
display
    apparel products, 217–224
    books, gifts, and accessories, 222–223
    budgeting for, 151
    cosmetics, 213–215
    hair, skin, and body products, 211–213
    impulse merchandise, 206
    shelf talkers, 215–216
    showcasing *vs.* mass merchandising, 209–211
    skin, body, and beauty products, 208–2011
    *See also* visual merchandising

## E

education
    defined, 179
    for effective selling, 178–180, 182–184
    about pilferage, 116–117
    training *vs.*, 179–180
electronic media messages
    email, 255–256
    website, 256–258
email promotions, 255–256
embroidery, of logo, 291–292
enlightenment, 184

entryway, welcoming, 196–197
environment, maximizing total,
    163–165
equipment rental, budgeting for, 150
essential oils, allergies to, 177
estheticians, selling by, 174
exclusivity, vendor support and, 71
expense variances, 155

## F

Facebook, 258–260
fads, trends and, 23
fashion, trends and, 23
"Feature Item," 5
financial goals, retail protocol and, 186
financial performance, 123–159
    inventory turnover, 142–145
    key business indicators, 123–130
first impressions of spa, 175
fitness trainers, 3
fixtures
    built-in, 289–290
    freestanding, 289–290
    for skin, body, and beauty products, 208
    types of, 289–290
    vendor-supplied, 224
floor layout
    photos of different layouts, 204
    product positioning and, 203–206
    supplies for designing, 205
floor plan
    criteria for designing, 205–206
    flow of, 197
flyers, 254
follow-up, as challenge area, 164
forecasting revenue, 145–147
401(k), 149
four-way fixture, 218
freestanding fixtures, 290
freight
    budgeting for, 151
    invoice discounts, 139

freight costs
    order frequency and, 133
    for private label products, 78
frequency, of marketing message, 250
frequent buyer programs, 274
front desk
    handout cards, 264
    marketing message, 264
front desk staff
    challenge areas for, 167–170
    objections to selling, 168–169
    as sale initiator, 185–186
    sales facilitation, 165

G
gift cards, 268–269
gift certificates, 268–269, 309
gift display, 222–224
gifting merchandise, 113
gift registry, 252
gift wrap
    budgeting for, 151
    select program for, 304–305
    as value-added service, 187
glare, lighting and, 201
"good-better-best" pricing philosophy, 54–55
Green Book, report on trends (2011), 24–25
grid retail design, 204
gross margin, 7, 141

H
hair, skin, and body products
    display by chronological order, 211–212
    display by hair or skin type, 212
    display by usage, 211
    shelf sculpting for, 212–213
hair designers, selling by, 174
hair products. See hair, skin, and body products
handout cards, at front desk, 264
hangers, 220–221
hangtags, 69
health and life insurance, 149

holidays
    merchandise markdowns during, 107
    monthly sales forecast and, 34
    promotions for, 303–304
hotel. See resort/hotel salon and spa
housekeeping tasks, 228–229

I
impulse items, 52
impulse products, displays for, 206
incentive
    selling, 169
    straight commission as weak, 41
industry events, 58–59
in-store demonstrations, 71
internal marketing staff, 265
International Beauty Show, 58
International SPA Association
    on purchase of spa products, 163
    Uniform System of Financial Reporting
        for Spas, 124
inventory
    uncounted, cost of sales percentage and, 135
    See also physical inventory
inventory management, 85–121
    automation of, 88–90
    average retail inventory, 89
    basic retail management and. See retail
        management, basic
    business transitions, 105
    desired turns, 92
    determining correct inventory levels, 100–101
    initial investment in inventory, 105
    inventory aging, 94–95
    just-in-time approach, 100
    manual recordkeeping, 107–113. See also
        manual recordkeeping
    markdowns and, 104–105
    order quantities, 103–104
    planning, 300–301
    replenishment strategies, 90–91, 101–104
    retail method of, 96

sell through percentage, 93

shrinkage, 114–117

stock-to-sales ratio, 90

storage and control procedures, 117

supporting the retail plan, 86–88

techniques for retail, 88

turnover, 89, 96–100. *See also* inventory
        turnover

inventory procedures, 300–301

inventory turnover, 142–145

days of inventory on hand, 144–145

physical inventory and, 142–144

ISPA

media query service, 263

Conference & Expo, vendor research at, 58

## J

jewelry, display of, 224

## K

key business indicators

cost of sales, 128–129

list of, 123

retail markdown percentage, 128–129

retail sales by service provider, 127–128

retail sales contribution by classification,
        125–126

retail sales percentage of revenue, 125

retail sales per square foot, 129–130

retail sales per ticket, 126–127

key item, 93

keystone markup, 137

key vendor, 56

## L

late orders, 67

liability insurance, vendor support with, 71

licenses and fees, budgeting for, 151

life coach, 3

lighting

as challenge area, 164

choosing, 290

direct, on products, 202–203

heat emitted by, 202

for makeup area, 200

for retail area, 201–202

as retail focal point, 199–200

listening, importance of, 26

location, monthly sales forecast and, 34

logo, creating, 291–293

loop floor design, 204

loyalty programs, 274

## M

magazines, advertising in, 261–262

mail order programs, 268

develop processes for, 304

maintained markup, 141–142

makeover contest, 274–275

makeup area, lighting for, 200

makeup events, 274

managers, sales facilitation by, 165

mannequin forms, 219

manual recordkeeping

chargebacks, 112

markups, 109–110

merchandise received, 110–111

recording markdowns, 108–109

temporary price reduction, 109

transfers, 112–113

manufacturer's suggested retail price,
        42, 64

margin

defined, 138

gross, 141

markdowns, 104–107

average retail rate of, 129

cost of goods sold and, 138

cost of sales percentage and, 134,
        138–139

defined, 138

reasons for, 140

recording, 108–109

slow movers and, 94

marketing, 235–279
  benefits of, 238–241
  brand awareness and, 240–241
  customer relationships and, 230–240
  defined, 235–236
  delivering your message, 253–263. *See also* marketing vehicles
  evaluation, 275–276
  marketing plan, 242–253. *See also* marketing plan
  people involved in, 264–266
  promotions. *See* marketing promotions
  put plan into action, 267
  year of promotions, 269–275
marketing budget, 247–251
marketing calendar, 251–253
marketing plan
  budgeting for marketing and, 247–251
  business plan and, 242
  defined, 242
  develop retail, 303–304
  goal setting and, 246
  identifying customers and competition in, 244–246
  marketing and promotion worksheet, 267
  questions answered by, 243
  retail marketing calendar, 251–253
  *See also* retail marketing plan
marketing promotions, 267–269
  gift cards, 268–269
  gift certificates, 268–269
  mail order, 268
marketing staff, internal, 265
marketing vehicles
  external
    billboards, 260–261
    broadcast media, 260
    electronic media, 255–256
    newsletters, 255
    postcards, 254–255
    press releases, 262–263

    print advertising, 261–262
    print media: brochures and flyers, 254
    social media, 258–260
  internal
    front desk message, 263–264
    handout cards at front desk, 264
    message behind front desk, 264
    on-hold message, 263
    retail area message, 264
    staff recommendation, 264
market research, paying for, 247
market survey
  conduct, 284–289
  customer demographics, 287
  marketing considerations, 287–288
  sample survey form, 285–286
markup
  initial, 141
  maintained, 141–142
markup/markdown record, 108
markups, 109–110
  initial, 137–138
massage therapist
  retail and, 172–174
  as sale initiator, 186
mass merchandising display, 209–211
maximum stock level, 91–92
media people, relationships with, 266
medical spas, cosmetics offered by, 52
merchandise display. *See* display
merchandise plan, 293–294
merchandise received, 110–111
merchandise tags, budgeting for, 151
metatags, 257
minimum order point stock levels, 91
min/max levels, 91–92, 103–104
mirrors, wall and free-standing, 221
mission statement, 21
multiple lines, 4
music
  as retail focal point, 199
  relaxation, 163

**N**

nail technician
   selling by, 174
   *See also* technician
net retail revenue, 124–125, 125
new product launch, 251
new service launch, 251
newsletters, 255
newspapers, advertising in, 261–262
news releases, 262–263

**O**

online marketing
   email, 255–256
   social media, 258–260
   website, 256–257
online retailing, 258
on-site services, 274
open-ended conversation, 180–181
open to buy (OTB), 101–103
operating supplies
   budgeting for, 151
   purchase, 308–309
order log, 67
OTB. *See* open to buy
over-assorted, 93

**P**

packaging
   budgeting for, 151
   private label products, 76
   select program for, 304–305
par stock, 99
partial shipments, 68
Paul Mitchell concept salons, 65
payroll expense, retail budgeting and,
   148–149
payroll variances, 155
peripheral vendor, 56
perishable goods, 94
personal trainer, 4
Phillips, Carol, 163

philosophy, 8
   purchasing products and, 49
   retail protocol and, 186
   synchronize retail with business,
      19–20
physical inventory
   cost of goods sold and, 139–140
   cost of sales percentage and, 134–135,
      139–140
   incorrect count, 134–135
   shrinkage and, 114
   turnover and, 142–144
pilferage, 115–117
   cost of sales percentage and, 134
   *See also* shoplifting
PMS. *See* property management system
PO. *See* purchase order
point-of-sale (POS) computer system
   find bugs in, 311
   identify minimum order point levels, 91
   inventory management and, 88
   order log for, 67
   selecting, 294–293
point-of-sale reductions, 108
POS. *See* point-of-sale (POS) computer system
postcards, 254–255, 266
posters, 225–226
preferred customer thank-you, 273
press releases, 262–263, 266
price tags, 69
pricing
   retail plan and, 54–56
   *See also* ticketing
pricing strategies, 310
print media, 254
private label product line, 72–78
   benefits of, 72–73
   guest loyalty, private label products and, 73
   marketing, 79–80
   profit margin on, 73
   risks associated with, 73–75
   storage for, 75

straight commission, 41–42
  *See also* commission
  types of products, 75–77
  vendor selection, 77–78
product classifications
  floor layout and, 205
  retail plan and, 53–54
product feature of the month, 252
product lines
  select, 65–66
  viewing, vendor selection and, 63–65
product positioning, 203–206
product return, due to skin reactions, 178
professional development, budgeting for, 152
professional use products, 112–113
profit margin, 138
  on private label products, 73
promotions
  big bang holidays
    Mother's Day, 270
    Valentine's Day, 269–270
    winter holidays, 270
  calendar of, 251–252
  monthly review of, 128
  plan, 303–304
  seasonal events
    back to school, 272–273
    bridal events, 272
    fall looks, 273
    Father's Day, 272
    graduates, 271–272
    Halloween, 273
    holiday dazzle, 273
    New Year, new you, 270
    post-winter blues, 271
    preferred customer thank-you, 273
    pre-spring, 271
    proms, 272
    secretary's day, 271
    spring cleaning, 271
    spring fling, 271
    summer slump, 272
season-less
  anniversary special, 274
  annual series sales, 273–274
  extreme makeover, 275
  face in a bag, 275
  frequent buyer programs, 274
  kiss and makeup, 274
  makeover contest, 274–275
  on-site services, 274
  reward/loyalty programs, 274
  vendor support with, 71
  year of, 269–275
property management system (PMS), 297
props, accessorizing with, 226–227
purchase order (PO), 302–303
  POS system generates, 88
purchasing, 49–84
  marketing and, 79–80
  private label product line, 72–78
  with retail plan, 49–56
  vendor partnerships, 70–71
  vendor selection and, 57–70
  vendor structure and, 56–57
purchasing plan, 52

**R**

racetrack floor design, 204
radio advertising, 260
reach, marketing, 250
receiving merchandise, start, 311–312
receiving system, 66–70
  common procedures, 67
  late orders, 67
  partial shipments, 68
  substitutions, 68–70
recordkeeping, delays in, 135
referral reward, 240
relaxation music, 163
reorder/restock procedures, 310
reorders, ticketing and, 69
replenishment strategies, 90–91. *See also* open
    to buy

resort/hotel salon and spa
  customer demographics of, 287
  guest promotions, 253
  internal marketing staff for, 265
  marketing considerations, 288
  retail forecasting for, 146
  sales per square foot, 130
retail
  additional revenue with, 7–8
  categories, 31–32
  defined, 8
  extends benefits of services and treatments,
    3–4
  fulfills client shopping desires, 5
  importance of, 3–8
  as one-stop shop, 4–5
  promotes brand identity, 5, 7
  retail consultants job description, 175–177
retail area, marketing message in, 264
  budget planner form, 153–154
  cost of sales percentage and, 148
  departmental income or loss, 152, 154
  forecasting revenue, 145–147
  payroll expense and, 148–149
  retail categories, 31–32
  revenue adjustments, 148
  variances and, 155–156
  See also Budget/budgeting
retail classifications
  creating, 30–33
  defined, 31
  monthly sales forecasts by, 37
retail consultant
  challenges for, in spa environment, 175–176
  job description, 175–177
  as sale initiator, 186
  sales facilitation by, 165
retail experience, understanding guest's, 184–185
retail fixtures. See fixtures
retail focal points
  cash wrap counter, 197
  dressing rooms, 197–198

  enhancing the basic space, 198
  fixtures, 199
  floor plan, 197
  lighting, 199–200
  overall decor, 198–199
  sound and scent, 199
  storefront windows, 195–196
  welcoming entryway, 196–197
retail inventory method, 96
retail layout, finalize, 289–291
retail management
  advanced, 95–107
    average turnover, 96–100
    determine correct inventory levels, 100–101
    inventory turnover goals, 96–100
    markdowns, 104–107
    replenishment strategies
      min/max levels, 103–104
      open to buy (OTB), 101–103
    retail method of inventory management, 96
  basic
    inventory aging, 94–95
    min/max levels, 91–92
    replenishment strategies, 90–91
    stock-to-sales ratio, 90
    top sellers/slow movers, 92–94
    turnover, 89
retail managers
  sales facilitation by, 165
  successful behaviors of, 166
retail marketing plan
  development of, 303–304
  See also marketing plan
retail mix, 51–52
retail opening, 281–317
  four months from opening
    begin merchandise purchases, 302–303
    develop direct mail and mail order
      processes, 304
    develop retail marketing plan, 303–304
    establish sales and inventory procedures,
      300–301

retail opening (*continued*)
 finalize opening inventory value, 302–303
 select packaging and gift wrap program, 304–305
 source remaining retail merchandise, 305–307
 four weeks from opening
  bring point-of-sale system online, 311
  hire staff and set training schedules, 310–311
  start receiving and ticketing merchandise, 311–312
 one week from opening, 313
 opening countdown, 283–284
 six months from opening
  conduct market survey, 284–289
  create logo, 291–293
  develop merchandise plan and budget, 293–294
  explore core retail treatment products, 298–300
  finalize retail design and layout, 289–291
  select point-of-sale computer system, 294–293
 systematic approach to planning, 281–284
 two months from opening
  determine pricing strategies, 310
  establish reorder/restock procedures, 310
  finalize gift certificate program, 309
  finalize retail commission structure, 308
  purchase operating supplies, 308–309
  recruit retail supervisor or consultant, 307–308
 two to three weeks from, 312
retail partnerships, 8–12
 clients, 11–12
 staff, 9–10
 vendors, 10–11
retail per service ticket, 126–127
retail per ticket, 126–127
retail philosophy, 8

retail plan
 budget and, 51
 defined, 49–50
 goal setting in, 246
 inventory management supports, 86–88
 key elements of, 19
 price points and, 53
 pricing schemes and, 54–56
 product classification, 53–54
 purchase with, 49–56
 purchasing plan, 52
 retail mix and, 51–52
 seasonal products and, 54
 synchronize with business philosophy, 19–20
 *See also* retail planning
retail planning, 17–47
 business vision and mission, 20–21
 clients and, 28–33
 compensation, 39–45
 core values, 22–27
 importance of, 18–20
 key elements of, 19
 questions to guide process, 17
 retail classifications, 30–33
 sales planning, 33–36
 synchronize retail with business philosophy, 19–20
 theme and, 19–20
 *See also* retail plan
retail protocol, 185–186
retail sales contribution by classification, 125–126
retail sales percentage, 125–126
retail sales percentage of revenue, 125
retail selling, as prescriptive, 4
retail supervisor, recruit, 307–308
retail trends, 22–23
retirement plans, 149
return policy, "100% satisfaction guaranteed," 137
revenue
 forecasting, 145–147
 retail supports additional, 7–8

revenue adjustments, 124, 133
    retail budgeting and, 148
reward programs, 274
round rack, 218
runway events, 252

## S

salaries and wages, budget for, 149
sales forecast
    evaluate accuracy of, 36
    monthly, by classification, 37
    seasonality and, 34–36
sales forecasts
    monthly, per employee, 38
    yearly, 33–34
sales leadership, as challenge area, 164
sales planning
    establish seasonality, 34–36
    evaluate sales forecast accuracy, 36
    forecast sales for year, 33–34
sales procedures, establish, 300–301
sales training, 180–181
sanitation, in cosmetic tester areas, 214
scent, as retail focal point, 199
seasonality
    establish, 34–36
    spa calendar, 36
seasonal products
    retail plan and, 54
seasonal promotions, 251, 303–304
season-less promotions, 251
selling
    education and training for, 178–186
    negative images of word, 2
"selling through service" approach, 2
sell through, 56
seminars, specialty, 252
service providers
    challenge areas for, 170–172
    retail per service ticket, 126
    retail sales by, 127–128
    seizing the sale, 165

services, retail extends benefits of, 3–4
shelf talkers, 215–216
shelving, for skin, body, and beauty products,
        208
shoplifting
    of cosmetics, 215
    lock cases to prevent, 213
    See also pilferage
showcasing displays, 209
shrinkage, 114–117
    calculating, 114–115
    paperwork errors and, 115
    pilferage and, 115–117
signage, 225–226, 247
silk screen printing, 292–293
skin, body, and beauty products
    fixtures and shelving for, 208
    prepping for display, 208–209
    private label products, 74
    successful display techniques,
        209–211
    visual merchandising for, 206–217
    See also hair, skin, and body products
slat wall, 219
slow movers, 93–94
social media, marketing through, 258–260
social trends, 23–24
spa seasonality calendar, 36
special orders, 187
specialty clinics or seminars, 252
staff
    daily housekeeping tasks for, 228–229
    hire, 310–311
    internal marketing, 265
    recommendations for promotions from, 264
    as retail partner, 9–10
    salon and spa, marketing by, 265
    support for products from, 64
staff incentives, commissions and, 44–45
staples, trends and, 23
Starbucks Coffee, 241
storefront windows, 195–196

store layout, pilferage and, 116
store planning, 193–202
    storefront windows, 195–196
    *See also* retail focal points
straight commission, 41–42
    *See also* commission
subclassifications, 32–33
    inventory turns for, 99
substitutions, receiving system and, 68–70
success, measures of, 187
suggested retail price, manufacturer's,
        42, 64
sun care products, expiration of, 77
sunscreens, recommending, 177
SWOT analysis, 244–246

**T**
tables, for visual displays, 219
target market, 30, 237–238
technicians
    sales facilitation by, 165
    as sale initiator, 186
telecommunications, budgeting for, 152
television advertising, 250, 260
temporary installments, 208
temporary price reductions, 108–109
tent cards, 266
    display products using, 80
theme
    retail, 19–20
    window display, 195–196
ticketing merchandise
    establish procedures for, 69
    start, 311–312
tiered commission
    based on productivity, 42–43
    based on profitability, 42
top-down budgeting method, 248–249
top sellers, 92
total retail revenue, 124
trade magazines, 58
trade shows, 59–62

training
    as challenge area, 164–165
    defined, 179
    education *vs.*, 179–180
    for effective selling, 178–181
    set schedules for, 310–311
transfers
    cost of sales percentage and, 134
    inventory, planning for, 300–301
    manual record keeping for, 112–113
treatment-oriented products, 177
trends
    categories of, 23
    in client demographics, 28
    life cycles of, 23
    retail, 22–23
    stages of, 23
    social and cultural, 23–24
    stay current on, 24–25
    *See also* retail trends
    life cycles of trends and, 23
    retail trends, 22–23
T-stand, 218
turnover
    financial performance and, 142–145
    inventory, 89
        average turnover, 96–100
        goals, 96–100
    product classification and, 97
Twitter, 258–260
two-way stand, 218
    *See also* display apparel

**U**
uniforms, budgeting for, 152
*Uniform System of Financial Reporting for Spas*, 124
    distribution of revenue, 294
    spa categories in, 31–32
    top-down budgeting method in, 248–249
UPC bar codes, 69
UPC label, 295
UPC tags, vendor-supplied, 209

# V

value-added customer service, 186–187

value proposition, 244

variances, retail budgeting and, 155–156

vendors

calendar, 34

classification, sample, 32

cosmetic, tester stands from, 213–215

education by, 183

manufacturer's suggested retail price, 42

marketing efforts from, 265–266

partnerships, 70–71

price changes, 155

for private label product line, 75

product positioning for key, 205

promotions, 251

questions to help choose, 56–57

relationships, bill paying and, 69

research, 58–59

as retail partner, 10–11

selecting. *See* vendor selection

support from, 71

vendor selection

attend trade shows, 59–62

establish receiving system, 66–70

meet with vendors, 61–63

private label product line, 77–78

research vendors, 58–59

select product lines, 65–66

view product lines, 63–65

vendor structure, 56–57

VIP gift cards, 253

VIP gifts, 113, 301

visioning, 21

visual experience, as challenge area, 164

visual merchandising, 199–233

apparel products, 217–224

clean and simple, 228–229

floor layout and product positioning, 203–206

fresh shopping experience and, 227–228

props, 226–227

signage, 225–226

for skin, body, and beauty products, 206–217

store planning and floor layout, 193–202

*See also* display

# W

wall unit, 219

website, 256–258

blog with, 251

development, budgeting for, 249

wholesale price points, 64

*Why We Buy: The Science of Shopping* (Underhill), 207

window display

as magnet, 306

theme for, 195–196

wish list, 187, 252

word of mouth

marketing, 248

vendor information and, 59

worker's compensation insurance, 149

# Y

Yelp, 259